The Screenwriter's Journey

From Starting Out to Breaking In

Hywel Berry

Lucas Alexander Publishing

Published by
Lucas Alexander Publishing

ISBN 9798611822500

Dedicated to Quinlan and Maksym, who mean the world to me.

Contents:

Introduction:

Let's get straight to the juicy stuff. Here is the journey you must take to become a screenwriter:

1) Buy Final Draft screenwriting software, or install the free version, Celtx, on your computer.
2) Plan out a story you are passionate about.
3) Start writing.
4) Keep writing every day and don't stop until you have written "**FADE OUT**".
5) Give the screenplay to people you trust for feedback—preferably, but not necessarily, people in the movie industry.
6) Rewrite your story according to their notes, while maintaining your vision.
7) Keep rewriting every day until you have written "**FADE OUT**" for the second time.
8) Write letters or emails to as many pertinent people as you can find and pitch the story of your screenplay.
9) Wait.
10) When someone replies, send the full screenplay.
11) Wait some more.
12) When someone recognizes your genius and wants to buy your screenplay, negotiate a good option fee against a great fee if the screenplay goes into production.
13) Move to Los Angeles (if you're not there already).
14) Wait for the call from agents who have heard about your screenplay sale.
15) Sign with the agent you liked the most.
16) Get sent out on pitch meetings with producers.
17) Dazzle them with your genius ideas for their project.
18) Get your first real writing assignment.
19) Get poached by a top-tier agency.
20) Write a summer blockbuster.
21) Congratulations! You are now a successful screenwriter.

Doesn't sound so hard, does it? That's because it's not. There is no reason the scenario above should not be exactly the way it happens for you. Except, of course, for one thing—reality. In real life, things are never that easy. And what would be the fun if they were?

That scenario above has genuinely happened for some people. Not many, but it has happened. Movie making is one of a very small group of industries in which experience can count for the grand total of zero. Not for all jobs, though—ironically, just for the high-profile jobs. No one gets hired as a director of photography without years of credits on increasingly expensive and well-known productions. You won't even get a job as a clapper loader without some sort of experience. But, actors, writers, and directors can just appear from nowhere and walk into the top tier of the industry, based on one audition, one short film, or one fantastic screenplay—and that's the killer here, everyone; your screenplay has to be *fantastic*. Not "good," not "better than most movies you saw this year," not "just as funny as *Trainwreck,*" (Amy Schumer) but *fantastic* in every way.

(As an aside, whenever it isn't too irritating, I will always try and list the credited writers of a movie the first time it is mentioned. Any working writer knows the horrible reality that most reviewers, critics, and fans will end up crediting the director as the sole creative force behind a movie. Let's redress that here.)

We need to get real and face one harsh reality: Our first screenplay won't be fantastic. It won't even be good. It will be average-to-poor, which puts it in the bucket with approximately 50,000 other screenplays that are registered every year with the Writers Guild of America. Not to mention the tens of thousands of screenplays that are copyrighted in other ways, or simply never registered at all. All these screenplays are vying to be one of the roughly 200 movies that are released annually by the major studios.

In fact, let's be even more realistic: 95% or more of studio movies are franchise pictures, book adaptations, sequels, or projects from famous writers and producers with a proven track record, which means all the new writers are fighting for perhaps three or four slots on studio slates. Will an average screenplay cut it? No. Even if we manage to get it into the hands of a reader, it will most likely be tossed aside by Page 10 (Page 30, if you're lucky) and never picked up again. A good screenplay may make it to Page 50.

Does this book exist to depress you and crush your dream of being a screenwriter? I hope not. This book is here to educate you that your journey to screenwriting success is just that—a journey. This journey will take you years, not months—and certainly not days, as some screenwriting books would have you believe. Such books only serve to perpetuate the myth that writing a screenplay is just typing words onto a page. I could paint a picture in a few days, but it would be awful. It would take me years to learn to paint a picture for which a stranger would pay me any money, just as it will probably take you years to write a script for which a studio will pay you hundreds of thousands of dollars.

Therefore, this book is a companion to your whole journey, from beginning to end. It is not a replacement for the myriad of other books on screenwriting that are out there. In fact, I will point you to the best books to help you at each stage of your journey. Some are more suited to the new writer, while others become much more valuable as you develop your talent and knowledge.

First, let's get something out of the way right now: I am not a working screenwriter.

In my early years, I wrote my one-million words (roughly, 12 feature-length screenplays, including rewrites), and I did all the things I *thought* I was supposed to do to put myself out into the industry. I marketed my spec scripts to agents and producers and eventually got requests for my work. After many rejections I had some scripts optioned. I even got hired to write a couple of screenplays, but none of the options or assignments ever made it to production. At the end of 10 years I had made some money, but never enough to support myself completely.

I would love to say the system was against me, and my genius was continually overlooked, but those things just aren't true. The truth is, I didn't make good choices, and I didn't work hard enough. As Woody Allen said, *"Seventy percent of success in life is showing up,"* and I stopped showing up.

Therefore, in a crazy scheme to stay alive, I had to work other jobs to pay the bills and eat food.

I did some acting. I worked in TV for a while as a production assistant. I then worked in sales for an international newspaper. Eventually, 10 years ago, I started working as a public speaker, a job I instantly loved. I began traveling the U.S. and the world, speaking to Fortune 500 companies on all sorts of topics, including creativity and storytelling. This work fulfilled my desire to inspire and entertain, and allowed me to be applauded by hundreds of people 3-5 times a week: Everything a failed actor and writer needs. It was the ultimate (and nicely paid) distraction for someone on their own screenwriting journey.

On stage, I would often talk about the fact that I had tried—and failed—to become a screenwriter. When I came offstage, people would tell me their own story of trying to break in as a screenwriter and the challenges they faced. In listening to them, I realized they were making the same mistakes I did. They felt alone on their journey and ready to quit.

Every successful screenwriter needs a healthy balance of ability and drive. One without the other is not good enough. Huge drive can get you a meeting, but without a quality script to back it up, the meeting will end quickly. Similarly, natural ability by itself will only get you so far; the industry is just too competitive. Huge natural ability *and* huge drive makes you Aaron Sorkin.

While speaking to these writers, I became aware of the myriad of reasons people drop off the journey to screenwriting success: The rejection, the time commitment, the loneliness, unsupportive friends and family, and, of course, the realities of having to make money to survive.

But, in many cases, they were good writers. Perhaps they could have even been *great* writers, if they persevered. I began coaching them, giving them feedback on their screenplays, and advising them on the steps to take towards success—but, more importantly, the steps to take to avoid failure.

There are some great books by working screenwriters, such as those by Blake Snyder, and Thomas Lennon & Robert Ben Garant (all of whom made A LOT of money), and to those people, I say, "Thank you." They give invaluable and real-life insight into the final game we are all trying to get to.

Instead, I offer all the advice in this book as someone who has taken the journey over the last 20 years and knows its pitfalls and perils. You will learn from my mistakes, and the mistakes of countless other possible star writers who fell by the wayside to make sure that you do not suffer the same fate.

We may sit by ourselves in front of our computer, but we are not alone. We are going to take this journey together. We will experience all the highs and lows this journey throws at us. We will make the most of each success and move on as quickly as possible from each failure so that our journey to a screenwriting career will be as short and successful as possible.

Stage 1:
Starting Our Screenwriting Journey

1.

I Want To Be A Screenwriter

Where are you on your journey so far? Planning your first screenplay? Or finishing your tenth? You may even be making money as a writer. Wherever we are on our journey, it is always worth remembering why we started in the first place.

My own inspiration—along with many of my peers—started with William Goldman. If you do not know of William Goldman, then firstly, shame on you, and secondly, your first piece of homework is to watch at least three Goldman movies in the next two weeks. It is not hard. He wrote many, and they are all (with very few exceptions) wonderful. They include *Butch Cassidy and the Sundance Kid*, *All the President's Men*, *Misery*, *Maverick*, and everyone's favorite adventure/love story, *The Princess Bride*. Before his recent passing he worked steadily as one of the highest paid script consultants in Hollywood and continued to be a creative force behind numerous movies and younger writers.

Goldman wrote a seminal book in 1983, entitled *Adventures in the Screen Trade*. This is our first book recommendation. It is the inspiration behind countless screenwriters working today. It is a brutally honest, funny, exciting, and not always appealing vision of a working screenwriter. Its references may feel slightly dated now, and the agent/studio system has changed over the years, but the genius behind the book is its balance of the glamor of the industry combined with the realities of a job behind that glamour. A job that is hard, no matter how good a writer we may be.

I first read *Adventures in the Screen Trade* when I was 18 years old. My love of the book and desire to become a screenwriter did not come out of thin air. I was already a huge fan of movies, and since the age of 13, I had worked professionally as an actor, even landing a few gigs in TV and film. Not enough to sustain a career, but enough to fund me very nicely as a teenager. However, the bulk of my acting was on stage, and this was where I saw my future. I had already written a play, produced it with some friends in a very small theater, and it had won some small, local awards.

Excited by Goldman's book, I wanted to read his movie scripts as well. However, this was the '90s; there was no internet to type in "screenplays" and become inundated with results. What *were* available in most bookstores (remember them?) were a few screenplays by famous writers that had been printed up in collections. Luckily, those by Goldman were one of the few that existed. I bought a book that included the original screenplay for *Butch Cassidy and the Sundance Kid*, which Goldman famously sold for $400k—a phenomenal sum back in the mid-'60s.

As I read the screenplay, two things struck me: It was very difficult to read—much harder than any play I had ever read—and it was unfathomably exciting. These were the images I had seen onscreen, described right there on the page. The words Newman and Redford had said—the words that made them seem so smart, cool, and exciting—they written right there, by Goldman. This screenplay would now exist forever as so much more than words on the page. It existed as a movie that had been watched by millions and would continue to be watched for generations to come. I wanted a piece of this action, and I wanted it right away.

What was your inspiration? What sparked the desire to sit down and start writing? A movie? A story? A book? A person?

Whatever it was, remember it, hold onto it, and write it down somewhere so that you don't forget it, for there are dark times ahead. Times when we will doubt ourselves, our talent, and the journey. Times when we will believe we are quite literally the least creative person in the world. Times when we want to cry, as people point out all the flaws in our screenplay we knew were there but hoped no one would notice. Times when anything will seem more appealing than sitting down at the computer and writing.

If you have jobs around the house you have been putting off, fear not. The moment you try and write a screenplay, they will all become immediately critical and will get done within a few weeks. Then you will move onto jobs that *don't* need to be done, and finally, onto jobs that have no earthly purpose.

Here is a list (in increasingly idiotic order) of some of the things I have found myself doing over the years to avoid writing a screenplay:

1) Tidying my desk.
2) Cleaning my computer screens.
3) Cleaning my computer keyboards.
4) Rearranging my DVDs by year/genre/color.

3

5) Clipping my cat's nails.
6) Painting a 1" patch of wall that was slightly discolored.
7) Swapping the couch and TV onto opposite walls to see if it looked better. (It didn't, and I had to switch them back immediately.)
8) Arranging all the coins in my change jar into the shape of a car.
9) Trying on a jacket that I knew was too small for me, just to confirm it was too small.
10) Writing a book.

On the other hand, when I don't do any writing, I feel tense and anxious. I don't sleep well. I feel unfulfilled in a way that is difficult for many people to understand. For most of us who start this journey, there is an innate and almost animalistic desire to create, to get our ideas out, to entertain, and to surprise.

I say, again: Remember why you started doing this. Know what drives you. There is no right answer; it is entirely personal and specific to you. Don't worry how stupid it may sound. It doesn't have to make sense to anyone else. This is just for you. Hold onto it and never let it go.

The reason we must never forget our inspiration is that there is a stark reality to face: Very few of us who embark on this journey will reach our goal and become working screenwriters.

It is very hard to be good enough to make a living as a screenwriter, and even if we *are* good enough, it is still difficult to get work and *keep* getting work. I know that is a very depressing reality, and it might seem like enough of a reason to give up this journey right now.

Do not give up!

Because here is the other side of that reality—no one knows who is actually going to make it. Successful screenwriters have come from all corners of the globe, and from a wide variety of backgrounds.

Sure, it doesn't hurt to be a Harvard graduate who wrote for the Harvard Lampoon. That's going to open some useful doors for us the day we turn up in Los Angeles, but it doesn't get us a job, and it doesn't sell our shitty script.

The hardest working, most resilient writer has the best shot at success.

Do we need talent? Yes. But, more than that, we need to *really* want this, and we need to be willing to work incredibly hard to get it. Any less than that, and you *should* give it up. Go and get a good job you enjoy and treasure your free time with your friends and family. You can still write screenplays if you want, but know you are doing it for fun, for a nice pastime, the same way you might write a blog or short stories to entertain yourself. But, don't, for one moment, believe that lazily writing a script every two years and sending it out to a couple of agents is ever, in your wildest dreams, going to get you the career you covet.

Look at the following diagram:

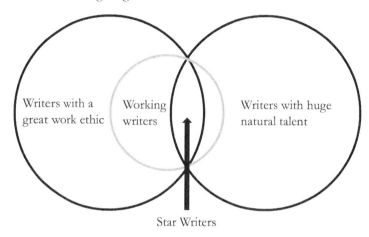

Star Writers

On the left are writers with a great work ethic. On the right are writers who have a great deal of natural talent. The tiny crossover in the middle are people who become star writers, win awards, and make millions.

However, the light gray bubble in the middle represents people who build a real career as a working screenwriter. For those who only have one of those attributes, the majority will come from the group with a great work ethic. We can't all be Charles Dickens, Shakespeare, William Goldman, or Quentin Tarantino. Those people are as elite in the field of writing as Tiger Woods is in the game of golf, or Babe Ruth was in baseball. But Babe Ruth didn't stop thousands of other people from becoming professional baseball players and enjoying wonderful and successful careers. They may not quite have become The Babe, but they were a lot happier than they would have been working in retail.

New writers emerge and create their own success *every single day*, and very few of them grew up around the industry, went to film school, or were writers before they broke in—but they *all* wanted this more than anything else. You need to want it *that much*.

I thought I wanted it, but when the chips were down, I was too easily distracted; by other writing (for five years, I made some money writing television comedy); by friends, by relationships, by reading imdbpro.com, and by the other work I had to do to survive. When an enjoyable career that matched my skillset presented itself and was *way* easier than writing a great screenplay, I turned towards it far too quickly. I was just another person who had the potential but let it slip away.

Don't be fooled into thinking people without talent and ambition are making money as screenwriters. They are not. The people making a living as screenwriters are phenomenally talented and desperately hardworking, and, for a variety of reasons, the movies they write sometimes end up being terrible, and sometimes end up being fantastic.

I know this sounds harsh, but I am saying this because I wish someone had been as blunt with me when I started out. If you want to be a screenwriter, then you have to *be* a screenwriter. Everything you do is designed to get you to your goal of working as a screenwriter.

Think of it this way: If you weren't going to be a screenwriter, what would be your second-most desirable job? A doctor? An architect? A lawyer? A game designer? An athlete? Whatever it is, no job people actually want is ever available from nothing. It's not possible. We must either put in years of study, or years of experience in shitty jobs to get to the place we desire.

Now, think of how difficult all those jobs are to achieve and multiply it by 10. In fact, multiply it by 100, and you will be close to realizing how hard this journey will be, because for any job you can think of that people would call a "good job", there are a hundred times more people trying to make movies. Filmmaking is the sexiest industry in the world. Even people who are staggeringly successful in other industries will drop what they are doing in a second if Hollywood comes calling and offers them a chance to be part of the glamor of filmmaking.

So, how do you start your own screenwriter's journey? By stating here and now that you are *going* to be a screenwriter, and that the only thing that can stop you getting there is you! I can't guarantee you will become a millionaire or an Oscar winner, but I *can* guarantee that if you truly fight harder for it than anyone else around you, you will enjoy some sort of success. Exactly what that will look like, I can't say, but I'm going to do everything I can so that one day, when someone asks you what you do for a living, you will be able to say, truthfully and with gusto, "I'm a screenwriter."

2.

The *Real* Screenwriter's Journey

If we can't just turn up Los Angeles and sell our 100 pages of paper for a million dollars, then what must we do to build a real career as a screenwriter?

Unfortunately, the real journey is much longer and much more difficult. There are eight stages to our journey that will be outlined in this book. Let's take a look at each of them now.

Stage 1: Starting Our Screenwriting Journey

You are completing this stage right now. Millions of people go through this stage, as it requires no actual writing. It is the nice part, when we get to dream about our impending screenwriting success without the nastiness of actually doing it. But, we do need to make some big decisions at this stage to get it right.

We must start building our life around a writing schedule. We must accept that "free time" is going to become a thing of the past. We must be comfortable telling everyone in our life that we are now a writer, despite the potential negativity and ridicule it may bring. We are not "giving screenwriting a go"; we "are a screenwriter".

Stage 2: Our First Screenplay

Millions of people *start* this stage, but few actually finish it. This is the stage when we realize just how hard it is to fill 100 pages with a story that works.

What seems like it will take a few weeks will end up taking many months and much frustration to complete. But, we must finish it, or our journey is dead before it's even started. To do so, we will explore the reasons people get blocked or stop writing, and how to avoid them.

Stage 3: Rewriting 101

This is when we try to improve the unholy mess of a screenplay we just finished. But, at least when we are finished, we will have our masterpiece, right? Wrong. This is also the stage when we will discover we weren't quite the literary geniuses we thought we were. We realize agents and studios are not falling over themselves to throw money at us. People who do read our script will undoubtedly rip our literary child to shreds and leave us to pick up the pieces.

This is the stage when reality sets in, and we must make the conscious choice to continue, aware of just how long and hard this journey will be.

Stage 4: Our Second, Third, Fourth, and Fifth Screenplays

After we realize one screenplay was never going to be enough, we must now learn to actually write. The writing of these subsequent four screenplays will allow us to hone our craft and improve immeasurably as writers.

This is also the stage when we must start to build our network of contacts, who will eventually help us break in.

Stage 5: Advanced Rewriting

Although each new first draft will improve, this is the stage when we truly learn that rewriting is what makes a good script great.

We are finally able to "kill our darlings" and delete the greatest line or scene we ever wrote for the betterment of the screenplay. We find layers and depth in the character and story we never realized was there.

We are now writers.

Stage 6: The Business of Movies

Most of us have not grown up in L.A. or as the child of a studio mogul, so although we may have a movie lovers' knowledge of the industry, there is still a lot for us to learn. We must understand what opportunities are available to us, how financing works, how we will make money, and the proper form for new writers to make themselves known to the filmmaking community.

Stage 7: Professional Level Writing

During this stage, we need to start making some difficult life choices. Do we move to Los Angeles? What is going to raise our screenplay above the pack of other new writers? What kind of writer do we want to be? What kind of career do we want to have?

Stage 8: Breaking In

This is what we've all been waiting for, so let's get real. It is going to take us at least two years—more realistically, 5-7 years—for us to get to this point. That's only if everything goes our way. Remember: It takes just as long to be a doctor or lawyer, and they have to pay hundreds of thousands of dollars for the privilege. All we've had to buy is Final Draft and some paper.

***

Many start this journey, but very few will finish it. Some will get there earlier than others; some will make more money than others. Some will have short-lived careers before moving on to other things; others will be names for decades. A very small group will become superstars, win Oscars, and command multi-million-dollar paychecks. But, if we truly persevere, do everything we need to do, and work harder than everyone around us, then we, too, can have a real career as a screenwriter.

That is the journey we are now going to take together.

3.

What is A Screenplay?

We live in a very different world now, compared to when I started out. Movie screenplays are so readily available that I doubt there are many people who would not recognize the format from afar:

INT. STARBUCKS — DAY

Suzie looks across the table at the HANDSOME STUDENT (21).

He taps away on his computer but looks up and catches her eye. She smiles. Then, she looks at his screen and sees he is writing a screenplay.

She turns back to her friend.

                    FRIEND
       He's cute.

                    SUZIE
       Forget it. Wannabe screenwriter.

They are also easier to read. The style of screenplay structure and format has favored a more readable screenplay over the years, with less description, more white space, and less unnecessary camera direction, such as "CUT TO:" and "ANGLE ON:".

If you have not read many—or any—screenplays, then you must start reading straight away. Start with the movies you love, as this shouldn't feel like a chore, but it is imperative you gain an innate sense of screenplay format and style. You should read so many, and become so familiar with it, that you start describing mundane, everyday incidents in your head as if they were in screenplay format:

INT. KITCHEN — DAY

Hywel opens the fridge. He rummages around for
something to eat and clumsily knocks a carton of
eggs onto the floor.

The carton bursts open, and broken eggs spill onto
the tile.

                         HYWEL
             Shit!

He grabs a wad of kitchen roll and begins the
laborious task of cleaning up.

Then, the door bursts open, and the TERMINATOR walks
in. It holds out its hand out to Hywel.

                       TERMINATOR
             Come with me if you want to live.

(That last bit didn't really happen. In reality, I just cleaned up the eggs and
had toast instead, but you also need to practice turning mundane moments
into drama.)

So, back to our heading for this chapter: What is a screenplay? A screenplay
is a dynamic blueprint for a movie. Like a blueprint for a building it needs
to be understandable by many different people, all of whom should be able
to envision basically the same thing. Not necessarily *exactly* the same thing,
but enough of a similar image in their mind to all work towards the same
goal in production.

It is dynamic because it is a living thing that is constantly changing. Many
people will be involved in the creation and production of a screenplay
throughout its life.

However, for those of us trying to break into the industry, the screenplay
has an additional and much more important purpose. It is a sales document.
It is there to sell *you*. Even if we are lucky enough to sell this screenplay, the
chances of it ever getting made are very slim. The chances of *any* screenplay
actually going into production are very slim, even those commissioned by
successful producers for major studios from world-class writers.

So, if it's not going to get made, what are we writing it for? The primary
purpose of this screenplay is to get us recognized. We are writing a spec
script. This stands for "speculative script", a screenplay written without any
fee up front that the writer hopes to sell after the fact or use to gain

attention. It is the recognized, industry-standard way for new writers to present themselves as a potentially hirable writer.

We are writing something that needs to say: "Look how good I am. Buy this script if you want, but I am the best, new, cheap writer you will find. Please hire me for your project that is already in development."

There is definitely the opportunity to sell the screenplay—potentially, for a lot of money. Some working writers make a good living by continuing to write spec scripts alongside their other assignment work. For instance, Blake Snyder—the author of the hugely popular screenwriting manual *Save the Cat*—sold many spec screenplays over his career, some for over $1M. However, he was still only credited with two films that actually went into production.

If this concept is anathema to you, and you have a story that *must* get out to the world, then there are other routes to take. Make the movie yourself or take it the indie route as a producer to find private financing. These routes become more and more viable each year, as costs on low-budget productions plummet, thanks to exponential increases in digital camera standards.

There are some very famous spec screenplay sales from new writers that *did* become movies. Andrew Kevin Walker worked at a record store (remember those?) when he wrote *Se7en*. He called David Koepp to ask him to read his screenplay. He did.

Danny Rubin was a new writer being pitched to Harold Ramis for a project he was working on. As a writing sample, Rubin's agent sent Ramis *Groundhog Day*. Ramis enjoyed it so much that he dropped the project he was working on, bought *Groundhog Day,* and got it into production, working with Danny Rubin on the rewrites.

Stories like these are very few and far between, though. For the vast majority of writers, their spec screenplays are fantastic pieces of work that open doors for them with producers and studios. These screenplays are soon forgotten, once the writer starts getting assignment work.

Therefore, our spec screenplay must do more than tell a story. It must tell it in a way that makes us stand out for all the right reasons. It must say:

1) I am totally adept at screenplay format.
2) I have a deep understanding of screenplay structure.
3) I am a natural storyteller.
4) My characters are authentic and engaging.

5) I can still surprise you and excite you, no matter how many screenplays you have read today.
6) You should hire me right away!

If you have written a screenplay already, does it say that? All of that? If not, we still have work to do.

One or two things on that list are not good enough. It's not enough to have some fantastic dialogue in a story that makes no sense. It's not enough to have a bunch of funny scenes if the set-up is illogical. It's not enough to have fantastic action sequences if the characters are dull and clichéd.

It would be great if we could send out our screenplay and have a major producer call us back and say, "Hey, I read your screenplay. Can't produce it as it is, but pages 32-36 were *fantastic*, and I want to buy it and work with you to make the rest of this screenplay as good as those 4 pages."

Why doesn't that happen? Because that producer has literally hundreds of other screenplays sitting on their desk, waiting to be read. It makes no sense to take a screenplay that doesn't work and spend time and money to try and fix all those problems, when they can just keep going through screenplays until they find one that has no problems and is already perfect.

Again, remember: The vast majority of the time, they are not even looking for a screenplay to produce; they are looking for a writer who has mastered their craft and is a lot cheaper than the star writers who already have produced credits to their name. That's the only way in, so that is the screenplay we are going to write.

I promise that reading screenplays (good and bad) will only serve to deepen your desire to be in the business of making these things.

Sites such as "Selling Your Screenplay" (www.sellingyourscreenplay.com), by Ashley Scott Meyers, or "Simply Scripts" (www.simplyscripts.com) offer free access to such screenplays.

Below is a list of screenplays that should definitely be on our immediate reading list. They are all exceptional examples of their craft. They may not be genres we usually enjoy, but that is not important here. What is important is they are impeccably crafted screenplays, and that is what we want to study and understand. So, track down these screenplays as soon as you can!

In chronological order, they are:

1) *Butch Cassidy and the Sundance Kid* (William Goldman)
2) *The Sting* (David S. Ward)

3) *Jaws* (Carl Gottlieb and Peter Benchley; Original Novel by Peter Benchley)

4) *Raiders of the Lost Ark* (Lawrence Kasdan; Story by George Lucas and Philip Kaufman)

5) *Die Hard* (Jeb Stuart and Steven E. de Souza; Original Novel by Roderick Thorp)

6) *The Shawshank Redemption* (Frank Darabont; Original Short Story by Stephen King)

7) *Pulp Fiction* (Quentin Tarantino)

8) *Se7en* (Andrew Kevin Walker)

9) *Fargo* (Ethan Coen & Joel Coen)

10) *Boogie Nights* (Paul Thomas Anderson)

11) *There's Something About Mary* (Ed Decter & John Strauss, and Peter Farrelly & Bobby Farrelly)

12) *The Sixth Sense* (M. Night Shyamalan)

13) *Election* (Alexander Payne & Jim Taylor)

14) *School of Rock* (Mike White)

15) *Mean Girls* (Tina Fey; Based on the Book by Rosalind Wiseman)

16) *The 40-Year-Old Virgin* (Judd Apatow & Steve Carell)

17) *Moneyball* (Steven Zaillian and Aaron Sorkin; Story by Stan Chervin; Based on the Book by Michael Lewis)

18) *Whiplash* (Damien Chazelle)

19) *Spotlight* (Josh Singer and Tom McCarthy)

Always pay attention to writing credits to make sure you understand the industry. Movies can have various writers credited on the production draft. If names are separated by an "&", it means those writers worked together as a writing team. If names are separated by "and", it means they worked on the screenplay separately on different drafts, but both contributed enough to the final product to receive a full credit.

Many additional writers could have worked on the screenplay but did not contribute enough to the final product to get credited.

Try to also get access to unproduced screenplays from other beginner and up-and-coming writers. Some of these screenplays will be very difficult to get through but trust me when I say the things that make you want to throw the screenplay across the room in anger will appear in our own screenplays. We need to read them in other people's work to give us the best chance of avoiding them ourselves.

4.

What Screenwriting Books Should We Read?

Other than mine? None! They're all terrible.

Not true, of course. There are some fantastic books on all aspects of screenwriting, and they each add something different to our journey.

This book is not designed to replace or overtake the message from any other source, but rather, to accompany you along the whole journey. Therefore, I will point you towards the best books at each stage.

That being said, I would not recommend reading any of the more famous "how-to" manuals *right now*. Books such as *Story* by Robert McKee, and *Screenplay* by Syd Field, and many others like them, are written by truly talented teachers and writers, but in my experience, their advice is much more useful once you have completed and rewritten *at least* one screenplay.

Let's say you wanted to build a car. A *great* car. But, you're building it from scratch, and you've never built a car before.

All you have to help you are owner's manuals from some of the best cars on the planet. You've got one for a Corvette, one for a Range Rover, and one for a Rolls Royce. Three very different cars, all of them wonderful and successful in their own way.

So, you read the owner's manuals for these three great cars, and then you try and build your own—with none of the hundreds of years of expertise and experience that went into the development of each of these cars. How useful would those owner's manuals be? Could they actually be more of a hindrance?

I bet you would get frustrated very quickly as you tried—and failed—to recreate the suspension of a Corvette. Eventually, you would throw those manuals away and just try and do it on your own.

That's what many screenwriting books are. They are owner's manuals for great cars. Cars we couldn't possibly build our first time out.

Although I am going to suggest lots of tools and tricks in this first section, they are all designed to get us writing, rather than trying to create some grand vision of perfection—which we are unlikely to achieve with our first screenplay, no matter how many books we read.

Once we have a finished screenplay in hand, we can come back to those manuals, and they will make much more sense, as we compare them to what we actually created.

If I really cannot stop you from reading one of the famous books, then the one I would point you to read first is *Save the Cat,* by Blake Snyder. The reason I would suggest it over the other popular writing manuals is that it looks at the wider picture of screenplays and genres, rather than the nitty-gritty of writing. It is inspirational (and fun) on many levels.

Don't worry; I will definitely recommend all the other books you've heard of when the time is right.

5.

When Do We Write?

Our writing habits will develop over the first few years of our journey, but there are some core principles that can be useful for us all:

1) Write every day

Writing must become a habit as ingrained as brushing our teeth or eating. It must become "what we do." Not "what we do *when we have time*," or "what we do *when inspiration strikes.*"

This is very smug advice from somebody who once went more than four months without writing a word, while still telling everyone I was a writer, but remember: I am here to help you avoid the mistakes I made, not allow you to suffer the same fate.

I know you have a myriad of other things in your life. You need to make a living, and maybe also have a family and children, and all those things take up time. But if you are even *remotely* serious about becoming a screenwriter, then get used to saying, "I'm just going to do some writing," at the most inopportune moments. Before breakfast, during a break at work, while sitting in the park with friends, immediately after sex—these are all perfectly good times to grab your computer, fire up Final Draft, *and write something.*

How much do we have to write? That's the beauty of it—not very much. It would be great if we could write 2000 words a day. That means we would finish a draft of a full screenplay in 10-15 days. What a great world that would be! But, it's simply not practical for most of us.

Let's set ourselves a much more manageable goal. How much do we have to write? Something. *Anything.* I don't care how much it is. What's important is that you—and everyone else in your life—gets used to the fact that you are now a writer, and it is as important as anything else that previously took up your time.

> **Writing must become as natural and regular to a screenwriter as cooking is to a world-class chef.**

2) Involve your friends and family

If we can, we should get the people around us involved in our writing. It will make it much easier when we need to end a dinner early or cancel a lunch because we choose to do some writing instead.

My wife is a very creative person, but not a writer. She is very supportive of my writing, but it feels like a different part of my life than that which I share with her so, wherever possible, I will try to involve her.

When we are out to dinner we play the "movie name game." The rules are simple. We each think of a word, choosing beforehand who will be the first word or second word. Then, on the count of 3, we shout out our words in sequence to create a movie title. If what comes out sounds like a potential movie, we try to think through a possible plot to the movie that matches the name. If what comes out is gibberish, then we move on and play again. Two spec screenplays I have written have come from the "movie name game."

Secondly, she proofreads all my screenplays for me. She is a much more detail-oriented and fastidious person than I am, and she attacks my screenplays with gusto and a red pen, marking spelling and grammatical errors, as well as offering simple rewrites to make my prose easier to read. If nothing else, it allows our partners and friends to see what resulted from all the times we have disappeared off to write.

Writing "every day" doesn't mean 365 days a year. Firstly, we are allowed weekends off. This is a job, and, like every other job, we will get burned out pretty quickly if we never have a day off. However, "weekends" doesn't necessarily mean Saturday and Sunday; it means we choose two days a week that fit our schedule and can become our non-writing days. This may be Monday and Tuesday, or Wednesday and Saturday. Whatever it is, we are allowed to *not* write on those two days. It does not mean we should actively avoid writing on those days; it just means if we do skip them, we are still on schedule and should feel no shame or embarrassment.

Also, like a diet, we are allowed a "cheat day" once a week. On a random day, we can skip writing altogether: Maybe because we're hung over, or because we have to visit the in-laws, or because we want to spend the night watching movies. However, if we don't write on the second day, then we are no longer "cheating," we are just not writing, and so, we are no longer a writer.

We will justify it, of course: We're just planning our next act; we've got a busy weekend, and we'll pick up again on Monday. But, two days becomes five, and five becomes a couple of weeks, and then we can't even remember exactly where we were in the screenplay. Going back to it seems intimidating, and frankly, it's so much easier *not* to write, so maybe we'll just take a break and come back in a few weeks. Then, we'll get back to working really hard every day.

You're lying to yourself!

Remember, all we need to do to truthfully answer the question "Are we writing every day?" is write one word in our screenplay. One word! That's it. We have no excuse not to write one word. Even drunk, coming home from a friend's birthday party, before we spill coffee everywhere and send a drunken text to an ex, we can open the computer and write one word! If we write one word, the screenplay grows. Not much, but it grows, and we have kept to our habit.

3) Always move forward

At some point (or every day) we will be inclined to sit down and edit what we've already written, rather than write anything new.

This may seem like a perfectly reasonable idea on the surface. Why shouldn't we improve what we've already written? We're going to do it sometime, right? The problem is that it is all too easy to fall into "rewrite paralysis." Every time we go back and edit what we have already written we are stopping ourselves from progressing. We will continually edit the first 15 pages. So, instead of having a full screenplay, and the chance to rewrite it into something wonderful, we have 15 pages of a screenplay that is slightly improved from the first draft we wrote.

I wouldn't even suggest reading what you've written before. Just sit down at your computer, move the cursor to the last thing you wrote, and start writing.

If you do have to go back and read (which you will, of course), don't start fixing it in any way. Not even spelling errors. They'll still be there when we come back to rewrite it properly; I assure you. We are not going to show this version to anybody. Leave the mistakes, get back to the bottom of the screenplay, and keep writing. It is the only way we will ever finish.

4) Find the right environment

This is very personal to every writer. The places I find most conducive for working are the main reading room of the NY Public Library, and at the desk in my bedroom, when my wife is sleeping next to me.

I am a night writer. The most productive hours for writing are 10 PM-2 AM. If I never had anything booked into my calendar before 11 AM, then these are the writing hours I would keep every single day of my life. Unfortunately, again, life doesn't work like that.

Time and place are something with which you should experiment to find what works best for you. Ron Bass, the Oscar-winning writer of *Rain Man* (Ron Bass and Barry Morrow; Story by Barry Morrow), started his screenwriting career while still working as a corporate lawyer. He would write before breakfast and while sitting on planes.

If you like listening to music while you write, do it. If you enjoy total silence, then hide in the basement. Write outside; write in the attic; I don't care—just find somewhere and some time you enjoy writing.

5) Be in control of your faculties

Is it possible to write something wonderful while drunk, high, or hallucinating? Sure, why not? Artists who enjoyed various legal and illegal substances as they worked have created great works of art in all fields. I'm making no moral judgment on this, but from a purely craft-oriented standpoint, writing while under the influence of any drug (including alcohol) has the potential to negatively affect our work. At the moment of creation, it might feel like we just bested Tolstoy in our writing—just as many a drunk person has decided, in their inebriated state, that alcohol has, in fact, made them a *better* driver—but it's not true.

Let's *become* an artistic genius before we start *acting* like an artistic genius. The best way to be sure of the quality of what we are writing is to be completely in control of our faculties as we write.

***

An excellent book I recommend reading on this topic is *The 101 Habits of Highly Successful Screenwriters* by Karl Iglesias. Interesting and useful to read now, it is something that we should come back to and read every six months for the first few years of our journey. Each time, you will discover some wonderful new nugget from the interviews with working writers about their method, or the choices they've made that worked/failed.

6.

Should We Write with A Partner?

If you need an answer to this question because you *don't* have a writing partner, then you should not seek one out.

Writing partnerships should grow naturally. You can't force two people to write together effectively. It only works if two people form a relationship. They don't need to be best friends, but they must love and admire the same types of movies, and both have a similar desire and work ethic to write those kinds of movies together.

If we find such a relationship, then writing with a partner can be a wonderful thing. I have never written feature scripts with a partner, but I did have a writing partner when I wrote sitcoms for television. In fact, our partnership joined forces with two other writing groups in a setup similar to Monty Python, and we created a TV pilot, which was optioned by a major production company and a television network.

When a partnership works, it offers all sorts of huge advantages. We have someone to share the workload. We have someone to commiserate with when things go wrong. We have at least one person in the world who truly understands how hard we are working. We have someone to laugh with, bounce ideas off of, get excited with, and share a glass of champagne with when something wonderful happens. We have people who can tell us when ideas aren't working. This makes rewriting *way* more effective. Those are all terrific things.

On the other hand, if we are even slightly unsuited to one another, if our ideas about what's good and what's not are misaligned, if one of us naturally writes 5,000 words a week, while the other struggles to put out 500, or if one of us is too honest, and the other one will never criticize, then the partnership is most likely doomed to fail. On some occasions, we are lucky enough to find a partner who fills in our missing pieces. We may work very differently from each other, but we can complement each other perfectly. One of us is good at coming up with ideas but terrible at structuring those ideas. The other is a genius at structure but can't find a good idea to save their life. Or, one of us is fantastic at dialogue but terrible at action, while the other's action is dynamite, but their characters all sound the same. One of us is a born salesman, and the other enjoys writing 24 hours a day. If we truly find someone who fills in our missing pieces, then we might have found gold.

Give it a go but understand that most partnerships won't work. It is a wonderful and joyous accident. It is not something we can ever *expect* to happen.

(Plus, we have to split our fee 50/50. Studios don't pay twice the money just because we enjoy writing as a pair, so we'd better be damn sure writing with this person is worth it!)

Stage 2:
Our First Screenplay

7.

How Do We Start our First Screenplay?

Don't skip this chapter, even if you have already completed your first screenplay. That experience will have taught you a lot, but there is always something useful in revisiting our early experiences and reminding ourselves of our key learnings.

So, how do we start? The best thing to do with our first screenplay is just jump in and start. We can be prone to using "learning" about screenwriting as a good tool to put off the business of actually writing.

Our goal with our first screenplay is not to write something as good as *The Grand Budapest Hotel* (Story by Wes Anderson & Hugo Guinness; Screenplay by Wes Anderson). We're not going to, so it's simply a fool's errand to try. All we are aiming to achieve is getting a story down on paper in a recognizable and readable screenplay format. That's it. If we set that goal for ourselves, then the chances of succeeding are very good.

I have met new writers who have spent up to five years "planning" their first screenplay. Oh, the research they're doing! The studying! The books they're reading! Boy, when this screenplay gets written, the whole world is going to stop and take notice. "Who is this great talent?" they will say. "Where has his genius been hiding?"

In reality, their screenplay is never going to get written. Even if it does, I guarantee it will be the same cliché-ridden, hammy-dialogued, plot-hole-filled mess the rest of us write the first time out.

We have so much to learn at this stage, but the best way to learn is to get on and do it. Is research useful? Of course. Does studying our craft make us better? Absolutely! But, none of that will teach us as much as putting finger to keyboard and crafting a screenplay from beginning to end.

Let's switch this up and make it about sports for a moment.

Let's say we wanted to become a professional golfer. Would we refuse to go out onto the course until we had spent years reading books about golf?

Studying the world's great swings? Watching videos of the masters? No. We'd pick up a club and get swinging. We'd be terrible, but if we stuck to our goal, we would get better and better, and we'd keep going until we were the best in our club, and then we'd try out for the PGA, and at first, everyone else would be better than us, but we'd keep practicing, playing, and studying, and we'd get better—*and we'd be playing golf the whole time!*

Is everyone's first screenplay terrible? Yes, to some degree. Some people are more natural storytellers, just as some people are more natural athletes.

My father used to play golf with a lovely guy called Owen. The first time Owen ever picked up a golf club he shot a round of five over par. For anyone who has ever hacked away at a golf course day after day, only to have their handicap plateau at 24, this is the most depressing concept in the world.

However, after a lifetime of playing, Owen's handicap was still a 5. He never got any better. He was born a natural five-handicap player and didn't care to improve. But, other people who were terrible the first time they played got better. They practiced; they learned; they challenged themselves to improve, and those are the people who became professionals and now make millions on the PGA tour.

This is exactly the same for screenwriting. We do not sit down and write *Being John Malkovich* (Charlie Kaufman). It is just as unlikely and unrealistic as picking up a golf club and beating Tiger Woods.

There are exceptions to any rule. If you hunt hard enough, you will find someone who sold their first-ever screenplay, but their journey and level of success has nothing to do with our own. We are seeking our own accomplishments on our own journey. For most of us, this is hard.

Lawrence Kasdan was 30 years old when a screenplay he wrote was finally released. That film was *Star Wars Episode V: The Empire Strikes Back*. The year after that, *Raiders of the Lost Ark* was released as his second credited movie (I believe he was actually hired to write *Raiders* first and got *Star Wars* off the back of his phenomenal script). That's not a bad couple of years. Did he just turn up in Hollywood and say, "Hi, can I write your sequel to the most successful movie in history, please?" No. He turned up, wrote and wrote, and pitched screenplays to anyone he could find, until someone recognized his genius and hired him to write the sequel to the most successful movie in history.

To become a screenwriter, we must always be writing. We are not going to care how good our first screenplay is, compared to all the other first screenplays in the world, because there will always be an Owen. There will always be someone whose first screenplay is lightyears ahead of their counterparts. That person might even be us, but we still don't care, because we are still nowhere near our goal. A first screenplay that is better than all the other first screenplays is still a massive way behind the best screenplays that are written each year, and that's what we are striving to achieve.

Successful writers don't just talk about writing; they write. Constantly.

Therefore, what do we need to get started? Very little, actually: An idea and some writing software.

The industry-standard writing software is Final Draft. Available from www.finaldraft.com it will cost you around $250. It is user-friendly and has all the formatting built in so that there is nothing to learn and very little to get wrong.

$250 is still a fair chunk of money, though, and our journey should not necessarily be an expensive one at this stage, so thanks to some very lovely people who believe resources should be free, you also have Celtx at www.celtx.com.

This has developed over the years from a free writing software program to a full suite of paid-for production tools, but the writing software is still free to download and does the same job as Final Draft. Therefore, for a few minutes of downloading and no money down, we have all the tools we need to start writing.

If you haven't done this yet, go and do it now, and then come back.

Done it? Good. Now, we need to decide what to write about. Let's not make our first day too difficult. Let's keep it really simple. All we need right now is to choose a genre. There is usually a genre of movies we love.

The following is an exchange I have been a part of more than once:

```
INT. CONFERENCE ROOM — DAY

Hywel stands with a WRITER, (23).

                    HYWEL
          So, what is your screenplay?

                    WRITER
          It's a low-budget horror.
```

> HYWEL
>
> Okay. Great. What's your favorite horror movie?

> WRITER
>
> Er... Well, I'm not really a horror fan, to be honest, but horror is really in right now, and I know that studios are looking for the next *Paranormal Activity*.

> HYWEL
>
> Right, but if you don't really like horror movies, then how do you know if yours is a good one?

> WRITER
>
> Oh, it's a good one; believe me.

I don't believe them. At all. Neither does anyone else.

Write what you love. Write what inspires you. Write what you would enjoy watching. Writing is hard enough as it is; don't make it any harder by writing to impress other people. If *Happy Gilmore* (Tim Herlihy & Adam Sandler) is your favorite movie ever, then write something that would entertain you just as much. If you can't go to sleep without enjoying 20 minutes of a Nicholas Sparks movie, then write a love story that would make you weep for a week. If *Melancholia* (Lars Von Trier) plays on strict rotation in your house, then get strapped in to create the bleak drama to end all bleak dramas.

So, that's it. Choose a genre, and we are done for the day. Well done; we have just started our first screenplay.

8.

What Shouldn't We Write?

This is a quick chapter but potentially a very important one, as I am going to save some of us a lot of time and effort.

We cannot write something that belongs to somebody else. That includes movies based on existing characters, or works we don't own, such as a new idea for a *Batman* movie, or an adaptation of our favorite novel. It's illegal and potentially very costly if the true owner of the work decides to sue us.

However, the main reason is: No one will *ever* read it. The moment a real reader or buyer sees a screenplay based on existing material from a new writer, they will throw it away immediately. There are two key reasons for this:

1) They could get sued for becoming involved with material that has contravened copyright laws. America is a litigious society. No one is going to put themselves in that position.

2) It screams, "Amateur!" It immediately says we don't understand the industry and are, therefore, not worthy of consideration, no matter how much talent we may have. I can't tell you how many writers I have met who have written a *Spiderman* movie, or an *Avengers* movie, and think this will be their ticket in. Sending those scripts to Marvel and expecting them to be read is the equivalent of standing outside the gates to Taylor Swift's mansion and shouting, "Taylor! I've written you a song. If you let me in, I'll let you buy it from me." It's *that* level of amateur.

So, please, don't do it. Until the day Spielberg calls you up and commissions you to write the new *Jurassic Park* movie, just leave other people's characters alone. Show how brilliant your own creations are. That is what will break you in.

9.

What Does A Screenplay Look Like?

Thanks to Final Draft (and Celtx), it is not as necessary as it was in the old days to teach screenplay format. Anything that Final Draft does not do for us, we'll learn by reading as many screenplays as we can. For now, let's just look at anything we really *need* to know.

Firstly, the font for *all* screenplays—and I mean *all*—is Courier 12pt. Our screenplay will not *stand out* if it's written in a different font. Instead, our screenplay will be *thrown out* if it's written in a different font.

Also, the format for a spec screenplay is slightly different from production screenplays. Remember, the production screenplay is the blueprint for everyone: Sound, lighting, makeup, continuity, actors, director. It needs to have everything that each department requires to do their job.

A spec screenplay is different. It just needs to tell the story for the reader. It needs to look like a screenplay but can be a lot more stripped down, in terms of the elements within it, to tell the story as succinctly as possible. People don't want or need to be bogged down with technical details at this stage.

That means we will not include scene numbers, camera moves, lighting requirements, editing techniques, a particular piece of music, or even the type of music we envisage. We are just there to get people gripped by the story.

Therefore, scene headings (or slug lines) should be as short and functional as possible:

INT. MUSEUM — DAY

That's absolutely fine. Nothing more is needed.

Similarly, action description should be punchy and succinct, with lots of short sentences and small paragraphs. Create some white space. It makes the screenplay much nicer to look at and much easier to read.

                        WRITER
            Why is that so important?

                        HYWEL
            Because when you have many
            screenplays to read, opening a
            screenplay and finding a full
            page of thick, black action
            description can be very
            overwhelming, and a good reason
            to put the screenplay to the
            bottom of the pile.

Action is *always* written in the present tense. For example:

Dave jumps over the desk.

Not:

Dave jumped over the desk.

Past tense is for novels.

It is also written with the active verb formation. For example:

Dave pats the dog.

Not:

Dave is patting the dog.

No verbs ending in "ing". Find the more active way to describe it.

If you are ever confused about how something should be formatted, then think of a film that does the same thing, track down the screenplay, and see how that writer formatted it.

If you want to study this in more detail, then I would suggest *The Hollywood Standard: The Complete and Authoritative Guide to Script Format and Style* by Christopher Riley.

We will look at dialogue in much more detail later, so I'm not going to cover it now. It's not important until we create some characters and get them talking. So, let's do that. Let's create our story.

10.

What is a Story?

Let's all get on the same page about one thing right now: Spec screenplays are about story and structure. They are not about spectacle; they are not about special effects; they are not about explosions or even snappy dialogue. Spec screenplays truly do their job when their stories work.

Modern movies make money for all sorts of reasons. There will always be movies that happily replace story with spectacle and see huge financial returns—even though most viewers would be unable to recall the actual story a week later. But here is why I bring it up:

We don't have that luxury.

Transformers: Dark of the Moon made over $1B worldwide. If we handed in an original screenplay that had just as much logic and structure to its story, the reader of our screenplay wouldn't get past Page 30. The success of such movies is based on brand recognition, savvy marketing, and a generation of 16-24 year olds who have become used to the following exchange as they leave the theater:

EXT. MOVIE THEATER — NIGHT

Two TEENAGERS walk out to the car park.

                  TEENAGER #1
     Wow. That movie was awesome.

                  TEENAGER #2
     Yeah.

                  TEENAGER #1
     I didn't really understand what
     was going on, though.

```
                      TEENAGER #2
          No, me neither, but the effects
          were amazing.
```

You can sell a movie to a teenager that doesn't make any sense, but you can't sell a screenplay to a studio that doesn't make any sense.

Our story must be bulletproof, because only writers who can write bulletproof stories will get hired. After that, our bulletproof script will be changed by everyone else into something that may or may not be terrible.

Back to our chapter title, then. What is a story? This topic is potentially vast, and many great books have been written just to answer this one question. The most justifiably famous book currently is *Story* by Robert McKee, a screenwriting guru so ingrained in the current writer's landscape that he appears as himself (although played by Brian Cox) in *Adaptation* (Charlie Kaufman). If that description confuses you (and I hope it does), it is one of the many reasons Kaufman's writing—and *Adaptation* specifically—are so wonderful.

I believe the reading of McKee's book should be made mandatory for anyone who wants to be a screenwriter, but as mentioned earlier, I would not suggest you read it just yet. It is an extraordinary book, but it covers the topic in such depth that it can be overwhelming for new writers.

I will bring us back to McKee's opus later on. For now, I want to start with a much simpler definition:

A story: We meet a person (or persons). Something happens to them, which forces them to accomplish something, but obstacles keep getting in the way.

That's it. Think of any great movie, and I promise the plot will fit this paradigm. Let's look at five screenplays from different genres and decades:

1970s—*Jaws*

A person: Sheriff Brody

What happens to them: A shark attack on his beach on July 4th weekend.

What they need to accomplish: Kill the shark and save the town.

The obstacles the face: The mayor makes promises Brody can't keep, and they reopen the beaches. The shark attacks again. This time, Brody feels responsible. Undertrained fisherman are trying to kill it, but end up causing more problems. Brody doesn't know anything about sharks. A real shark hunter exists, but he wants $10K. Brody has to go along on the hunt, but he hates water. The outside help he brings in doesn't get along with the shark hunter; it's old-school vs. new-school fishing. When they finally find it, they realize that this shark is HUGE, and now the shark is hunting *them*. The shark hunter starts to go crazy, and a member of their party gets lost at sea. The shark starts to win and smashes their boat, eating the shark hunter in the process. Brody is left alone on a sinking boat with the shark getting ever closer.

1980s—*Die Hard*

A person: John McClane

What happens to them: His wife is taken hostage by terrorists. (I know, they're thieves, really—but terrorists, for all intents and purposes.)

What they need to accomplish: John must save his wife.

The obstacles they face: John is alone in a locked-down building, facing off against 30 terrorists. He can't call the police, and when he does, the police don't believe him. John has no shoes and no resources, while the terrorists are smart and well-funded. The terrorists nearly catch him. To escape, he must jump down a thousand-foot-tall air vent. The police finally arrive but think John is either lying or one of the terrorists. One of his wife's co-workers pretends to be John's friend and gets himself killed. The police blame John. John encounters one of the terrorists, and they realize he has no shoes on, so they cover the floor of the building in glass. The terrorists try to blow up the roof with the hostages on it. John gets shot at by the FBI and has to jump off a 60-story building attached to a fire hose. The terrorists work out who his wife is and use her as leverage against him. John has to give himself up to save her.

1990s—*Reservoir Dogs* (Quentin Tarantino)

A person: An undercover cop, Freddy/Mr. Orange. (I know it's a multi-protagonist story, but Mr. Orange is our star.)

What happens to them: He infiltrates a gang of thieves, who are about to pull off a jewelry heist.

What they need to accomplish: Go through with the robbery, and then take down their bosses, Nice Guy Eddie and Joe Cabot.

The obstacles they face: The robbery goes wrong. Mr. Blonde starts shooting everyone. A gunfight erupts, and the gang escapes. Mr. Orange has to leave with Mr. White to keep his cover. Some of the gang die during the robbery. Mr. Orange tries to steal a car and gets shot in the stomach, then he kills the driver on instinct. Joe and Nice Guy Eddie have not arrived on schedule. Mr. Orange begs to be taken to a hospital, where he knows he will be safe, but he still can't reveal his true identity, so the others refuse. Mr. Blonde has kidnapped a cop to torture, but Mr. Orange can't stop them without giving himself away. The rest of the gang start to turn on each other. No one knows who they can trust. Mr. Orange shoots Mr. Blonde to stop him from killing the cop. When Joe and Nice Guy Eddie finally arrive, they accuse Mr. Orange of being a cop. Mr. White defends him, and the situation becomes a standoff, with everyone holding guns on each other.

2000s—*The 40-Year-Old Virgin* (Judd Apatow & Steve Carell)

A person: Andy, a 40-year-old virgin

What happens to them: His work colleagues find out his terrible secret.

What they need to accomplish: He must get laid.

The obstacles they face: Andy doesn't know how to talk to women. He is terrified of sex. He doesn't even know how to put on a condom. His friends keep pushing him into it. They set him up with very inappropriate women. He can't drive. He tries to make himself more handsome but fails miserably. He meets a woman he really likes, Trish, but is scared to tell her the truth. Trish's daughter finds out he's a virgin. Trish wants to have sex with him, but he is scared and tries to avoid it. His refusal to have sex with Trish leads to her breaking up with him. Upon finding a stash of porn a friend gave him, she assumes he is some sort of sex pervert.

2010s—*The Lego Movie* (Screenplay by Phil Lord & Christopher Miller; Story by Dan Hageman & Kevin Hageman, and Phil Lord & Christopher Miller)

A person: Emmet

What happens to them: Accidentally gets stuck to the "piece of resistance."

What they need to accomplish: Must fulfill the prophecy of the Special and place the "piece of resistance" on the Kragle and save the whole of Lego-kind from Lord Business.

The obstacles they face: He is not really the Special. He is not a master builder. He doesn't even know what a master builder is. He's a nothing person with no outstanding qualities whatsoever. Even his co-workers barely remember him. Bad Cop is tracking him through the worlds. No one wants to listen to him or his ideas. Lord Business is engaging his plan to unleash the Kragle and glue everyone in place so that people stop messing with his stuff. He doesn't realize he has been tagged with a tracker and leads Bad Cop right to Cloud Cuckoo Land and all the remaining master builders. All the master builders are captured. When he does finally come up with plan, it fails, and everyone is captured inside the Octan Corporation. It turns out the prophecy is a lie. Emmet is captured and held by the open window at the top of the Octan Tower.

***

There you go. Five movies from different decades with very different genres, tones, stories, and characters, but each one following a similar structure.

Are there exceptions? There are screenplays and screenwriters who are so adept at their craft, they can create what seem like much more complicated and surprising stories—but at their core, they are no different. They are just created by people who understand the rules enough to break them.

There are many more nuances to great stories of course, like subtext, subplots, antagonists, and internal flaws—all of which we will come to. Remember: This is just to get us started.

What didn't we cover here, though? We didn't cover the endings, of course. All the story descriptions above end at the worst possible time: The pinnacle of the hero's troubles. Sheriff Brody sits on the bow of a sinking ship, as the shark tries to eat him. John McClane, bloodied battered, and out of ammo, with his feet torn to shreds, walks out to give himself up. Mr. White, Nice Guy Eddie, Mr. Orange, and Joe are in a Mexican standoff. Andy watches Trish run out of his apartment—and out of his life—forever. Emmet wakes up in the void (i.e., the basement).

So, why wasn't the ending included in the description? Because the ending is dictated by the events that led up to it.

When the shark appears on Sheriff Brody's beach, we know Sheriff Brody is going to kill the shark. When John McClane's wife is captured by terrorists, we know John McClane is going to rescue her (and probably kill all the terrorists in the process). When Mr. Orange becomes part of a gang that survives on loyalty, and he then betrays that loyalty, we know he (and the gang) are going to get their comeuppance, in one form or another. When Andy is discovered to be a virgin, we know he's going to lose his virginity. When Emmet finds out he has accomplished nothing in life and is given the chance to be the Special, we know he is going to rise to the challenge, defeat Lord Business, and save everyone… somehow.

These are not clichéd endings. These are the endings to the stories being told. We are not shocked when it ends that way. We are *satisfied* it ends that way.

For the best explanation of endings, we must go back to the master, William Goldman, who explains, *"Give the audience the ending they always expected on a route they couldn't possibly have imagined."*

30 minutes into the some of the greatest movies ever made, you could stop the projector, turn to the audience, and say, "How is this going to end?", and most of the time, the audience would be absolutely on the money. Do we really think Andy and Trish aren't going to end up together? No. *How and why* they end up together is the important element. What obstacles do they overcome to make that happen? *That's* the story we want to watch.

Imagine a different version of *Die Hard*: Hans Gruber turns up and kidnaps John McClane's wife and the other hostages. John is left alone in the building. He realizes he is outgunned but for 60 minutes, he kills off Gruber's men, one by one, taunting Hans all the time on the walkie-talkies. John even starts to get the upper hand and gets hold of Hans's detonators.

Then, 90 minutes in, Hans realizes Holly Genarro is John McClane's wife, so he holds her hostage and orders John to come out. John doesn't, so Hans shoots Holly. John is devastated. He hides in a bathroom, while the thieves take their money. Some of the gang are killed by the FBI, but Hans gets away with most of the $650M in negotiable bearer bonds. John comes out and goes home to his kids to explain their mother is dead. The end.

How do you feel walking out of that theater? Confused? Let down? Angry? Empty inside? Of course, you do. It's a surprising ending; I'll give you that, and no way would I have predicted it, but that's because that ending has nothing to do with the story we were watching. The story was about a man who had put his job before his marriage. Therefore, the story we are watching ends when he puts his wife before everything else and saves her.

Does that mean all stories have to have happy endings? No, we know that's not true. A famous example that is justifiably cited is *Se7en*. Detective Mills' wife is dead, along with his unborn child inside her. Mills fulfills John Doe's terrible prediction, and, in doing so, guarantees himself life in prison. A famously "down" ending in the sense that everyone didn't walk away smiling into the sunset. *However,* Mills and Somerset caught John Doe, and that is the important element of a mystery: The perpetrator is identified and caught. Had Somerset just retired without solving the case, and Mills took over, and then the murders stopped one day, and no one ever found out who did it—*that* would be a "down" ending.

The extra element required from *Se7en* was for all seven deadly sins to be played out. It's right there in the title, and we got it. *Se7en* is the living embodiment of the ending we always wanted, on a route we couldn't possibly have imagined. We needed the final deadly sin, or we couldn't leave the theater. But, no one saw the head in the box coming. It's an astonishing piece of writing that shocks, surprises, excites, and satisfies—all at the same time.

So, let's go back to our definition once more and complete it.

A Story: We meet a person (or persons). Something happens to them, which forces them to accomplish something, but obstacles keep getting in the way. *They find ways to overcome these obstacles and achieve their goal.*

The breadth of ways we can bring this definition to life is what makes storytelling so wonderful, but this definition is true of all the greatest stories that have ever been told.

Truly great storytellers make it hard to see this structure, but when we go looking hard enough, we realize it's still there; it's just dressed up in a way we've never seen before.

11.

How Do We Create Our Story?

"Learning by doing" doesn't mean we are going to sit down and start writing randomly. It is important to have certain elements in place before we begin. We want to know whom our story is about, and our basic structure. Anything less, and I can guarantee we will write 5-10 pages and stop, realizing we have no idea where we are going.

We want to keep it simple at this stage and plan out a simple story that makes sense.

Don't worry about writing something as nuanced and genre-busting as *Se7en* right now. That was not Andrew Kevin Walker's first screenplay; it was just the screenplay that got him justifiably noticed by Hollywood. For now, we are going to create a story that we like and that excites us.

Let's remind ourselves of our story definition:

A Story: We meet a person (or persons). Something happens to them, which forces them to accomplish something, but obstacles keep getting in the way. They find ways to overcome these obstacles and achieve their goal.

There is no one way to create a story. Experiment and find what works for you, but until you have something better, please feel free to use *The Screenwriter's Journey* story questions to help create the basic structure for any story.

These can be downloaded in an editable PDF format at my website: www.screenwritingjourney.com

The questions are:

1) Who is the story about? (i.e., our protagonist)
2) What is their flaw or flaws? (i.e., What needs fixing?)
3) What happens to them that changes their life for better or worse?
4) What must they now achieve? (i.e., their goal)
5) What could get in the way of that goal? (Write down as many things as you can think of.)
6) What's the worst thing that could happen to the protagonist?

7) How must this story end?

8) What must the protagonist do to achieve that ending?

That's it. With these eight questions, we have the basic elements of any story. It gives us our protagonist, as well as our beginning, middle, and end.

Let's look at what each question does for us:

1) Who is the story about?

This is our protagonist, or "hero."

Every story needs a protagonist. Most movies have a single protagonist who drives the action. However, we can have dual protagonists. Romantic comedies are nearly always dual-protagonist stories, as we are watching two people falling in love, and thus, following both of their stories. Alternatively, we can have multiple protagonists, such as those in *Pulp Fiction* (Quentin Tarantino), *Love Actually* (Richard Curtis), and *Ocean's 11* (Ted Griffin, based on the 1960 movie by many other writers). Although, even in true multi-protagonist movies, there is usually one character who holds just that little more of the screen time and weight of the story. In *Pulp Fiction,* it is Vincent Vega; in *Love Actually,* it is Hugh Grant as the Prime Minister; and in *Ocean's 11,* it is Danny Ocean. His name is in the title, and although we follow legitimate stories of many of the gang, it is still Danny who primarily drives the story and the resolution.

Active vs. Passive Protagonist

Our protagonist must make their story happen. Things can't happen *to the protagonist*. They must happen *because of the protagonist.*

I have read many scripts by new writers that rely on event after event happening *to* the protagonist, leaving them as nothing more than empty vessels being pushed around by the supporting characters.

We can *start* a story on a coincidence. In fact, many stories are started this way. But, the moment the protagonist is aware of their situation they must start to make active, deliberate decisions that move the story forward. They must be in charge of their destiny.

2) What is their flaw?

Every protagonist needs a flaw (or flaws) that will be fixed by the end of the story. Again, this is not hackneyed writing; this is storytelling. It can come across as hackneyed if we make it too obvious or just cram it in for the sake of it, but it is the protagonist's flaws that make them interesting. It is the reason we are watching their story. If they are perfect and have no flaws and nothing to learn, then why should we give them two hours of our time?

To illustrate this, let's look at some movies that have very likeable protagonists and analyze their flaws.

In *The Wizard of Oz*, (Noel Langley & Florence Ryerson, and Edgar Allen Woolf), Dorothy is one of the sweetest girls in the world and good at heart. She is a "good" character, but she is complacent about her boring Kansas home life. She doesn't appreciate what she has. This is her flaw, and it will be fixed by the end of the movie, when she clicks her heels together and states the theme of the movie: *"There's no place like home."*

Similarly, in *It's a Wonderful Life* (Frances Goodrich, Albert Hackett, and Frank Capra), George Bailey puts everyone and everything ahead of his own needs. He gives up on his travels to save the family business, gives up his honeymoon to help the townsfolk, marries his childhood sweetheart, treats her well, and loves his kids. So, what's his flaw? His flaw is he thinks he has settled and achieved nothing in his life. He thinks the town is beneath him, and he deserves something more. As the phenomenal resolution plays out, he finally realizes how much his life has achieved for others and just how valuable his life has been. His small town is where he belongs. He does, indeed, have a wonderful life.

For the ultimate in likeable protagonists, let's go to everyone's favorite everyman—Tom Hanks. As Sam Baldwin in *Sleepless in Seattle* (Nora Ephron & Delia Ephron, and David S. Ward) Sam is the greatest guy in the world. He's a successful architect, he has raised a great kid whom he loves completely, and he has wonderful friends who care about him. His flaw? Because of the recent passing of his wife, he no longer believes in true love. This is what will be fixed when he meets Meg Ryan on the top of the Empire State building.

The flaw has to have *something* to do with the rest of the story, because it's going to be fixed *by* the story. In *Liar, Liar* (Paul Guay & Stephen Mazur), Fletcher Reid's flaws are dishonesty and being a bad father. His son wishes for him to be unable to tell a lie for 24 hours, which is going to teach Fletcher two things: How to do things honestly, *and* how much he loves his son. If Fletcher Reid's flaws were gambling addiction and being a bad father, then it would have felt much more contrived (and a bit weird) to try and fix both problems during the movie, because the gambling problem would seem unconnected to what is happening.

Find the flaws that fit the story.

3) What happens to them that changes their life for better or worse?

This is the start of the protagonist's story. Until this thing happens, the protagonist's life is ticking along as normal. This is the moment that makes their life significantly better or worse. You may have heard this moment referred to as "the inciting incident."

In *Monsters, Inc.* (Andrew Stanton, Daniel Gerson; Original Story by Peter Doctor, Jill Culton, Jeff Pidgeon, Ralph Eggleston), as in all Pixar movies, the setting and the world are impeccably created, but the fantastic idea of monsters scaring children to generate power is not a story. James P. Sullivan's story doesn't begin until Boo, a deadly child, escapes through her door and into Sullivan's life. Now he has a problem to fix.

In *Pitch Perfect* (Kay Cannon, Based on the Book by Mickey Rapkin), Beca would have avoided the *a capella* groups forever—until her father makes her a deal: Join in and try to make friends, and if it doesn't work out, then he will pay for her to go to Los Angeles and work in the recording industry. Against her better judgment, she joins the one group she has had any contact with: The Barden Bellas. As far as she is concerned, this makes her life worse, and thus, this starts her story.

In *Pretty Woman* (JF Lawton), Vivian stands on her usual spot on Hollywood Boulevard when Edward Lewis stops next to her, lost and unable to drive his European sports car. This moment is about to make her life significantly better and set her on a path she couldn't have imagined.

Drama scripts can sometimes have an inciting incident that is much smaller, in terms of its initial effect on the protagonist.

In *12 Angry Men* (Reginald Rose), all that happens to Henry Fonda's character is he is the only juror who thinks the defendant is not guilty. A small moment, but still one that makes his life worse, even if just for a short time, and enough to start Fonda's story. He must now convince the other 11 jurors that he is right.

In *The Artist* (Michel Hazanavicius), the thing that makes George Valentin's life worse *and* starts his story is the invention of sound in motion pictures. It happens offscreen, and when he learns about it, George laughs it off, believing it to be a fad that doesn't affect him—but we know that's not true. We know his life is changed forever.

So, it may be small, but don't kid yourself; that moment is still there in every great story.

A fatal flaw of many beginner screenplays is they vastly underestimate this element of storytelling, and they have nothing that starts the story. They think stories are all about recreating real life. You meet their protagonist, and then you learn about the world of the protagonist, and then you meet some of their friends and family, and then you see them at work, and then they meet up with some friends for drinks, and then you're 45 pages in, and all you're thinking is: *When is this story going to start? Nothing is happening.* That's not a story. That's just a snapshot of someone's life—and not a very interesting one.

If we don't have something happen that makes the protagonist's life *significantly* better or worse, then we don't have a story.

4) What must they now achieve? (i.e., their goal)

Now that their life has been changed, it will have done one of three things:

1) Created a goal
2) Made a current goal harder
3) Made a current goal easier

Let's look at an example of each.

Created a goal: In *The Bourne Identity* (Tony Gilroy and William Blake Herron), after Jason Bourne is pulled out of the water, unconscious and near-death, he wakes up and has only one goal: To find out who he is, and why he was floating in the sea.

Made a current goal harder: In *The Artist*, George's goal doesn't change. He wants to remain the biggest movie star in Hollywood—but he is the only one who doesn't see how difficult that is now going to be.

Made a current goal easier: In *Bruce Almighty* (Steve Koren & Mark O'Keefe, and Steve Oedekerk), Bruce Nolan already has a goal: He wants to have a materially successful life. When God gives him all His powers, Bruce now has the chance to achieve his goal and get everything he ever wanted.

The goal can change as the story progresses. A goal that might seem immediately desirable to the protagonist may reveal itself to be unappealing later on. Alternatively, our protagonist's desires may change as they grow and develop as a person.

Bruce Nolan wants onscreen success. With God's powers, he gives himself a sexy sports car. He makes his girlfriend's boobs bigger. He makes himself the world's greatest lover, and he tricks his bosses into giving him the promotion he felt he deserved. However, as the story progresses, he discovers such material possessions and successes are irrelevant. His final goal—and the one he achieves at the end—is to build a happy life with his girlfriend and go back to the job he was born to do: A goofy, on-the-spot reporter.

Therefore, although the protagonist's goal may change, to answer this question, we are going to choose what the protagonist's goal is *immediately following* the inciting incident. That's what drives the story forward right now.

5) What could get in the way of that goal?

We are now going to make that goal as difficult as possible, because without obstacles, there is no story.

Let me say that again: *Without obstacles, there is no story.*

In *Speed* (Graham Yost), if all Jack Traven needed to do was find the bus, stop it, and defuse the bomb, then there isn't much of a story. BUT, if the bus can't slow down below 50mph without blowing up, then we have a *huge* obstacle, and a wonderful story.

Drama is created out of conflict. Conflict is created out of obstacles. Therefore, all stories need obstacles.

Weak screenplays have the protagonist doing "stuff." Let's say our hero is a professional football star who has just suffered a career-ending injury. He realizes the only way to maintain his lifestyle is to become a TV football analyst. So, we have 50 pages of him practicing broadcasting techniques with friends and other broadcasters, then creating audition tapes and sending them out to major networks. Finally, ESPN calls him in for an audition. He goes to the audition, and he blows them away and gets the job as their new onscreen analyst.

Is this a story? No. This is just watching someone go through the normal motions of starting a new career in broadcasting. There's no drama here, no obstacle. Instead, what if he was infamous for being the player that never gave interviews? What if he has pissed off, ignored, or even assaulted everyone from the major networks during his time as a player? Now, he has an obstacle to overcome. At every turn, he is now going to find people who are against him, wanting him to fail, and even sabotaging him. Even if, deep down, we know he is going to succeed, we are excited to see *how* he does it.

Therefore, to answer this question, we want to just let our mind go and write down any potential obstacle that pops into our head. We're not going to use all those ideas but better to edit them down later than start writing and realize we don't have enough (or any) obstacles.

In many cases, a person will drive the obstacles. If so, this is our "antagonist." They are the opposite of our hero. They are the person trying to stop the hero from achieving their goal. A simple example is any James Bond movie. James Bond is our hero. His story starts when he is introduced to the latest supervillain (e.g., Blowfeld, Goldfinger, Le Chiffre, etc.), and the details of their dastardly plot to blackmail/blow up the world. The villain is now the antagonist. Our protagonist and antagonist are at complete odds with each other for the rest of the movie—until one of them (Bond) is victorious.

Wherever possible, we want to try and give our antagonist a human face. It makes it more interesting and easier to write. It also creates some of the more memorable movie characters: Hans Gruber and The Sheriff of Nottingham (both Alan Rickman in his first two movie roles), Darth Vader, Freddie Krueger, Annie Wilkes, Dr. Hannibal Lecter, Nurse Ratched, Lex Luthor, Cruella De Vil, Prince Humperdinck, Dr. Evil, Bill Lumbergh, Magneto, Regina George, Mugatu, Lord Voldemort, Loki, The Joker, and Lord Business. All fantastic characters that any actor would relish playing.

However, other things can be the antagonist and the driving force for the obstacles, such as the location itself. The recent YA adaptation of *The Maze Runner* (Noah Oppenheim and Grant Pierce Myers and T.S. Nowlin, Based on the Novel by James Dashner) is a good example of this. The maze is the antagonist. We assume there is someone behind it all, but we never see them. The obstacles the boys must overcome are the maze, and what they find in the maze. We see a similar antagonist in the hotel room in *1408* (Matt Greenberg and Scott Alexander & Larry Karaszewski, Based on the Short Story by Stephen King), or the hotel in *The Shining* (Stanley Kubrick & Diane Johnson, based on the novel by Stephen King). Obviously, Stephen King knows a thing or two about locations as antagonists.

The antagonist could also be the setup. In *Groundhog Day,* there is no one who puts Phil Connors in this situation (other than Phil Connors), but the fact that he will wake up and live Groundhog Day over and over again is what drives the obstacles.

In *When Harry Met Sally*, the antagonist is an idea: Can men and women really be friends without sex getting in the way?

6) What's the worst thing that could happen to the protagonist?

At some point, things must become completely impossible for our protagonist. You will see this moment called different things in different books, but whatever we call it, it is the moment when our protagonist is the furthest from achieving their goal—so it needs to be *really* bad.

We may find this in our list of obstacles from Question 5. We are looking for the obstacles that are the hardest and most impossible. The obstacles that might legitimately make our protagonist think, *Oh, forget it. I'll just lay down here and die, rather than keep going.*

Sometimes, this moment can feel inevitable, given the setup. For instance, in *National Lampoon's Vacation* (John Hughes), Clark Griswold is taking his family on a cross-country vacation to visit Wally World. The vacation is plagued with one catastrophe after another. Nothing goes the way they expect.

My guess would be that as soon as it was decided the goal of the movie was to get to Wally World, then the idea was floated pretty early on that when they finally arrived, they would find it was closed. Despite everything that happened, arriving at Wally World and finding it closed means they are as far from their goal as they can possibly be. It's insurmountable. There is no way they are going to open a theme park just because the Griswolds want them to.

I may be wrong. I don't know during what stage of the screenplay development between John Hughes and Harold Ramis's rewrites they decided on Wally World being closed, but it seems to me to be a natural and inevitable moment, given the setup.

Or, in *School of Rock* (Mike White), as soon as Dewey Finn pretends to be Ned Schneebly and takes over the class as a substitute teacher, we know he has to get found out at some point. We are not shocked when he is caught, and in doing so, loses the class, the money, his friendship with Rosalie, and his chance to win Battle of the Bands.

So, although this moment may not be altogether surprising, that's not a problem—as long as our protagonist's solution *is* surprising and inventive enough to keep us going, as it is in both *Vacation* and *School of Rock*.

45

In other stories, this moment can be much more unexpected for the writer and the audience, and it will develop from the other obstacles we create.

In *Legally Blonde* (Karen McCullah and Kirsten Smith, Original Novel by Amanda Brown), the worst thing that happens to Elle Woods is when Professor Callahan, her law professor and lead counsel, appears impressed by her skills and talents—only to hit on her in private. It is the moment when Elle realizes she is as far from her goal as she could possibly be. As Elle says, despite everything she has done, despite all her work, and all the uptight clothes, Callahan still just sees her as a "piece of ass." This moment is perfect, but it could have been something else. This moment with Callahan wasn't inevitable in the same way as the moment in *School of Rock*. It could have been something else and still worked, and so, it developed out of the other obstacles and characters created along the way.

This moment is definitely not set in stone. It may change as we write, and it has a very good chance of changing in rewrites, so for now, just answer this question with something that feels genuine and honest. Something that could legitimately make our protagonist want to give up.

7) How must this story end?

You may read or hear the phrase "know your ending" from some books and teachers. It is argued, by some, that we shouldn't start writing until we know how the story ends. I both agree and disagree with this. I agree we should know how our story will change our protagonist. Are they a better person at the end? Have they found their place in the world? Have they fixed the relationships that were broken? However, the *exact* details do not need to be set in stone as we start writing.

To answer this question, write down all the things we want to be true at the end, as well as things that *may* be true.

For instance, in *Chasing Amy* (Kevin Smith), we meet Holden McNeill. He is a comic book writer who has an unhealthy, codependent relationship with his best friend and work partner, as well as a slight misogynist streak that he justifies by comparison to his best friend's extreme misogyny. Holden falls in love with a girl but quickly finds out she is a lesbian, and he feels slighted. He continues to pursue her, until they start a relationship—only for him to ruin it, thanks to his own insecurities and pride. At the end, they are not together, but Holden is happy, and more importantly, a better person with a deeper understanding of women, thanks to his time with Amy. It's an interesting romantic comedy because in most cases, the protagonists have to get together for the ending to work. The goal is typically true love. That's not true here. I don't know if this happened, but I wouldn't be shocked if Kevin Smith wrote a version of this screenplay in which they *did* end up together. It feels like either one could have been a satisfying ending, if Holden and Amy ended up better people for their time together.

We also want to include any *new* goals the protagonist may have developed as the story progressed.

Let's go back to *Bruce Almighty* for a moment. Along with a lot of wish-fulfillment stories, Bruce starts out very happy with his new powers, as they allow him to fulfill his immediate goal of fame and financial success, but as he fulfills what he *thinks* he wanted, he starts to realize it doesn't bring him the happiness he expected. As things fall apart, Bruce realizes the anchor job and financial success are not his goal at all. His goal is to put right everything he has messed up—primarily, his relationship with Grace. So, his *new* goal is the one that must be fulfilled by the end of the movie. That is what should be included here.

Remember, what is the ending that the audience expects? That's what we want to give them, but if the journey to get there has been surprising and unexpected, they will be satisfied.

8) What must the protagonist do to achieve that ending?

The rule here is that it must be our protagonist that makes it happen. They must be the one that chooses and carries out the actions that turn things around. Remember, we can start a story on a coincidence, but we can't end one on a coincidence.

So, when our hero is trapped on Everest in a terrible storm, trying to get home, and she has broken her leg and run out of food, and her friends have stopped looking for her, and she is starting to hallucinate, and she is ready to just give up and die, we can't suddenly have a helpful Sherpa pass by and say, "Gosh, you look tired and underfed. Here's some water and food. Let me help you get down to base camp." It's a cheat, a cop-out. Our protagonist must to turn it around and make it happen *themselves*.

Interestingly *School of Rock* appears to break this rule, as it is not Dewey who makes the ending happen. After losing his job, he goes home and hides in bed. It is the kids who make it happen by escaping from school, lying to the school-bus driver, going to pick up Dewey, and getting to the Battle of the Bands. Usually, this wouldn't work, but it *does* work beautifully because

Mike White has done something very smart. Dewey was the kids' teacher and inspired them. They are now an extension of him. When he met them, they were a bunch of goody-goodies that wouldn't break the rules. Now, they are rebels, desperate to be rockers. Together they turn his life around.

And be under no illusion folks, this part is hard to answer and much harder to write. If we have done our job well, the obstacle they just faced was so insurmountable that the audience genuinely has no idea how the protagonist is going to get out of it. Which means that we may have no idea how they are going to get out of it either.

It's got to be surprising and brilliant, but also completely honest and authentic to the character, which is a tall order. So, don't feel it needs to be perfect at this stage. Just answer it with something they *could* do to get to the ending we need. This is something that will likely be changed and adapted a lot as we write and rewrite.

And that's it. With 8 questions, we can map out our potential story. And the answers don't have to be long. This is not an essay. It should be just enough for us to start building.

Let's look at what this might have looked like for some existing movies.

Toy Story (Joss Whedon, Andrew Stanton, Joel Cohen and Alec Sokolow, original story by John Lasseter, Peter Doctor, Andrew Stanton, Joe Ranft):

1) **Who is the story about?** Woody, a cowboy doll that comes to life when his owner, Andy, is not around.
2) **What is their flaw?** Woody has become conceited about being Andy's favorite toy.
3) **What happens to them that changes their life for better or worse?** Andy gets Buzz Lightyear, a flashy space toy that usurps his love for Woody.
4) **What must they now achieve?** Woody must get rid of Buzz and become Andy's favorite again.
5) **What could get in the way of that goal?** Everyone loves Buzz. They are all impressed by him. Woody lets his jealousy get the better of him and accidentally knocks Buzz out of the window, turning the other toys against him. He tries to save Buzz but instead they get into a fight in the car and fall out, getting left at a gas station. They are now lost toys. They have to get to Andy, but he has already driven away. When they finally get to the same location they are captured by an evil kid, Sid, who takes them home

to torture them. They get trapped in Sid's bedroom with the mutant toys he has created. Sid's house is right next to Andy's. They have a chance to get home, but Buzz discovers he's just a toy and not a real space man and loses motivation to get home. Andy's other toys refuse to help, thinking that Woody has killed Buzz.

6) **What's the worst thing that could happen to the protagonist?** Woody is stuck in Sid's bedroom. Buzz has a rocket strapped to his back. Woody is waiting for the morning when they will be blown up/pulled apart. The same day that Andy will move away to a new house and be gone forever.

7) **How must this story end?** Woody must get back to Andy before he moves to a new house. He must convince Buzz that being a toy is just as special as being a spaceman, and he must also accept that he is no longer Andy's only favorite toy.

8) **What must the protagonist do to achieve that ending?** He must break the rules and come to life when a child is watching. He must also do it *with* Buzz so that the other toys will forgive him.

Shaun of the Dead (Simon Pegg & Edgar Wright)

1) **Who is the story about?** Shaun. A 20-something Londoner.

2) **What is their flaw?** He is an underachiever in every area of life. He is in a dead-end job and cannot properly commit to his relationship with his girlfriend Liz, instead choosing to spend his life playing video games and drinking in the local pub – The Winchester - with his equally listless roommate, Ed.

3) **What happens to them that changes their life for better or worse?** A virus causes the city to be overrun by zombies.

4) **What must they now achieve?** Get the people he loves to safety from the zombies.

5) **What could get in the way of that goal?** He doesn't even know about the zombies. Ed keeps leaving the front door open, allowing zombies into the house. Their third roommate is infected and becomes a zombie. He has to get through London to Liz's house. He has to convince Liz to come with him. He has to also collect his mom, and his stepdad, who he hates. His stepdad is infected and will soon be a zombie, so he has to convince his mom to leave him. He has no plan to save everyone. The best he can come up with is to go to The Winchester. They now have to travel without a car, through the zombies to the pub. His mom gets infected without him knowing. Once at the pub the group starts to turn on

each other. The zombies find them, and the group must barricade themselves in against the approaching zombie hoard.

6) **What's the worst thing that could happen to the protagonist?** The zombies break in and almost everyone he loves is either dead, infected or already a zombie.

7) **How must this story end?** He must at least save Liz, get out of this alive and finally commit to a real relationship.

8) **What must the protagonist do to achieve that ending?** He must finally be a grown up and make difficult choices. He must kill people he loves to stop them from killing more. Leading to the fantastic line "I don't think I've got it in me to shoot my flat-mate, my mum and my girlfriend all in the same evening!"

***

Go away for a moment and think of your favorite movies. What would the answers be to these questions? Write them out. Get used to thinking about how great stories break down.

We are going to use these eight questions to create potential stories until we hit on one that excites us enough to write it.

We do not have to answer the questions in sequence. We can start with a character that interests us and create a dramatic situation that makes their life better or worse. Or, we may have a fantastic dramatic idea for which we then need to find a character. Either one is fine. In fact, it's good to jump around the questions and answer them out of sequence. All we need is a coherent set of answers at the end.

And remember, none of this stuff is set in stone. We can change it as we go along, and we will almost certainly make big changes in rewrites, but having it now means we always have somewhere to go next, rather than just an empty abyss of nothingness.

I may answer these story questions 10 times before I hit on an idea that really excites me, or maybe 20 times, or maybe 50 times. That's still only a few days or weeks. That's a very worthwhile investment of time to find a story that excites us enough to spend the next three to twelve months of our life writing it.

Woody Allen famously writes any story idea on a scrap of paper and stuffs it in a drawer in his house. When he gets ready to start a new screenplay, he goes back to his drawer and rifles through it, until he hits on one that he wants to write up. Similarly, we will discard many, many more ideas for screenplays than we will ever write. Just because something *can* be a story doesn't mean it's worth writing.

Every writer will find their own process for deciding which story to finally write, but for what it's worth, my own process is based on how many ideas for images and scenes and lines of dialogue start popping into my head as I am answering the questions above. Does question number 5 start filling up with ideas for obstacles without my having to even try? Am I thinking of ideas faster than I can get them down on paper? If so, then there is a good chance that I've got something that can sustain me for the work ahead, something that will give me more ideas than I need so that I can edit down, rather than struggling to think of obstacles and ideas when I am deep into the writing of it.

However, when we have made our choice of what to write, we must stick to it, no matter how difficult it gets, or how many challenges we find along the way. If we stop this screenplay and start another one, the next idea will have just as many challenges and story problems. No matter how good the concept, at some point it will feel like our story was written by a five year old. We will weep as we wonder what on Earth possessed us to choose this story, and question why we have given up weeks of our life to the creation of this stupid idea. We will delve into these rather depressing thoughts in more detail later when we are into the writing of the screenplay.

12.

What Is A Logline?

A logline is a one (or two) sentence description of the story of our film. It will be used when we describe it to people verbally. It will also be used when we send out inquiry emails to people. And a version of it will be used by studio and marketing people all the way through its development right up to its description on IMDB or rottentomatoes.

If you followed my book recommendation and read *Save the Cat*, then let me say that I completely agree with Blake Snyder; creating our logline before we start writing will greatly increase the quality of our screenplay as it will help us nail down the core of our story.

Remember what we have learned so far; drama is created out of conflict. Our logline needs to define the elemental conflict at the heart of our story. Without that conflict, we have no story.

For instance:

When the head of a mafia family is shot, his second in command takes charge of the family.

There's nothing of interest or note in this logline. It's exactly what we would expect to happen. It's exactly what *should* happen. There's no conflict of character, expectation, or setting, and therefore, no drama.

However:

When the head of a mafia family is shot, the one son who wants nothing to do with the family business is forced to step up and take charge—The Godfather (Mario Puzo and Francis Ford Coppola)

Now we have conflict. *Now* we have drama. The son who wants out of the family is dragged in, and who knows what he will change, or who he will clash with along the way.

Let's look at some other loglines. (I'm taking these from IMDB, so these are not written by the original writers, but I want to show just how easy it is for anyone to write a logline for a film that has clear conflict.)

A suburban psychiatrist acquires a new patient; the head of the New York crime family—Analyze This (Peter Tolan and Harold Ramis and Kenneth Lonergan)

When a blonde sorority queen is dumped by her boyfriend, she follows him to Harvard Law School—Legally Blonde

Both describe very clear conflicts of character, setting, and expectation. They're both comedies so let's look at some dramatic loglines:

After an explosion severely injures their spacecraft, NASA must devise a strategy to return the Apollo 13 astronauts safely to the Earth—Apollo 13 (William Broyles Jr & Al Reinert and John Sayles, based on the book by Jim Lovell and Jeffrey Kluger)

A small-time boxer gets the chance to fight the heavyweight champion of the world—Rocky (Sylvester Stallone)

Or some horror loglines:

After moving into a suburban home, a couple becomes increasingly disturbed by a nightly demonic presence—Paranormal Activity (Oren Peli)

Five friends visiting their grandfather's house in the country are hunted and terrorized by a chain-saw-wielding killer and his family of grave-robbing cannibals—The Texas Chainsaw Massacre (Kim Henkel and Tobe Hooper)

Talk about conflict! These films weren't staggeringly successful by accident. They were built on fantastically strong foundations of conflict.

What is the conflict in our story? If we don't have any, then we don't have a story yet.

I see loglines from new writers all the time that simply state a situation but don't explain the drama. For instance:

After the unexpected death of her father, a woman moves back to her hometown to reconnect with the life she left behind.

Er… okay. Isn't that what people do all the time? What's that film about? Maybe there is a great story in there filled with drama and conflict, but that's definitely not clear in the logline. If we cannot see the conflict clearly and definitively then we are making it much harder for ourselves when we get into the meat of the second Act.

And when it comes to selling, we are trying to hook people in, to make it so that they cannot say no to reading the script. I can say no to the script above *very* easily.

The Screenwriter's Journey   Hywel Berry

Our sales logline may be completely different from the version we need now to get us writing, but in all cases our logline should contain some, or all, of the core story elements:

-   Our protagonist
-   His or her flaw
-   The inciting incident
-   Their goal
-   The antagonist (or the main thing that stops them from achieving their goal)

For instance, the sales logline of *Get Out* (Jordan Peele) could be:

A young African-American man, who wants to believe that racism is a thing of the past, visits his white girlfriend's parents for the first time. He becomes increasingly uneasy about their outwardly liberal attitude and tries to get away, but instead becomes the victim of their twisted family secret.

That covers all the elements of the story without revealing the fantastic twist. But the logline that we use to keep us on track as we write would be very different:

A young African-American man visits his white girlfriend's seemingly liberal parents for the weekend, but becomes a victim of their sinister, racist experiments.

This is more than enough to keep us on track through our first draft. Many elements can change as we develop the story and create the details, but this is the underlying drama that will remain at its core.

Keep your logline in front of you as you write. Write it out on a post-it and stick it to your screen. If we get it right, our logline will help keep us on track through our first draft and our rewrites.

54

13.

What Are Subplots?

Every time we introduce a new character that interacts with our protagonist, we have created a subplot. How much time it takes up and how deep that subplot goes is debatable, but it begins the moment they cross paths with our protagonist.

How many subplots should we have? A great rule of thumb for all screenwriting is: no more than necessary. No more description than is necessary, no more dialogue than is necessary and no more characters than are necessary.

By answering our story questions, we have not necessarily created all the characters we may need. We may have created an antagonist, who is trying to stop the hero, and maybe a friendly character, such as a best friend, a mentor, or maybe a love interest.

There are no characters we *must* create. It is only necessary to create characters who help or hinder the hero on their journey. Any more than that, and we are overcomplicating things for no reason. It's not necessary for every hero to have a love interest, just as it is not necessary for every hero to have a comedy sidekick. We should only create those characters if they help or hinder our hero.

It can be a good idea with our first screenplay to create a story within a small world, such as *Clerks* (Kevin Smith), set almost exclusively in a convenience store, or *Rope* (Hume Cronyn & Arthur Laurents, from the play by Patrick Hamilton), the classic Hitchcock thriller that is set in a single apartment. Two killers host a dinner party where, unknown to the guests, the dead body of their friend lays inside a trunk in the middle of the apartment.

These are not small movies. They express very big ideas, but they do it in a limited setting with a very manageable number of characters.

We should write what excites and inspires us, but the act of limiting ourselves can be a useful tool in learning our craft as a writer.

If our first screenplay is about an intergalactic policeman seeking the head of a rebel force from another galaxy, then the sheer volume of choices available to us in terms of character and setting might be overwhelming.

Interestingly, the first draft of *Ghostbusters* was about a team of intergalactic ghost hunters roaming the universe. General opinion was that the budget for such a movie would have been astronomical (in 1984). When stripped down and limited to New York City the budget became feasible, but more importantly the true brilliance of the idea became clear.

So how do we choose the characters we need? We do it with two simple questions:

1) Who could help our protagonist achieve their goal?
2) Who might get in the way of the protagonist achieving their goal?

That's it. Again, there are many more nuances to creating great supporting characters, which we will look at later, but for now we just want to know who is going to help or hinder our protagonist.

Jaws offers a wonderful example of necessary characters. Let's list all the key characters and see if they help or hinder Sheriff Brody in catching the shark.

- Sheriff Brody (Hero)
- Quint, the shark hunter (Help. Expertise with the act of catching the shark)
- Hooper, the oceanographic expert (Help. Expertise with sharks in general and helps him deal with Quint)
- Ellen Brody, his wife (Help. She helps him research, but also as motivation to keep his family safe)
- Vaughn, the Mayor (Hinder. He refuses to accept there is a shark and reopens the beaches)
- Chrissie, the girl who dies in the opening (Hinder, in the sense that she gets attacked)
- Ben Gardner, and all the other fishermen (Hinder. They go out half-assed and ill-equipped and cause trouble, or get themselves killed)
- Mrs Kintner, whose son dies and who blames Sheriff Brody (Help. Her blaming Brody is motivation for him to pay Quint and go out himself to catch the shark.)
- And lastly—The shark (Hinder. The shark is the antagonist and is trying to eat as many people as it can before hunting Sheriff Brody)

So, there we go. All the key characters. Anyone else listed in the credits is either unnamed on screen or is so incidental that we wouldn't even remember them, such as other fishermen, police or townspeople. These are the characters that get real screen time and affect the story, and each one has a specific role to help or hinder Brody in achieving his goal.

We want to create a similar list for ourselves of our key characters and how they help or hinder. This will most likely not be our final list of characters. Others may be necessary as we are writing, or characters may become obsolete once we start. That's fine. Just create the people we think we need right now so that we have a world of people available to our protagonist. As more come along, add them to your list and make sure to name whether they help or hinder.

The size and complexity of their help or hindrance determines the size and complexity of the subplot. Some subplots are very small, just one or two scenes; we introduce someone, they present a challenge or help to the protagonist, we accept their help or overcome the challenge and the character leaves never to be seen again. Others run through the entire script in conjunction with the main plot. In each case, how they interact with our protagonist becomes their subplot.

For now, we are not going to go into any more depth in creating each subplot other than to make sure we follow two guiding principles:

1) Does every character we introduce help or hinder the protagonist?
2) Do we close off each of these character's stories by the time we end the film?

If we have a 'yes' answer to both these questions, then our characters have a reason to exist and the subplot has an ending, which is more than enough to get things moving on our first screenplay.

14.

What Is Screenplay Structure?

We now have all the key elements of our story, but that's only half the equation. We also need to structure those events and characters properly.

Modern screenplays have quite a rigid structure that readers and buyers expect to see. This gives them confidence that we understand screenplay structure and can apply it to their own projects.

New writers can be quite skeptical, or even defensive, about this need for structure, worrying that our true creativity is being restricted. It's true that it would be a lovely world where stories could be told in any form and in any structure that the writer desires. So nice in fact that such a world has existed for thousands of years—the world of poems.

Poems can be any structure we want. They can rhyme or not, they can have a fixed or random number of syllables per line, they can be 2 lines long or 10,000 words long. They can be anything.

How do poems get away with this? Because it doesn't cost $50m-$400m dollars to produce and distribute a poem to its intended market. To protect and see a return on their investment, distributors want to know that their product is in a format that audiences understand and enjoy, and that fits with multiplex distribution. If you want total creative freedom then write poems (or novels, which have a more flexible format and structure) but if you want to write movies it's best to just get over it now and learn the structure that the industry expects.

The desired structure has changed and developed slightly throughout the history of moviemaking. You only need to watch movies from each decade to see that development, but what has been consistent since the advent of sound and the two-hour feature movie is the three Act structure.

Three Acts gives us a beginning (Act One), a middle (Act Two) and a resolution (Act Three).

It is generally accepted that a page of screenplay equates to 1 minute of screen time, so for a 120-minute movie, we need to write roughly 120 pages.

I am going to push you to challenge your sense of brevity and try to create 100-page screenplays, but to learn and understand the model it is easiest to look at a standard 120-minute model.

You may have seen this model elsewhere, but our three Act structure breaks down as follows:

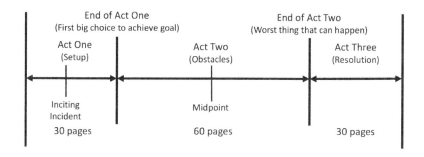

It basically breaks down into quarters. The first Act setup is one quarter. The second Act is two quarters separated by the Midpoint. And the third Act is the last quarter.

In a three Act structure, there are two big turning points in the story; one at the end of Act One, when the protagonist will start their new quest. And then again at the end of Act Two, when it looks like the protagonist is going to give up on their quest.

Along with the big strokes of the protagonist's wellbeing, there are other elements that must exist. Here are the moments our story must have and the guideline pages on which they should happen in a standard 120-page screenplay.

Act One – Setup:

1) Meeting our protagonist and discovering their flaw(s) that needs to be fixed. (Pages 1-10)
2) The inciting incident. The thing that starts the story. (Usually around page 10-15 but definitely before page 25)
3) Refusal to act. (Immediately after the inciting incident. No fixed number of pages but at least one scene.)
4) The end of Act One. When the protagonist chooses to act or is forced to act to achieve their new goal. (Page 30)

Act Two – Obstacles:

5) The first major obstacle. (Approximately pages 30-45)

6) The second major obstacle. (Approximately pages 45-60)
7) Midpoint. (Approximately pages 60-65)
8) The third major obstacle. (Approximately pages 65-80)
9) The fourth major obstacle. (Pages 80-90)
10) The end of Act Two: The worst moment the protagonist faces. (Page 90)

Act Three – Resolution:

11) How the protagonist turns it around and solves their problem. (Pages 90-100)
12) The resolution. (Pages 100-120)

None of these page numbers are set in stone. They are a guideline to help us picture the structure of our story, and they adapt accordingly for shorter or longer screenplays, but they should be close to these numbers. We can't have an inciting incident on Page 60, and we can't have the worst thing that happens to the protagonist on Page 35.

The second Act is the biggest in terms of screen time and material that we need, as well as the choices we must make. That is why the second Act is so difficult to write.

This may seem intimidating if we've never done this before, but by playing the story game we've already got most of it planned out. Let's go back to our story questions:

Act One:

1) Who is the story about? (Meeting the protagonist)
2) What is their flaw? (Learn it at the beginning and fix it during the resolution)
3) What happens to them that changes their life for better or worse? (Inciting Incident)
4) What must they now achieve? (Refusal to act, the end of Act One)

Act Two:

5) What could get in the way of that goal? (Many obstacles to the protagonist's goal, including 4 *major* obstacles to overcome, each one more difficult than the last.)
6) What's the worst thing that could happen to the protagonist? (The end of Act Two)

Act Three:

7) How must this story end? (The resolution)

8) What does the Protagonist do to achieve that ending? (How the Protagonist turns it around and solves their problem)

In the next few chapters we are going to look at how each of these Acts affects our protagonist, and what we need to structure each piece properly.

15.

The Protagonist's Journey

We can give the journey of our protagonist a visual representation if we steal from the world of psychology and look at the theory of change curves.

Built out of various research including the five stages of grief by Elizabeth Kubler Ross and David Kessler, the change curves show us the highs and lows that people (our protagonist) go through as they experience change.

The Negative Change Curve:

If we experience a negative change in life, we must go through the negative change curve:

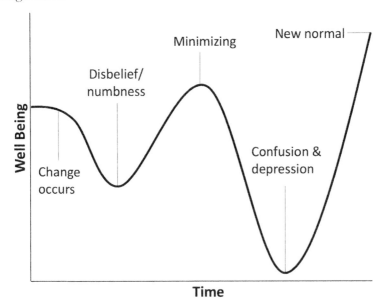

In real life, this may be when we are fired or made redundant. We have an immediate loss in confidence and well-being. We are angry and confused.

However, we bounce back, as we minimize the situation and set about finding a new job, convinced we will be gainfully employed at a new, *better* job in a matter of days.

When that doesn't happen, we go down a slippery slope. We lose motivation. Our well-being drops quickly. We may even give up job-hunting, convinced the whole endeavor is futile.

Then, we have our crisis moment. Maybe we are at an economic breaking point, or someone in our life forces us to reexamine our choices. Either way, we are forced to find a job, and it may not be the job we want, but it can be the steppingstone we need. As we start working, we grow in confidence and well-being. Maybe we change jobs quickly, but this time, we are choosing each job to be more suitable than the last, and we don't stop until we find a job we enjoy more than the one we originally lost. This may take some time—maybe even years—but our journey is not over until we are happier than we were before. It is why you will hear many people say a variation of, "Losing that job was the best thing that ever happened to me." They sure didn't feel that way at the time, but eventually they realize that the change, horrible as it was, led to them bettering their situation.

It is the same for our protagonist.

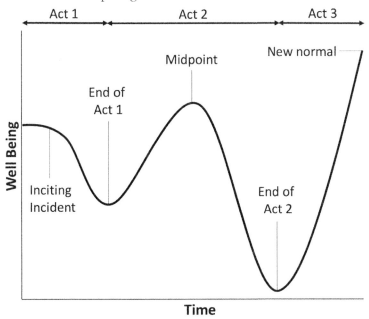

When the inciting incident happens, they suffer an immediate drop in well-being. This continues throughout the first Act as they struggle to understand this change.

But the end of Act One brings a moment that offers new possibilities, and with it the chance to regain their sense of self as they start to enjoy this new situation, minimizing the greater threats they face.

However, the midpoint throws their real situation into stark relief. The fun is over and reality kicks in, and with it comes real threat.

Act Two culminates with our protagonist at their lowest point. The crisis that they must overcome.

But when they do overcome it, they quickly rise past where they started and into a new, better situation.

Most movies take place on the negative change curve, so let's look at this in practice with some real examples.

The Lego Movie:

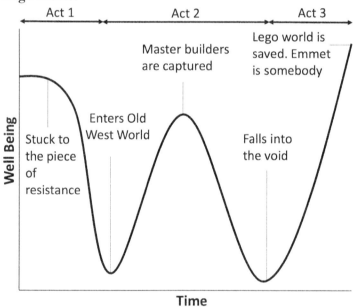

Emmet's life is going great. Great job, great friends (at least in his mind), great tunes. But then he follows Lucy and gets stuck to the piece of resistance.

Waking up, he is strapped to a laser and being interrogated by Bad Cop. His well-being plummets.

Lucy helps him to escape and they make it out to Old West World. He is falling for Lucy and everyone keeps telling him that he is The Special. He is finally going to make something of his life. But then he accidentally leads Bad Cop right to Cloud Cuckoo Land and all the master builders are captured.

Emmet now has to do something amazing to save everybody. He tries to create plans to defeat Lord Business, but they all go wrong. He is finally captured and banished to the void. Their world is doomed. Emmet must unite the two worlds and bring the boy and his father together to save Lego world. When he achieves this, he unites Lego world, *and* becomes a somebody. Now he is truly happy, unlike his delusional self at the start.

In this case, Emmet starts off at a high wellbeing, but that might not necessarily be true.

Bruce Almighty:

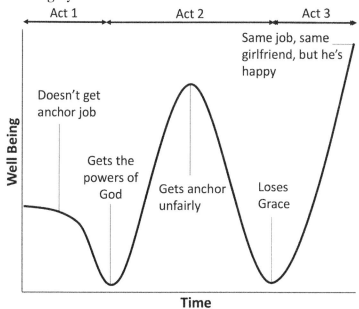

Bruce starts off unhappy and just gets more miserable throughout the first Act until he receives the powers of God. He then goes through the same curve, which in this case has a more noticeable high until the midpoint because of where he started.

The Positive Change Curve:

If our protagonist experiences a positive change, they go through the positive change curve:

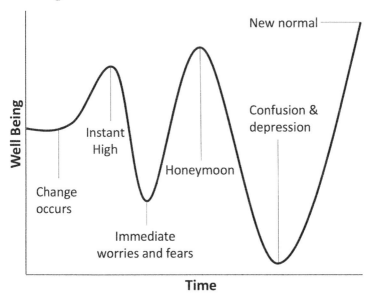

An example of a positive change curve in real life is getting a new job. When we are offered a new job, we have an immediate upswing in well-being. We are excited and happy, keen to start this new chapter in our lives. However, we then have the immediate problem of quitting our old job. Saying goodbye to all the people we like. All the fears and worries kick in as to whether we have made the right choice.

After starting our new job, however, everything is great—at first. We settle in; everyone is polite and nice; we have more money. But at some point we start to lose our sense of happiness. Things are different. We don't understand the politics; we have lost our old friends; expectations are higher. Our sense of well-being plummets, potentially even falling into sadness and depression.

Then, something happens. Maybe we finally pour out our feelings to our new boss, or we have a breakthrough in our new relationships. Either way, something happens that starts us on our road to recovery, and eventually, we end up happier than we did at the start, with everything we used to have *and* a new, better-paying job.

It's no different for our protagonist.

Pretty Woman:

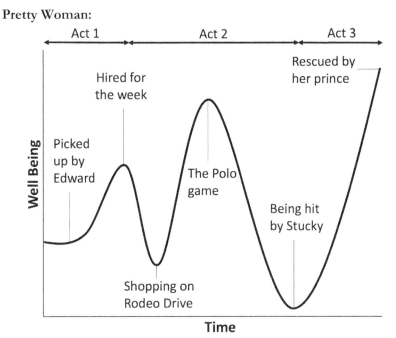

Vivian's life as a hooker in Hollywood is far from what she desires. She doesn't even have the money to make rent.

Then she meets Edward. Her life takes an immediate upswing. She is spending the night in a five-star Beverly Hills Hotel. He then offers to pay her $3000 to spend the week with him. She's on a high.

But immediately, reality kicks in as she tries to go shopping on Rodeo Drive and is ridiculed and belittled by the salespeople.

Getting back on track, Edward takes her shopping and she starts to enjoy the spoils of life in the rich set—private jets, opening night at the opera, fancy restaurants.

But at the Polo game, Edwards lawyer, Stucky, finds out who she really is and propositions her. Her old life is thrust back into focus. Their burgeoning relationship crumbles. They are too different and can never really be together.

Finally, as the week closes, Stucky comes to the hotel room and attacks her. Edward fights him off and fires him, but Vivian knows she has no choice. She has to leave.

The final upswing comes when Edward realizes the person he really wants to be and travels to her apartment to climb to the tall tower and rescue her right back, giving her a level of happiness that she never experienced before.

However, all of these curves so far speak to stories that end on a high—what we know as "happy endings". But as we discussed earlier on, this is not necessary for a story to work. So, what about "down endings"? Well, actually there are two types.

They both follow the standard route of the change curves, with the same crisis at the end of Act Two, and a possible redemption in the third Act. But this time, to facilitate the negative ending we see a new peak in the third Act.

At this point the protagonist can go one of two ways. In both cases the end will be *sad*, in that the characters (and most likely the viewers) do not leave the movie theater with big smiles on their faces, but the choices they make could lead to them ending up with either higher or lower well-being than they started the movie.

Thelma & Louise:

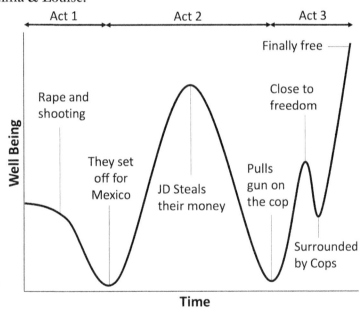

In the first kind, exhibited here by *Thelma & Louise* (Callie Khouri), the ending is sad, in that Thelma and Louise die by driving off the cliff into the Grand Canyon. But they do this willingly because they will finally be free of the lives that made them so unhappy. They will die together—their way. At that moment, this is the choice that gives them a greater sense of well-being. They end happy, even though we lose two characters we have fallen in love with.

We see a similar story curve in *One flew Over the Cuckoo's Nest*, or *Million Dollar Baby* (screenplay by Paul Haggis), where the death of the protagonist is a relief or freedom of some kind.

So, in the first kind, the ending is definitely sad, but the protagonist themselves is better off.

In the second version, we see the same peak in the third Act, but this time the protagonist makes a choice that sends their wellbeing plummeting.

Se7en:

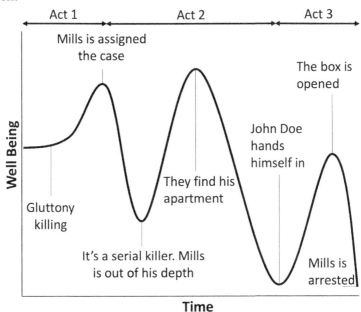

In *Se7en*, it's actually a positive change curve, as Mills is keen and eager to make his mark as a detective, so finding and being assigned the first murder sends him off on the positive track.

He suffers the expected troughs and peaks until at their worst moment John Doe hands himself in. The mini peak now is when John Doe agrees to take them to find the remaining bodies. Everything appears fixed, until he makes his gruesome delivery to Mills.

Mills makes his choice, kills John Doe and condemns himself to prison. It is a "down" ending for both us *and* Mills.

Interestingly, in an earlier draft by Andrew Kevin Walker, it is Somerset who kills John Doe and knows he will go to jail. But the effect is ultimately the same in a movie with such clear dual protagonists.

We see similar endings in movies such as *Leaving Las Vegas* (Mike Figgis, based on the novel by John O'Brien), *Fight Club* (Jim Uhls, based on the novel by Chuck Palahniuk), or *An American Werewolf in London* (John Landis).

Interestingly, the recent *Parasite* (Bong Joon-Ho and Jin Won Han), offers an ending that could be read by the viewer as both high or low wellbeing for the Kim family, and I think that is one of the reasons it had such an emotional effect on its audience and made it the best picture winner.

With these pictorial depictions of our protagonist's journey we can give ourselves a clear visual plan for the big movements of our story, determined by the three Acts.

16.

Act One

Act One is the most fun to plan out, and the most fun to write. We have lots of structural pieces that give us a solid backbone for where our character needs to go.

1) Meeting our protagonist and discovering their flaw(s) that needs to be fixed. (Pages 1-10)

We must let our reader know who the story is about. We have roughly 10 pages to build an affinity with our protagonist(s), learn their situation, and reveal the flaw that needs to be fixed.

We *may* also need to meet the other side of our story—our antagonist, so that we know what they are trying to achieve and what our protagonist is going up against. Or, that part of the story may be revealed later.

There will probably be a few pages more before we get to the inciting incident, but these first 10 pages are the most crucial in making sure we have set up everything we need to know about the protagonist and their world.

I am going to use *Ghostbusters* (1984) as the example to show how each of these structural pieces are brought to life in a real screenplay. It's always difficult to choose something that everyone has seen and knows well enough to understand, but hopefully this includes most of us. If you haven't seen or read it, you are missing out so do so as soon as possible.

In *Ghostbusters* we open on the New York public library. An elderly librarian is in the bowels of the building restacking books. Behind her, weird things start to happen. Cards start flying out of drawers. She is scared and runs away through the stacks. Finally, she is faced with a terrifying site – that we can't see. She screams.

Now we know the world of this movie. It is modern day New York, but it includes supernatural elements.

On page 3 we meet Dr. Peter Venkman, our protagonist. (I know all the Ghostbusters are important, but Peter is the driving force of the story).

Peter is in a laboratory conducting an experiment on ESP with some student volunteers. Part of the experiment is to give electric shocks. Very quickly we realize that Peter is not running the experiment honestly. He is cheating to flirt with the pretty girl while unnecessarily electrocuting the dweeby guy. Peter is a fraud; using science to pick up girls.

He is interrupted by his colleague, Dr. Ray Stantz. Ray tells him about the ghost at the library. Peter tries to get out of it but is forced to go. "This one's for real, Peter," he tells him. Ray is a dreamer, desperate to find their breakthrough.

At the library they meet the last colleague, Dr. Egon Spengler. He is studious and serious to the point of dangerous. "Egon, this reminds me of the time you tried to drill a hole in your head," says Peter.

They speak to the librarian and she tells them about the ghostly figure. Ray is super excited.

They go downstairs to try and see it. They find ectoplasmic residue and finally come across the ghost – a free floating apparition of an old lady reading a book – and they have no idea what to do.

Peter tries to talk to her. Nothing. Ray has a "plan." He tries to grab it and it transforms into a hideous demon.

The guys scream and run away. They are cowards. Clueless, useless, cowards.

That happens at the bottom of page 11. Now we know the world, the key characters and their flaws in a succinct, funny and exciting first 10 pages.

2) The inciting incident. The thing that starts the story. (Usually around page 10-15 but definitely before page 25)

This is the moment that makes our protagonist's life significantly better or worse. Remember, without this moment, the protagonist's life would just carry on as normal, whatever normal may be to them.

The reason for making sure that it appears as early as possible is so that we hook readers into our screenplay and make it difficult for them to put down. That doesn't mean it has to appear on page 1 though. The reader expects a certain amount of setup of the character and the world in which they live, but once they have those details, they want the story to get moving asap. It can appear anywhere up to page 25 without looking out of place, but anything later than page 15 and we'd better have a good reason for it.

What is set in stone is that something MUST happen that starts the story by making the protagonist's life significantly better or worse, and this must happen as early as possible for the story we are telling.

In *Ghostbusters*, this happens almost immediately after leaving the library.

They head back to Columbia University. Along the way Egon tells them that with his new readings there is a good chance of "…catching a ghost and holding it indefinitely."

They reach their lab to find it being cleared out. The Dean is there to inform them that they have had their grants terminated and are being fired: "You are a poor scientist, Dr. Venkman."

The life they had is now gone and forces them to start their new story, whatever that will be. A negative change. That is on page 15.

3) Refusal to act. (Immediately after the inciting incident. No fixed number of pages but at least one scene)

This moment can be very small, but it is necessary. The protagonist must resist this new situation, even if just for a very short time. If they want this change, then where is the conflict?

Whatever is happening to them *must* be undesirable in some way. They must be *forced* to accept their quest.

When they do, they will set in motion two goals:

1)   Their conscious goal. *The thing that must be achieved.* This goal will be the backbone of the movie we are watching.
2)   Their unconscious goal. *The thing the protagonist needs to fix to become a better person.* This goal gives the movie its emotional core.

The protagonist will be completely aware of their conscious goal and completely unaware of their unconscious goal.

In *Ghostbusters*, the three colleagues go and sit in the quad of Columbia University where Peter pitches the idea to save them – "To go into business for ourselves."

The refusal to act lasts for three scenes, and the refusal comes primarily from Ray. He is scared. He fears being outside of the University. Fears working in the private sector where they "expect results" and fears how much money it will cost to set up their own business.

Peter now becomes the dreamer and sees only opportunity.

The next scene is the three of them walking out of a Manhattan bank where Peter has convinced Ray to mortgage his childhood home at an extortionate interest rate. Again, Ray is lamenting the situation, but Peter is sure about their ghost catching business: "The franchise rights alone will make us rich beyond our wildest dreams."

The last refusal scene takes place in the Firehall that is to become their home. This time Egon and Peter are skeptical until Ray gets so excited about the firepole that it is clear they are going to take it.

Now they are all in. They have got the money and their new headquarters. The refusal is finished. We are on page 17.

Now they have their conscious goal:

Conscious goal: To make a success of their ghost catching business.

Their unconscious goal comes a little later.

4) The end of Act One. When the protagonist chooses to act or is forced to act to achieve their new goal. (Page 30)

The end of Act One culminates in the first big choice by the protagonist. It is the choice they need to make, or are forced to make, to achieve whatever goal they have now accepted.

We have probably met the antagonist by now, but if not, this is our last opportunity to meet the antagonist and understand why they are acting against the protagonist.

The end of Act One regularly involves a change of location. If so, this new location should be the protagonist's primary world for the rest of the movie.

Examples include the arena in *The Hunger Games*, or Beverly Hills in *Beverly Hills Cop* (Daniel Petrie Jr., Story by Danilo Bach and Daniel Petrie Jr.), Harvard Law School in *Legally Blonde*, or the 1920's in *Midnight in Paris* (Woody Allen).

Whether it's a choice, a change in situation, or a change in location, there is no going back. Once this big thing happens, the protagonist *must* move forward to achieve their goal or put their life right.

In *Ghostbusters*, we now meet the other half of our story when we pick up with Dana Barret as she comes home to her upper west side apartment, meeting her nerdy neighbor, Louis, on the way.

Dana goes into her apartment to unpack her groceries when weird things start happening. Her egg box opens on its own and the eggs start to cook themselves on her counter. She hears voices from her fridge, and when she opens it, she sees a fiery temple, and hears a voice shout, *"Zuul!"*

She screams and slams the door.

Dana comes to the Ghostbusters headquarters and tells them of her experience. They have no idea how to act or what to do – but they take the case.

Now we have our unconscious goal:

Unconscious goal: To save New York from this unknown demon, and for Peter to do something that *isn't* selfish.

That is on page 27.

And that's the end of Act One. We know our protagonist(s). We know what's wrong with them. We know what threw their life out of whack. We know what their new goal is, and we know why they don't want to take it on. We know who or what their antagonist is and why they are trying to stop our hero.

They have started their new quest, and so we move into Act Two.

17.

Act Two

Act Two is the most difficult to plan out and the most difficult to write. It is the place where we are likely to get stuck and give up. Why? Because it's the biggest chunk and it's less clear what we are supposed to do with it.

Act One had loads of moments that we needed to include, and they are mostly dictated by the setup of the movie. Act Two is all choices. So many choices that we can spend hours, or days, or weeks just thinking of all the different ways that our story can play out.

Therefore, we need to give ourselves a clear and easy structure that helps us to see this section as smaller, more manageable chunks.

A great second Act is all about obstacles. Specifically, 4 major obstacles for most movies running 100-120 minutes.

Importantly:

The obstacles must keep getting more difficult.

Every time the protagonist moves closer to achieving their conscious goal, new, unexpected obstacles appear that set them back.

We should look over all the ideas we have put down for obstacles and pick out the easiest one to overcome. That's our first obstacle, then select them in order of difficulty. By structuring the obstacles in this way our protagonist is always learning and growing as they move forward. If they are faced with an obstacle that is easier than one that they have already overcome, then it's no longer an obstacle. They're better than that now.

5) The first major obstacle. (Approximately pages 30-45)

Though difficult, the first major obstacle is going to be "fun" to overcome. "Fun" doesn't necessarily mean "funny," but it *does* mean it will embody the premise of the movie with only minimal threat. We know the protagonist will overcome this first obstacle—it's not that difficult—but we also know we will enjoy watching *how* they overcome it. This is what Blake Snyder calls the "fun and games" section.

This obstacle will not improve or fix the protagonist's flaw, in fact it may even increase or indulge their flaw.

In *Ghostbusters* their first obstacle is simple – they have no idea what they're doing. They have no idea how to run a business, and no idea how to catch a ghost even if anyone asked them to do so.

Peter visits Dana's apartment but is clueless as to what to do. He doesn't even understand the equipment he's using. Instead he uses it as an opportunity to hit on her and is thrown out, leaving them close to broke with only one client who hates Peter.

Then the alarm goes. It is a call from the Sedgewick hotel where a ghost is harassing a honeymooning couple.

The guys have their first real ghost. They tear off to the hotel. Once there, carnage ensues. They shoot up their corridors with their proton packs. Peter gets "slimed." And then they destroy a hotel ballroom as they try pathetically to catch the ghost.

The whole time though, Peter never loses his bravado. We also learn something very important; "Don't cross the beams!" ("streams" in the final movie).

Once they catch the ghost, they fleece the hotel manager for $5,000. In doing so they overcome all their current obstacles. They have some money. They have finally proved their business works and they are now actual ghostbusters.

This sequence ends on page 44 and has been everything we wanted from the promise of this premise; selfish idiots trying to catch ghosts in New York.

It has not changed them one bit. They have learned nothing about themselves but are achieving their conscious goal. To run their ghost catching business.

6) The second major obstacle. (Approximately pages 45-60)

This must be more difficult and more threatening than the first, but we are still not really worried about the physical or mental health of the protagonist. We know they are not going to die or give up yet. They can't. We still have 50-60 minutes left to fill. Again, it will rarely fix or improve their flaw. Indeed, they might revel in their flaw and even use it as a tool or justification to try and overcome the obstacle.

In *Ghostbusters*, the second obstacle is that their business is a huge hit. They are famous and over worked. They are on the news and on magazine covers. The phone is ringing off the hook. In the screenplay they even nab a ghost at Yankee stadium.

Of course, they don't realize yet that all this is because the city is seeing a huge increase in paranormal activity thanks to the impending coming of Gozer.

Peter meets up with Dana again and this time she agrees to a date. Everything is going great. To solve their problem of success they hire a new ghostbuster – Winston Zeddemore.

All this fun, success and frivolity ends on page 55.

7) Midpoint. (Approximately pages 60-65)

Something must happen that changes the tone of the story. After this the obstacles are no longer whimsical or threat free. From now on our obstacles are scary, dangerous and hazardous to the physical or mental health of the protagonist.

From now, until the end of Act Two, we must be scared for our protagonist(s), either for their health and mental well-being, or at the very least for their success in achieving their conscious goal.

In *Ghostbusters*, this sequence begins with the arrival of Walter Peck from the EPA on page 55. Not supernatural at all, Peck is a pencil pusher and determined to take them down. Peter embarrasses and ridicules him and Peck leaves, promising to return with a court order.

Peter goes to tell the others of the visit when he is informed that the current amount of psychic energy in New York would be represented by a Twinkie "35 feet long weighing approximately six hundred pounds."

The last scene of this sequence takes us back to Dana's building where the stone statues on the roof magically transform, and we see the glowing eyes of real-life terror-dogs underneath.

Everything is different now. The whimsy and fun are over. Now we know that what is to come will be difficult and dangerous.

That happens on page 59.

8) The third major obstacle. (Approximately pages 65-80)

This obstacle must therefore be genuinely hard, genuinely threatening and something that is going to force the protagonist to assess themselves and their choices.

The protagonist will start to see their own flaw, and to overcome this obstacle will have to make a choice that highlights this flaw.

This choice will change the protagonist in a way that the first few obstacles did not and will start them on the road to fixing their flaw.

In *Ghostbusters*, the third obstacle is that Gozer is starting to break through into the city. To do this, Louis and Dana are attacked by the terror-dogs, and their bodies overtaken by the demons inside. The sequence is still funny, but much darker in tone from what has come before.

To fix this, Louis, now the Keymaster, is taken in by Egon at their headquarters. Peter discovers Dana as he picks her up for his date and instead finds Zuul in Dana's body (the Gatekeeper).

Zuul tries to seduce Peter and he has to resist the temptation to take advantage of Dana. Not a completely selfless act, but something that he might have happily succumbed to before. Instead, he sedates her and heads back to headquarters. For now, the problem is solved.

There is also another ghost catching sequence in the screenplay that was rightly cut from the final film. That all ends on page 76.

9) The fourth major obstacle. (Approximately pages 80-90)

This obstacle must continue the downward trend even further. Things must get bad. Really bad. And our protagonist may begin to doubt the choices they just made to try and improve themselves. Indeed, they may even doubt the entire quest that they are on.

They will finally start to see their own flaws and realize how these flaws have brought them to this low point.

This last obstacle before the end of Act Two is never solved. Instead, the protagonist's failure is what pushes them into the end of Act Two.

In *Ghostbusters*, this last problem starts on page 76 as Walter Peck returns to the Ghostbusters headquarters with police and a warrant.

He forces the authorities to shut off the protection grid. Peter arrives back and tries to stop it, but Peck points out that this problem is of Peter's making. "Forget it, Venkman. You had your chance, but you thought it would be more fun to insult me. Now it's my turn, smart-ass." Peter's bravado and selfishness has brought them to the brink.

They shut off the protection grid and all the ghosts escape. So does Louis. Peck has the Ghostbusters – the only people who can stop Gozer – arrested and thrown in jail. That is on page 80.

All Peter wanted was to be a goof and get girls, and now the city is in danger and he is under arrest. Time to question why they started this at all.

10) The end of Act Two. The worst moment the protagonist faces. (Page 90)

This is the last piece of Act Two and sees our protagonist at their lowest point. The point at which even we feel that maybe they should give up.

Things must look impossible. The protagonist is not only contemplating giving up on his conscious goal, but also contemplating whether they can be, or should be, a better person.

I say page 90 but it does end up being in different places. Act One structure is much more rigid than Act Two and the Act Three resolution. If we have a short resolution, then we do have some extra time to play with in Act Two to extend out the obstacles, as long as we are not repeating ourselves or making the obstacles easier than before.

You will also see this moment referred to in some places as the "death moment" or equivalent. This is because a lot of end of Act Two moments are about death, physically or metaphorically. Interestingly, family/ comedy films do not shy away from literal death at these moments.

As well as being the worst moment the protagonist faces, this is also the moment that subconsciously tells the audience that the end is nigh. We are building to the resolution and eventual climax.

In *Ghostbusters*, all hell breaks loose in the city. Ghosts are everywhere. Louis is on his way to the Gatekeeper. If they get together it will facilitate the arrival of Gozer.

Locked in jail, the Ghostbusters realize that Dana's building is the epicenter of psychic energy for a cult that intended to bring about the end of the world.

They are as far from all goals as possible, conscious or unconscious. Their business is in tatters, Dana is in danger, the city is overrun, and they are stuck in jail. That is on Page 86.

***

And that's Act Two. A daunting 50-60 pages when you start, but hopefully a lot easier when you think about it as small chunks of overcoming each obstacle.

18.

Act Three

Act Three is pure frustration. If you think you had choices to make in Act Two, just wait. Now we need to give closure to all of our characters, our subplots, and the journey of our protagonist.

11) How the protagonist turns it around and solves their problem. (Pages 90-100)

I've given an outline of 10 possible pages here, but again, it takes as long as it takes. It could be less than 10 pages; it could be a few more. This is not the resolution remember, this is just the instrument the protagonist uses to get out of their worst moment and get back on track for a suitably surprising and satisfying resolution.

This is usually the moment where the protagonist has to make their biggest choice. Are they going to keep being the person they were, or choose to be the better person they could become?

It is with this choice that the protagonist will either see the solution to their current problem OR realize that overcoming their current problem is not necessary. Indeed, the goal they have been chasing the entire movie may suddenly seem irrelevant and unnecessary. Instead, they switch their conscious goal completely to align with their unconscious goal. They may fail in their original goal but succeed in their unconscious goal and become a better person.

In many cases they find the solution *because* they give up on their conscious goal. By abandoning what they thought they wanted they reveal the path they must actually take.

Either way, they find a solution that gets them out of their figurative hole, and onto victory.

In *Ghostbusters*, the guys are brought before the mayor to explain what is happening. Walter Peck is there trying to blame them for everything.

The Ghostbusters, specifically Peter, must make a choice. There's very little to gain now from getting involved. Their business is ruined. Facing off against Gozer means they could all die, but Peter must make a choice. He gives up on his conscious goal of money, fame and women, and into his unconscious goal – to so something selfless for the good of others. He must save New York City.

The mayor sides with the Ghostbusters and Peck is sent away.

Dana then wakes up and the Keymaster and Gatekeeper get together. This is what facilitates the arrival of Gozer and sends us flying into the resolution. That ends on page 90.

12) The resolution. (Pages 100-120)

As soon as our protagonist has turned around their worst moment, everything else is resolution.

This is where everything is fixed—or not. It is the sequence of scenes that puts the world right again, or at least closes off the stories we have created. They may end well, they may end badly, but they will end.

Things will still go wrong in this section. It's not that everything here is puppies and Jell-O, but everything from now until the end is moving the story to its satisfying conclusion. There are no more *major* obstacles.

The resolution needs to fix all the flaws we set out at the beginning, *and* close off all the stories we introduced throughout the movie, and it needs to do it in a way that is believable, logical and satisfying to the audience.

The protagonist may or may not have achieved their conscious goal, but thanks to the journey they have taken and the choices they have made they will have grown and developed as a person and fixed the flaws that held them back at the beginning of our story.

In *Ghostbusters*, the guys suit up and drive over to Dana's building.

As they arrive a sinkhole appears and nearly sucks them all up. Whatever is going on is very real and very dangerous.

They trudge up to the top of the building where they see Dana and Louis turn into terror-dogs.

Gozer arrives, ready to destroy the world. The Ghostbusters try to reason with it. They try to shoot it with proton packs, but to no avail. Gozer forces them to choose the form of their destructor and Ray thinks of the Stay Puft Marshmallow man, creating one of the greatest film images ever as the 100ft marshmallow man plods through Manhattan.

Finally, they have no choice. Nothing is working. Egon suggests a plan. They cross the beams. It will most likely kill everyone. In a final act of selflessness to complete his journey Peter loves the idea and the guys cross the beams.

Everything explodes, including the marshmallow man and Gozer is sent back through the portal.

They did it. They are alive. They beat Gozer. All is right with the world. Except that Dana and Louis are still terror-dogs, but now they are charred and burned. Then one of them moves. Inside the charred dogs are Louis and Dana, alive and well.

The city is saved, Dana is alive, and Peter is no longer the selfish huckster we met at the beginning. He is now the hero who risked his life for the safety of others. All done on page 108.

***

And that's your 3-Act structure. Producers, directors, studio execs and even audiences all know, love and expect this structure. Our job is to deliver it in a way that is fresh, exciting and new.

Two big notes here though:

1) You will never hit these markers on a first draft, so don't bother trying. For your first draft, just have fun and get writing. Getting the structure and page count correct is something that we will worry about in re-writes. Don't stress yourself about it now.

2) The 120-page screenplay is accepted as industry standard, but you should challenge yourself to be as concise as possible. If the Ghostbusters can rid the world of Gozer in 108 pages, then there is no reason we can't write most stories in 100-110 pages.

19.

Planning Our Screenplay

I know you're dying to get writing but trust me when I tell you if you start writing without having planned out your story, then you will get stuck and stop very quickly. It seems simple in our heads, but when we try to put a story down on paper, it becomes *way* more complicated.

The more we plan before we start writing the more likely we are to finish our first draft.

A screenplay is made up of scenes; how many scenes will be dictated by the story. There is no ideal scene length and there is no ideal number of scenes for any screenplay. A scene happens in one location at one time. The moment we change location or change time period and require a new slug line we (usually) start a new scene.

A scene can be a few seconds long or many minutes long. It can be full of dialogue or completely silent. It can be in a single room or moving through a jungle by helicopter. There are no rules or set expectations for a scene.

The more pertinent question, is what constitutes a *good* scene? A good scene is where something happens. To know if something has happened, we want to ask three questions:

1) Has the protagonist's journey been aided or hindered by what happened in the scene?
2) Do we know something we didn't know at the start of the scene?
3) Has something changed from the start of the scene?

If we have a yes answer to at least one question—but ideally all three—then the scene has achieved something. If we have learned something we didn't know, or someone has changed during the scene, or the protagonist has been moved closer/further away from his goal, then we have moved the story forward.

If two characters meet up and exchange no information, learn nothing new about each other, don't change in any way, and don't affect the protagonist's journey, then what on earth was the point of the scene? The story has stayed stagnant. Every scene must move the story forward. If it does, it's a useful scene.

But how do we structure our scenes?

If you have read other books on screenwriting, you will know that the two most famous methods of planning our screenplay are the treatment, or the card wall.

The treatment is a detailed synopsis of our story but written in prose rather than script form. It will detail the action and plot and may include the odd line of dialogue to support the characterization. Such outlines can run anywhere from 10-100 pages, but 20 pages is a good guideline of the kind of detail we want. Some very good examples of such outlines are included at the end of *Writing Movies for Fun and Profit* by Robert Ben Garant and Thomas Lennon; writers who swear by this method.

The argument in support of such a treatment is that with a detailed synopsis when we come to the actual writing of the script, all we are really doing is filling in some action and dialogue into our scenes, rather than structuring scenes and outcomes.

The other method is the "card wall." Literally a wall of 3"x5" index cards, each one containing brief details of a scene that we then place in order on the wall to map out our story. The advantage of the cards being that we can pick them up and move them around to keep restructuring our story to perfection. This method is proposed by Blake Snyder in *Save the Cat*, and indeed, a computerized version is available with his *Save the Cat* software.

Both these methods seem logical and useful, but in my early days I spent many hours siting at my computer trying to write a treatment, and then I spent many hours staring at a wall trying to create the scenes on cards. But in both cases I was simply unaware of exactly what it was I was supposed to be doing, and so neither method yielded much more than frustration. I believed that I had a more natural sense of story when I could just sit down at my computer and start writing. Something that I have encouraged you to avoid. Because although I started off great, as soon as I got stuck (usually around page 35-50), I had no way out. No backup. No structure to rely on. And eventually I would give up on the whole script realizing that I simply didn't have the correct underlying structure for the story to work.

Eventually, I was introduced to a game that saved me. It taught me everything I needed to know about how to create scenes by creating natural conflict while moving the story from point A to point B to point C, or in this case, from inciting incident, to end Act One, to first major obstacle etc.

If it works for you—great. If not, find your own way of planning. There is no "right" way, there is only what is best for you.

My method is a game that improvisational comedians call the "So…But…" game.

Let's see how it works by breaking down a section of a movie moment by moment:

I just accidentally travelled back in time in a time machine made from a DeLorean. I have crashed into a barn.

So, I try to apologize to the people who own the barn.

But in my futuristic radiation suit they think I am an alien and shoot at me.

So, I get back in the car and tear off as quickly as possible.

But as I drive, I see my own housing development being built.

So, I stop, and realize I have indeed travelled back to 1955.

But the car won't start.

So, I hide the time machine and walk into town.

But when I get there the town square is completely different. The 1950's version of the world I know.

So, I check a newspaper. It is indeed 1955.

Conscious goal: I have to get back to 1985.

First major obstacle: I am stuck out of my own time and need help.
So, I need to find the 1955 version of the scientist who created the time machine.

But I don't know where he lives in 1955.

So, I go into the diner to check the phone book and I find him listed.

But once inside, my modern clothes and accessories are gaining me unwanted attention.

So, I try to fit in and order something.

But I am lost as to how to order in this bygone age, and just make things worse.

So, I just order a coffee and the guy leaves me alone.

But some bullies come in and harass the guy next to me. I realize the man being bullied is my own father, at 17 years old. And he's the same pushover as the man I know.

So, I try to talk to him.

But before I know it, he disappears.

So, I follow him.

But when I catch up with him, I discover that he is a peeping tom. Then he falls into the street and is about to be hit by a car.

So, I push him out of the way and save him.

But I get hit by the car instead. And when I wake up, I am in the bed of my 17-year-old mother – and she has the hots for me!

And so on.

Each "so…" is positive move. Either it is an increase in the well-being of the protagonist, or it is a positive step towards their goal. Equally, each "but…" is a negative movement in their well-being or in achieving their goal.

Obviously, it is much easier for me to write out these story beats from a finished film than it is to plan them from scratch for our new story. We may change them many times as we plan and re-plan our story but trust me when I tell you that it is much easier to make those changes now than it is to try and make them when we are writing our screenplay.

A single scene may contain one or more of these positive and negative movements. Or, we may have a few scenes in a row that build a larger positive or negative move.

For instance, in the section from *Back to the Future* above, the diner scene covers eight "so…but…" movements. However, the "but…" moment when he sees his housing development until he gets to the diner is a sequence of four scenes, each one building a deeper negative move as he accepts the reality he now faces.

The enormity of each "so…" or "but…" moment will also vary wildly. In the *Back to the Future* sequence above, looking stupid at ordering is a very small "but…," however waking up in the bed of your own teenage mother is a very big "BUT…."

As we move through the story, the degree to which a scene affects our protagonist's life and their quest will increase. At the start we have relatively small changes each time (other than our inciting incident), but by the end, the choices they make, and the obstacles they encounter will have a huge effect on their well-being and their chances of success.

Let's go back to our change curves for a moment and see how this might look placed onto the larger emotional moves our protagonist goes through:

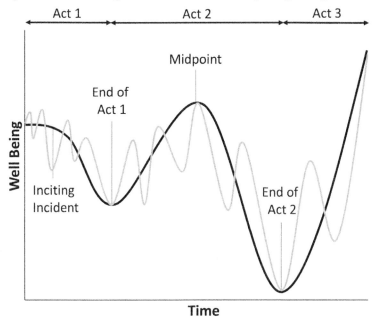

The light gray line represents the constant emotional change our protagonist goes through as each "So..., but..." moment moves them up and down.

Scenes build together to build a sequence. A sequence culminates in a bigger movement. Sequences can be about anything, but most of them will achieve one of our major structural elements, which are:

1) Meeting our protagonist and discovering their flaw(s) that needs to be fixed.
2) The inciting incident.
3) Refusal to act.
4) The end of Act One: When the protagonist chooses to act or is forced to act to achieve their new goal.
5) First major obstacle.
6) Second major obstacle.
7) Midpoint.
8) Third major obstacle.
9) Fourth major obstacle.

10) The worst moment the protagonist faces.

11) How the protagonist turns it around and solves their problem.

12) The resolution.

So, to recap:

- Within scenes are moments that have a small effect (positive or negative) on our protagonist.
- Each scene has a medium size effect (positive or negative) on the protagonist.
- Scenes build up sequences that have a large effect (positive or negative) on our protagonist.
- And sequences build up Acts that have an enormous effect (positive or negative) on our protagonist.

This process of building our scenes is where we will spend most of our time as we plan out our screenplay. But if we do it effectively, we get a big payback, because by the end of it we will have created a substantial and detailed treatment.

Playing the "So…But…" game doesn't stop you from then transferring those ideas and moments onto cards and using the card wall method to structure and restructure your screenplay if you feel that method would work better for you.

We will likely end up changing these movements once we get into the actual writing, but for now we want to plan a story that works in outline to give us the best chance of success once we sit down and start writing.

20.

Writing Our First Screenplay

Have we finished all our planning? Do we have our card wall or outline? Is every scene broken down so we know what is going to happen and why?

Great. Then we get to write our screenplay. All the musing and the brain dumps and the notes must end, and the actual writing must begin. On the positive side, when we tell people we are writing a screenplay, it's now true.

This is the stage of our journey where we buckle down and do it. Where we learn the realities of the physical act of screenwriting.

If you've never written in any volume before then you might be shocked to discover how hard it is to put 25,000 words down on the page.

If you have been writing, but in other mediums, you may still be shocked by how hard it is to get those 25,000 words to make sense and be of a quality that we require.

We can expect to experience the screenwriter's paradox; we will spend the first few weeks struggling to fill pages, hoping to make a dent on the expected 100 pages, only to reach page 60 and realize that our problem is no longer trying to fill 100 pages, but instead trying to *not* fill 300 pages.

This is the stage that offers the biggest single jump in our learning as a screenwriter. Everything we will ever need to learn as a screenwriter will be learned during the actual act of creating our first screenplay. From here on out we are finessing everything that we learn now.

All the books we've read and research we've done up to this point mean diddly squat. We will get stuck, we will get frustrated, we will want to give up, and we will be immensely proud when we finish.

So, let's not delay any further. Let's get writing.

Start a new Final Draft (or Celtx) file and save it as "Screenplay name—Draft 1" No matter what happens now we are only working on this file. Until we type the words FADE OUT: on page 100 we are working on our first draft, so do not save the file as anything else. Do not save it as Draft 2 or any subsequent draft. There is no rewriting and no Draft 2 until we have finished Draft 1.

You can create a file called "Screenplay name—deleted material" or something similar. As much as I tell you otherwise, you are going to do some rewriting as you go along, but I strongly encourage you to make deletions only. Any material you delete, copy and paste it into this new file. That way, it's not lost and if the opportunity comes to reinsert it into the screenplay you still have it available.

The first time we sit down at our computer and write FADE IN: it is going to feel very intimidating.

We are talking about a 100-page screenplay and we are right at the top of page 1. It seems like an impossible challenge, but as we know, the journey of a thousand miles begins with a single step, just as the screenplay of 100 pages starts with a single word. So just write a scene heading and see how it feels. Including FADE IN: we are 5-7 words in. That's not bad. We're moving.

How else can we make it a bit easier? Well, do we have any scenes that we've already written or planned, or got excited about? If so, go and write them up properly. We don't have to write in sequence. If we're lucky enough to have a burst of inspiration for a scene, then get it down on paper. Use that moment of inspiration.

Also, feel free to write out a scene as notes rather than action and dialogue. For example:

```
EXT. CAR PARK — DAY

Jack meets up with the thief and they make the deal
when a cop car cruises by.

Jack hurries back off to his car, but the cop has
seen him and follows him.

Maybe the cop chases Jack for a bit or maybe he just
pulls him straight over. Either way, Jack gets
arrested with the stolen painting.
```

The best scenes for this are the key scenes that we've already planned out. Our inciting incident, the end of Act One, a few key obstacle scenes and probably something in the resolution that we've been thinking about.

Even if we just shorthand out 5-8 scenes we should have a good solid 3-10 pages, and maybe 2000 words. That looks way less intimidating. We've made a very solid dent on the screenplay. Plus, for every scene we plan out, all we need to do is go back and fill in some dialogue and action details. Do that over a couple of days and the pages will start racking up before we know it.

Once we get to page 30, I promise that we will feel all warm and cuddly inside.

Just to warn you, though—it will slow down. The first 30 pages will be the fastest we write. The last 10 pages will be the next fastest. The 60 pages in between will be hard. There's no point sugar-coating it. We may even get stuck (see the upcoming chapter), but the advice is always the same. Keep writing!

21.

Writing Is Hard

We are writing, and that is the main thing. If writing were easy, everyone would do it (and other clichés that might make you feel better).

The point is, we are now a writer. A writer is somebody who gets words down on paper and has a hard time making their story work. That's us right now.

Let's look at the key issues that are going to appear during the actual writing of our screenplay.

1) Getting stuck, or "writer's block"

Two major issues will cause us to stop writing. Either we haven't planned out our story properly, or an idea doesn't work when we try to bring it to life.

Don't worry. Here is a little secret that will make you feel better: *Every writer gets stuck.*

There is no screenwriter in the world that sits down, bangs out 100 pages, stands up and says, "Well, there's another one done." It's just not that easy.

Aaron Sorkin gets stuck. Shakespeare got stuck; I promise. At some point, William Shakespeare put his quill down and thought to himself: *Aw, shit; I don't see how I can finish this without Romeo and Juliet both killing themselves. What a downer ending!* Then, he stared at the page for 20 minutes. Then, he got up and tidied his room a little. Then, he rearranged his other quills on his desk. Then, he stared at the page some more. Then he went to the mead shoppe, where everyone was working on their own plays. Then he came back and realized he was still stuck.

When we get stuck, we doubt ourselves. We want to give up. We worry that we've lost our talent, or whether we had any talent in the first place. These are the horrible thoughts of a writer.

Being stuck is a natural part of writing. It is not a problem. We don't need to stress about it. Instead we must accept that it's going to happen and discover the best way out of it.

Here it what it does *not* mean:

1) It does *not* mean we are a bad writer.
2) It does *not* mean we picked the wrong story.
3) It does *not* mean we should give up.
4) It does *not* mean we should start a different story.
5) It does *not* mean we should quit writing for a few days to "get a fresh perspective."

Here is what it *does* mean:

1) It means an idea needs more thought.
2) It means great stories are complicated and difficult.
3) It means some parts of our screenplay *are* working, since we can see this part *isn't* working.
4) It means by fixing this block, we can make the story even better.
5) It means we are a writer.

In my early years, I started and stopped roughly 10 screenplays within the first 40 pages. That's potentially 300-400 pages of wasted writing that taught me very little. Why? Because I didn't have anyone giving me this advice, and instead of just pushing through, I stopped writing, waiting for some divine intervention that would magically fix the problem for me, but it never came. *We* need to fix it, but we don't need to fix it *now*.

Therefore, this is how we are going to fix it: We are *not* going to fix it. We are going to write something that may not make any sense at all, but we are going to get past the moment that is blocking us—even if we just write shorthand notes.

For example:

```
Bob was supposed to be angry with Susan here, but
now that doesn't seem to make sense, but they need
to have a fight so let's say they have a fight about
the cake.
```

And then we are going to move on.

For your viewing pleasure, I now give you the most useful lesson a screenwriter can ever receive:

There's no such thing as a story problem until someone else reads it.

The process of creating our screenplay is just for us. It doesn't matter how many mistakes or problems it has, it's just for us. If we write with a partner, then the two of us become one unit. Together we can share and discuss the problems all we want, but it does not go outside of that partnership.

What we mustn't do is stop writing. The longer we stop, the harder it is to get started again. We might have written 40 wonderful pages, and then on page 41 we get stuck. We stop writing for days or weeks or months, because we convince ourselves that until this moment is perfect, we can't continue—but we can.

Painful as it is to know this, we are going to have to rewrite all this stuff many, many times. That fabulous 40 pages we just wrote, we'll be lucky if 4-5 pages of it remain in the third draft, so to stop writing because of one story or character issue is ridiculous.

Write *something* and get moving again.

In most cases, we'll move on to page 42, and then, as we get to page 50, we'll think of a solution and come back and drop it into page 41. But even if we don't, it doesn't matter. This is a first draft and it will be seen by only us.

Now go away and get back to writing.

2) "I'm on page 30 and have only just got to the inciting incident."

Again, don't worry. Remember, those were guideline page numbers for a shooting screenplay. The odds of those moments landing anywhere near the right page in a first draft is virtually zero. *All* first drafts are too long. We will visit this idea again later when we finish our first draft and think every one of the 165 pages is necessary, but for now, rest easy in the knowledge that even great screenplays were structural nightmares as they were being written. Again, just get the ideas down on paper and know we have plans in place to deal with it all at the right time.

Now go away and get back to writing.

3) "I've been writing for 3 months and are I'm nowhere near finished."

There is a difference between "planning" and "writing." "Planning" can, and should, take a while, weeks or months even. If we have done the planning properly then the actual writing should be a lot quicker. Have you been writing every day? If so, well done and don't worry, there is no time limit. However, there are some useful guideline times to have in mind. Let's look at a few scenarios, but remember, these times are just for the actual writing of our first draft. This is not a draft to be shown to other people. This is just to get the story down on paper.

1) I am a full-time writer. I have no other work commitments and am entirely funded by my parents/ inheritance/ rental income/ savvy investing, and I can write all day, every day if I want to.
   Goal time for first draft: 1-3 weeks

2) I work part time to survive and pay my bills, but I live cheap and have a lot of time to write my own spec screenplay.
   Goal time for first draft: 2-4 weeks.

3) I work a full-time job to pay bills, but I am single and have a lot of spare time to write at night and weekends.
   Goal time for first draft: 3-6 weeks

4) I work a full-time job. I have a family and can only write once the kids are asleep and during the lucky weekends when my spouse is with their parents.
   Goal time for first draft: 1-2 months

Again, these are just guidelines, but much less than this and we should be very proud of ourselves, much more than this and we need to give ourselves a good kick in the ass and get writing. There is very little correlation between the time it takes us to write our first draft and the quality of that first draft, so there is almost nothing to be gained from taking longer to write it. If you followed my advice from earlier on, then you are not rewriting as you go. The time it takes us to write our first draft should be the exact time it takes to type roughly 20,000-25,000 words. (The time it takes to rewrite that draft can be infinite, but we will worry about then when we get there.)

If you need to, go back to the chapter on "When do we write?" and remind yourself of just how important it is to get everyone in your life on board with the idea that you are now a screenwriter. Those little chunks of time that can be offered by those around us can make all the difference to making a dent in the screenplay and sticking closer to our deadlines.

A self-imposed deadline is a very good idea, as is giving ourselves a witness to those deadlines. Agree on weekly or monthly deadlines with your friend/ girlfriend/ boyfriend/ wife/ husband to finish 5000 or 10,000 words. It gives us a deadline to hit while also showing them that the time we are spending away from them is producing something tangible.

However, *do not let them read it yet*. This is an exercise in hitting deadlines, not getting feedback. We don't want feedback yet—especially not from someone who might be a bit pissy we keep disappearing every night to write. There is no way the script can be good enough yet to justify the time we are spending on it. They will get to read it very soon, when we have a draft that is ready for feedback.

Now go away and get back to writing.

4) "Did I pick the wrong story?"

Of course not. Everyone thinks this at some point. *Everyone*. It's all part of the same challenge as getting stuck. It's not a bad story; it's just not coming together the way we'd hoped.

The reason we are so depressed about our story is that we are deep in the writing of it and every scene presents its own challenges. Characters are saying stuff that feels contrived and stupid. We have to force characters to do things that don't make sense just to fit the story we planned out. Ideas for obstacles that seemed so wonderful at the beginning now seem clichéd and obvious.

Meanwhile, we are comparing it to other movies in the same genre, or movies we admire, which are so much more mature than our story. But great stories don't just appear fully formed. What looks so natural when we see it on screen took the writer months of struggling over the first draft and countless rewrites to make it so perfect. It also took time for the idea to mature into a complex story. That's what we are doing now. By writing it and finishing our first draft, we are giving the idea the chance to grow. It may feel clichéd and stupid right now, but it can't get any better if we give up on it and stop writing.

One of the many bonuses of being commissioned to write a screenplay is we can't just stop writing, as we've already taken the money. The problem with writing spec screenplays is we *can* give up on it, because no one has given us any money, but every idea will look like a bad idea *at some point*. Every idea will look clunky and cheap, with poor characters and no logic, *at some point*.

If we start another screenplay, I guarantee that the same problems will rear their ugly heads.

I am also going to remind you of something we discussed earlier: the chances of this screenplay being made/bought/or even read by anyone other than best friends and family is very small indeed.

Remember, this is our first screenplay. Our goal is to get a story down on paper that looks and reads like a screenplay.

I'll take this further and give you a scenario. Let's say we came up with an idea that could be independently verified as the greatest idea for a movie anyone has ever come up with in the history of humanity. If we really had that idea, then the *last* thing we'd want to do is write it for our first screenplay, or even our third—or even our tenth!

The idea is not enough. It has to be executed perfectly, and we are nowhere near good enough yet. The difference in the quality of our writing between our first screenplay and our fourth will be enormous. So, in reality, even if we could genuinely prove that we had better ideas than this one—save them. Finish this screenplay with the crappy idea and use it to make us a more accomplished writer for the better ideas we have.

However, the truth is what I said at the beginning of the chapter: it's not a bad idea. We're just stuck.

Now go away and get back to writing.

5) "I showed the first 30 pages of our screenplay to someone and they hated it!"

Of course they did. Not only is it not the full screenplay, but it's the first draft.

Never show an unfinished first draft to anyone! As I mentioned above, the first draft is just for us. Any feedback we get at this stage will only serve to confuse and depress us.

I wouldn't even tell people too much about what you're writing. It's like telling people potential names for your unborn child. If they love it their reaction will be neutral. More likely, they won't love it because they don't understand it. They don't understand the hours of thought that went into it and the evolution of the idea. And even if they don't outright criticize it the look in their eye will tell you everything you need to know, and you will start second guessing your choices.

I can't say this too many times—the first draft is just for us. Now go away and get back to writing.

***

On the off chance that we're not suffering from any of these problems and are just breezing through our first draft then great, keep going. It's rare, but it's not impossible. I would say enjoy it while you can, but let's not be pessimistic. Let's just assume that we have the right idea at the right time and the ideas are pouring out of us. Long may it continue.

Stage 3:
Rewriting 101

22.

We've Finished Our First Draft

If you haven't yet finished your first draft, then put this book down! Go and finish your screenplay. Nothing else in this book is useful until you have a finished script in hand. Remember:

**Successful writers don't just talk
about writing; they write. Constantly.**

If you *have* finished, well done! You should be very proud. You have achieved something millions of people say they are going to do, but a much smaller number achieve.

I have a friend who is a senior producer at a major movie company. You can imagine that as soon as people find out his job, they are all too ready to pitch him what they know is the "greatest movie idea ever." My friend is not going to waste his life listening to all their idiotic ideas, so he graciously stops them before they start and says: "Please send me the screenplay and I'll read it." And he means it. He has read at least 15 pages of every screenplay that has ever been sent to him, but what he knows is that most people will never sit down and do the work it takes to finish a full draft of a feature screenplay, and so he remains polite and friendly while saving himself a huge amount of time and trouble.

However, you have finished your screenplay, so you should take some time right now, give yourself a huge pat on the back, and relish your accomplishment.

1......... 2........... 3............4........

Okay, that's enough relishing. Now, we have work to do.

First:

Do not send this screenplay out!

I know you want to. I know selling this screenplay is all you can think about; the riches and fame are so close. I hate to be the bearer of bad news, but we are *far* from finished.

First, be aware that after finishing a screenplay, our emotions can be quite surprising. We might expect a sense of elation and satisfaction, but our real feelings can be very different. They can range from feeling incomplete to frustrated, even angry and lost. We have spent so long being consumed by our screenplay that free time suddenly feels odd and unwelcome.

Upon assessing the actual material, our feelings can range from, "What the hell kind of gibberish have I just churned out?" to, "That's the greatest piece of perfection ever committed to paper."

Any and all of these feelings are correct. They're not always fun, but we are not experiencing anything different from every other writer who has poured their soul into a story for months.

Fortunately, or unfortunately, depending on how you want to see it, we still have a lot of work to do. We now need to get out of writing mode and into re-writing mode.

Let's go back to our definition of a screenplay for a moment. A screenplay is a dynamic blueprint for a movie. The key word here is *dynamic*.

Here is a sample journey for a screenplay inside the studio system. Let's say a named producer with a deal at a studio decides she wants to make a family comedy.

- She hires a writer based on his story pitch about a lawyer that inherits a petting zoo from a long-lost uncle.
- The writer goes away and takes between 4 and 8 weeks to finish his first draft.
- Then he rewrites it. A lot. Sixty percent of the original text is changed. 20 percent is cut out completely. The love interest is changed from one of the female workers in the petting zoo to a mother who visits the zoo with her daughter.
- Then he shows the official first draft to the producer and her team. Everyone has their own thoughts on what works. The writer rewrites it again. 40% of the last draft is changed. It gets 20% longer. The lawyer now has two kids of his own and they need storylines.
- It goes back to the producer. She believes the original writer has run out of ideas and fires him. New writers are brought in to get a fresh perspective. They rewrite it again. Eighty percent of the last draft is changed, and 20 percent is cut out completely. The guy is now a banker and it's not a petting zoo but an aquarium.

- It goes back to the producer who likes it and sends the script up the line at the studio. Eventually, the screenplay is greenlit.
- A director comes on board. He gives notes to the writers. The romance needs to be changed. It's not believable. They rewrite it again. Thirty percent of the last draft is changed. The love interest is now the animal rights activist who is trying to shut the aquarium down.
- By this stage, only 6 words remain from the original screenplay; a single line by the star character that everyone has liked at every stage.
- The director doesn't like the changes and fires the writers, bringing in his own team that he trusts. They rewrite the screenplay with the director and request the old drafts of the screenplay. Forty percent is changed, and the kids are cut out again. Some lines from the original draft by the first writer are put back in.
- A star actor is found and signs on. They meet with the director and writer and give notes. The writers rewrite it again. This time 10% is changed. Primarily lines and moments involving the star actor that weren't funny/interesting enough. He also requests more of a "father lesson" element for his character, so the child subplots are put back in.
- A start date is set for production and pre-production begins. More studio notes come in and the writers go back to the script once more. 10 percent is changed. Mostly curse words being taken out and any moment that could push it into an R rating.
- A week before production the writers are fired, and a famous comedy team is brought in to "punch up" the dialogue with a lot more "fish/finance" jokes.
- Production begins. The lead actors feel that the lines are too wooden. The director suggests they just "wing it" and see what happens. They shoot one version from the screenplay and 22 takes with completely different ad-libs each time.
- The whale that is needed for the emotional final scene gets sick and is unavailable for shooting, so the director chooses to use a stingray instead and stays up all night to rewrite the screenplay himself.
- They finish production and the footage goes to the editor, who doesn't feel that the first Act works so cuts out the opening sequence in the bank.

- Then the director joins the editor and together they cut out the child subplots and all the footage of the long-lost uncle.
- An early cut is shown, and everyone agrees that the ending doesn't work without the whale. The stingray is just not funny enough. Reshoots are agreed and a new whale is found.
- They reshoot with the new whale and since they have booked the whale for three days, they also shoot some extra "whale footage" in case it's useful.
- Back to the editor who cuts in the new (original) ending. They also put in a lot of the "whale footage" into the end credits.

Let's stop there for a moment. These are not, by any means, *all* the stages it could have gone through, or all a movie *needs* to go through to make it to the theater. In fact, I am being generous with this journey. For some true horror stories, read *Tales from Development Hell: The Greatest Movies Never Made* by David Hughes.

Let's look back at what has happened to this screenplay. Would the original writer even recognize it as their own creation?

That's why screenwriting is a *dynamic* art and is not carried out by the writer alone. In fact, the only time we will ever have complete and total control over our work is now, as we start our journey and try to create one great screenplay that can break us in. This is the last time we can say, "No, I disagree with that idea. I'm going to leave it as it is," because after we break in, the people giving us their notes will be paying our salary, and if we don't agree with their changes, they will find someone who does.

So, what's the big lesson from all this?

Nothing is sacred in a screenplay.

Not a location, a character name, a line of dialogue—nothing. Even if it stays in the screenplay all the way through to production someone might just decide to change it on set because the indoor lighting looked weird that day, or the star actor was a bit drunk last night and is having trouble remembering any line over twelve words.

If it's not sacred later, there's no point treating it as sacred now. As we embark on rewriting our first screenplay, or even our second, third or fourth, we will be inclined to treat every word, every moment, every scene as perfect. Once we put it down on paper, we fool ourselves into thinking that there is no possible way it could be improved, and we will fight anyone who argues against us.

This is just not true.

There are literally infinite ways of depicting the same moment. Infinite lines that could be chosen to convey the same meaning.

Get this fixed in your brain right now:

A screenplay is not a document to write, but a document to re-write!

The sooner we allow this idea to become normal in our mind, the faster our screenplays will improve. If we are some way along our journey and we have started to learn this on our own, then simply say it louder: "I can—and must—always improve my screenplay."

The single greatest mistake new writers make is to write 100 pages and send it out into the world as if perfection has just poured from their fingers. It hasn't. Even the most brilliant writers in the world know that a first draft is just that—a first draft. The phrase means that there must be subsequent drafts.

Have you heard the phrase, "You don't get a second chance to make a great first impression"? Well, that is never truer than with screenplays. Sending out a poor screenplay to whatever contacts we do have, that might get us noticed by the industry, means that we have just closed the only doors we had to make it happen.

Our screenplay is a dynamic document. Love it, believe in it, argue for it, but remember that we can always improve it.

23.

Rewriting Our First Screenplay

First, let's be clear on the goal here; we are not trying to re-write this screenplay to production standard. We are re-writing it to make it as good as we can right now, and to learn the dark arts of re-writing.

This is our first screenplay, and its purpose was primarily for us to learn our craft. We are going to rewrite this screenplay to make it as good as possible, and then we are going to be realistic about its value in the market. If every reader and script consultant tell us we've written the next *Godfather,* then we will go out and try to sell it, but we are going to gauge reactions, and if everyone *doesn't* think it's the next *Godfather,* we are not going to be put off. We are going to keep writing because we understand success in this industry is a journey that is more than one screenplay long.

So, let's get re-writing.

First, let's start with the easy stuff: Spelling mistakes, missed words, and sentences that don't make any sense after cutting and pasting them from somewhere else.

The way to fix this stuff is to sit down with a *printed copy* of our screenplay—do not do this on the computer—and read it through in one sitting with a red pen in your hand.

This process can be very enjoyable. First, we get to read the whole screenplay and see which bits work. Second, every mark you make with a red pen feels like a solid improvement—even if it is as simple as correcting a spelling error.

The other thing we are going to do during this read through is make notes about other problems. The trick here is to write a note on the side of the page that is as honest as possible at the exact moment that we read it. If we read something and it doesn't make sense then write, "This doesn't make sense." Or, if we are bored during a few pages then write anywhere on the page, "This is boring." If a question pops into our mind, then write that. Such as, "Why wouldn't Doug just buy the bike?"

Make a note of anything that jumps out at you as you are reading. The pages might be covered in red by the end, but *don't stop reading*. This all has to be done in *one sitting* to get the most from it, so give yourself a clear gap of three hours to do it. Once we've been through it, we'll take our printed copy back to our computer, but before we make any changes, we are going to resave the file as "Screenplay name—Draft 2".

That's right; we are now starting Draft 2. This is only Draft 2 as far as *we* are concerned. When we finally have a draft that we feel is ready for other people to read, we will still call it Draft 1 for the outside world, but internally, we are now starting Draft 2. We do this now so that our first draft will sit untouched in its raw, unfinished form, and that's exactly what we want. Although sloppy and riddled with flaws, there is something honest about a real first draft. We sometimes have a passion and truth to a first draft that gets lost along the way, and if we rewrite that first draft without saving it, then we have lost it forever. Many drafts later, we may come back and read that first draft again and remember what made a character or scene so good.

Once we have Draft 2 open, we will transfer all the edits from the printed screenplay. For the moment, just do the actual text edits. All the other big ideas we will get to later.

Done it? Good. At minimum we have made the screenplay neater and easier to read and we have started rewriting. Well done.

Beyond simple spelling and grammar, there are three key things we are trying to achieve when we rewrite our screenplay.

1) Fix any story problems.
2) Make it shorter.
3) Make it better.

The first two are easier to achieve, though, so let's start there.

24.

How Do We Fix Story Problems?

If you followed my advice, then you kept writing even if you encountered a story problem. In some cases, we could have gone back and fixed it, but I promise you that there are still story problems in our screenplay.

The reality is that we will never fix all the story problems in our screenplay at this stage. We are simply too close to the material. It's nearly impossible to see all its flaws. Have you ever met a parent with an ugly baby who keeps sending you photos of their baby being "cute"? They just don't see it.

That's us right now. It doesn't matter how ugly our screenplay is, we just don't see it, but we must do what we can, and we must get used to the idea that we can always make the screenplay better.

By reading our screenplay straight through we will have noticed when our story wasn't "flowing" for some reason. It became boring, or we had 20 pages of good things happen to the protagonist, or the obstacles were not getting any harder, or it felt like the protagonist was just killing time to get to the end of Act Two.

As we discover these problems, we will think to ourselves, "Hmm. That doesn't really work the way I hoped. Still, I only notice it because I wrote it. No one else will notice that. I think I'll leave it alone."

It is a naïve and vain hope. In reality, readers will notice *every single error* we found. They will also find many, many more.

Story problems break down primarily into two categories:

1) Structural problems: Key story elements that we needed have ended up happening in the wrong order, in the wrong place, or not at all.
2) Logic problems: Characters do things because it fits our story, not because it's honest to the character.

Hopefully, the full read through of our screenplay brought some of these issues to light and we made notes about them in the margin. If we did, we are going to fix them.

1) Structural problems

Go back and check the script against the twelve basic elements of screenplay structure:

1) Meeting our protagonist and discovering their flaw(s) that needs to be fixed.
2) The inciting incident. The thing that starts the story.
3) Refusal to act.
4) The end of Act One: When the protagonist chooses to act or is forced to act to achieve their new goal.
5) The first major obstacle.
6) The second Major obstacle.
7) The Midpoint.
8) The third major obstacle.
9) The fourth major obstacle.
10) The end of Act Two: The worst moment the protagonist faces.
11) How the protagonist turns it around and solves their problem.
12) The resolution.

Are all these elements in the screenplay?

You'll notice that I've taken the page numbers away. That is because we haven't made the script shorter yet, so we are still not worrying about the elements appearing on the correct page. All we are worried about is whether they are there at all.

Even if they are all there, if we think a moment can be improved, then improve it. If a moment should be moved around to make it more powerful, then move it. If something doesn't work at all then cut it out and see what must be written to replace it.

The bulk of our structural problems will appear in Acts Two and Three. We will want to make changes to Act One as we struggle to make our first 30 pages perfect, but it is Acts Two and Three where the real problems will lie. In fact, screenplays will regularly have third Act problems right up until the day they go into production, or beyond.

Think of how many movies you've bought over the years with an alternate ending. Think of just how much time and effort the writer—and everyone else—put into the end of the movie, and they *still* had to go back and completely reshoot it.

But there are very few alternate *openings*. Why? Because it's a lot easier to agree on how a story should start, than how it should end. Once we have spent 90 minutes with our characters, there are just so many choices they *could* make.

We need to challenge ourselves to see the script from the perspective of an independent reader. Will they get increasingly excited and enthralled as they read the script, or will they get bored during Act Two and confused by Act Three?

A few other questions we should challenge ourselves with now are:

1) Do we learn what we need to know (and nothing more) about our protagonist before the inciting incident?
2) Does something happen that makes our protagonist's life significantly better or worse?
3) Do they have a clear goal?
4) Do the obstacles they face get increasingly difficult?
5) Does something happen that would make any normal person give up?
6) Do they get themselves out of that problem on their own?
7) Are all the stories closed off?
8) Is the protagonist's flaw fixed by the end of the movie?

Again, we will not see all the issues at this stage, but if we do see them, then it's crazy not to fix them.

2) Logic Problems

This is the real killer for new writers. This is what makes our screenplay stand out as being written by an amateur, and the main reason for it being thrown away before the reader gets to the end. The moment a character does something that isn't true to their personality, the reader loses all confidence in us and our writing.

Let's look at some common logic problems that come up in screenplays from newer writers (as well as movies that cost $200m).

I'll give you one that makes me cringe every time it happens. There was a time in spy movies when a genre convention allowed (if not encouraged) a logic problem. We've all seen it many times in Bond movies and beyond. The uber-criminal catches the super spy, and rather than just killing him, he ties the super spy up, explains to him in graphic detail the rest of his dastardly plot and then leaves the room to let the super spy die in some contrived and over-complicated way.

So famous is this movie trope that it was mocked perfectly in *Austin Powers: International Man of Mystery* (Mike Myers). Austin and Vanessa are caught by

Dr. Evil and rather than kill them Dr. Evil ties them up and hangs them on a platform above a pool of mutated sea bass with laser beams attached to their heads. Dr. Evil's son, Scott, the voice of the audience, can't understand what his father is doing. "Why don't you just shoot them? I have a gun in my bedroom, I'll go and get it now and we'll just shoot them." Dr. Evil turns to his son and delivers the perfect line "You just don't get it, do you, Scott?"

That movie came out on 1997. That should have spelt the end for that movie cliché. And yet movie after movie still does it. The antagonist and his goons are shooting people left and right, happily blowing up whole busloads of kids, but the moment they finally catch the Hero—the person they want dead more than any other—the first words out of their mouths are, "Tie them up!" Or they hold a gun to the hero's head (definitely not staying a safe distance away) and start "monologuing," as it was called so eloquently in the wonderful spy satire *The Incredibles* (Brad Bird), allowing the hero to do some sort of stupid spin move, knock the gun from the antagonist's hands and continue the fight to victory. It is so ludicrous that any time it happens in a modern movie the audience should groan in unison, stand up and leave the theater in protest.

Want to see it done properly? Watch *Lethal Weapon* (Shane Black). In the end, Riggs and Murtagh must deliver themselves to the bad guys to rescue Murtagh's daughter. There is a quick gunfight and Riggs kills a few of them, but they are finally overpowered and the two of them are captured. Why not killed? Because Riggs and Murtagh may know details of an incoming heroin shipment, the details of which they may have told to other cops. They must be captured and tortured for information—not killed. This allows a perfectly logical and believable face-to-face showdown between Riggs, Murtagh, and the bad guys. That's screenwriting.

Another big logic problem that appears in numerous screenplays by new writers is for people to fall in love for no reason. We want two people to be in love, so by the end of the screenplay they are in love, but nothing has happened that justified them falling in love.

Our hero wants the love interest, the love interest does not want the hero— a perfectly good obstacle to overcome, but we cannot overcome it by just having the love interest change their mind at some stage. This is especially true if the man has been set up to be in any way self-involved, shallow, uncaring or potentially misogynistic. There must be a real, tangible reason as to why any woman, given these character traits, would completely change her opinion about this man and fall in love with him. As Billy Crystal says in *City Slickers* by the legendary comedy writers Lowell Ganz & Babaloo Mandel: "Women need a reason to have sex. Men just need a place."

But these types of logic problems can rear their ugly heads for any number of reasons. A character we have set up as noble and good screws the hero over so that we can create a good end of Act Two moment. A hero that is nerdy and timid suddenly jumps into a fight with a drug dealer. A young heroine, that is safe in a closet from the killer outside, moves for no reason and the ensuing noise alerts the killer to her whereabouts. It doesn't matter what it is, it's poison.

We need to find them and get rid of them as soon as we can, and we'll know them the minute we read them. It will have felt wrong when we wrote it and wrong when we read it, but as previously mentioned, the voice in our head will be saying, *"I know it's illogical, but no one else will notice."* They *will* notice. I promise. Change it!

Logic problems such as these are one of the main reasons that our screenplay will be put down, or more likely, thrown across the room in anger. On the other hand, if a reader truly believes the motivation of every character at every stage of our story, then they will assume us to be a real writer, even if this screenplay didn't grab them emotionally on this occasion.

It won't be easy to fix all these issues. Every change we make may have unintended consequences for many other characters and moments throughout the screenplay. I never said that rewriting was easy, just necessary.

25.

How Do We Make Our Screenplay Shorter?

Now the big question—how many pages is our first draft? I'm going to bet it's more than the 100 pages we were aiming for. That's okay. In fact it is completely normal. If it's less than 100 pages, that's okay, too. It just means that we will have a lot of extra space to play with once we are done editing, because even if it is under 100 pages, we are still going to make it shorter.

One of the key skills of great screenwriting is brevity; saying the greatest amount in the fewest words. To paraphrase Mark Twain, "Sorry for the long letter, I didn't have time to write a short one."

It is also a skill that is innate within very few of us. Some people can create great characters. Others can write witty dialogue, but almost nobody is as succinct as possible, primarily because we have never really been trained to be. Essays we wrote in our youth were never given higher marks for being shorter. In fact, all we've ever really been taught is to pad out our writing to get to the 2,000 or 5,000 words that were required of us. To relearn the opposite is difficult, but we are going to do it.

What is your page count? We can cut it down by 20% in one go. That's right—20%. If we currently have 135 pages, we can lose 27 of them in one fell swoop leaving us with a much more manageable 108. If we have 95 pages, then we'll be down to 76 giving us a lot of space to build the story up.

How do we do this? By learning to cut down our overwriting. Everybody overwrites their first draft. Everybody. To what degree will vary slightly by the person, but no matter who we are we can lose 20% by editing down the unnecessary elements. This is the single most useful skill we will ever learn as a screenwriter.

Let's have a go. Here is a scene from a first draft screenplay of mine:

EXT. MOUNTAIN SHACK — DAY

KAI, (60), walks out of the shack and places a bowl full of vegetables on the ground, rubbing his aged back as he stands back up and looks up to the mountainside.

There is a cave entrance in the mountain about a hundred yards up with a pathway leading to it.

He grabs a small gong that is hanging on the wall. The back door to the shack bursts open and MAI LING, (23), runs out.

> MAI LING
>
> Father!

> KAI
>
> What?

> MAI LING
>
> The dagger of Mun-Tai has been stolen from America.

> KAI
>
> It is your brother.

> MAI LING
>
> We don't know that.

> KAI
>
> I know it, Mai Ling. I knew the day your brother left us that if he returned, he would return with the dagger.

Mai Ling looks up to the cave in the mountain.

> MAI LING
>
> Is Luong okay?

> KAI
>
> She's fine, Mai Ling. If she was in trouble, we would have felt it. As protector, you must learn to trust your instincts.

Kai strikes the gong. The sound echoes out across the mountains. A ROAR comes back from within the cave. A second later an enormous DRAGON emerges from the cave. She is LUONG. She is twenty feet tall with thick green scales.

She launches into the air, extends her wings and soars down to the shack. When she lands and sees Mai Ling, she bounds over with the excitement of a newborn puppy and licks his face. Her tongue is enormous and covers him in green tinged Dragon saliva.

There is an enormous stick lying by the door that is covered with tooth marks. Mai Ling picks it up and throws it off down the mountain for her. She tears off after the stick, her feet throwing up massive stones that fly at Mai Ling.

                    MAI LING
          What should we do? Shall we
          leave?

                    KAI
          No. We shall wait for him.

That is 320 words and about a page and a half.

I want you to go through it and cross out all the action that is not necessary and all the dialogue that does not move the story forward.

We want to try to lose 20% and get it down to no more than 260 words, or less than one page, but without losing any pertinent information. And, if possible, we want to try to make it look easier to read with more white space.

Go and have a try before you look at my second draft below.

EXT. MOUNTAIN SHACK — DAY

The shack sits on a remote mountainside with a cave visible above it.

KAI, (60), walks out and places a bowl full of vegetables on the ground, rubbing his aged back as he stands back up.

The back-door bursts open and MAI LING, (23), runs out.

>   MAI LING
>   Father! The dagger of Mun-Tai has
>   been stolen.

>   KAI
>   It is your brother.

>   MAI LING
>   We don't know that.

>   KAI
>   I knew the day he left us that if
>   he returned, he would return with
>   the dagger.

>   MAI LING
>   Is Luong okay?

>   KAI
>   She's fine. If not, you would
>   have felt it. As protector, you
>   must learn to trust your
>   instincts.

Kai strikes a gong. A ROAR is heard from within the cave.

LUONG emerges. She is a beautiful DRAGON, twenty feet tall. She launches into the air and soars down to the shack.

She bounds over to Mai Ling like a puppy and licks his face. Mai Ling grabs an enormous stick covered with tooth marks and throws it. Luong tears off after the stick.

>   MAI LING
>   What should we do?

>   KAI
>   We shall wait for him.

There we go. One page and 190 words. Better than I expected, since the goal was 260 words. I lost over 30%. What did you get it down to?

Let's break down what I took out.

1) A lot of description that added nothing. Just extra details of setting and characters that pour out of us in a first draft. When we are being strict on ourselves, though, most of this stuff is irrelevant.

2) Unnecessary dialogue. Such as:

MAI LING

Father!

KAI

What?

This adds nothing. Meaningless chitchat. Get to the point and lose anything that isn't necessary for the story. Such dialogue mostly shows up at the beginning of a scene, but not always. Anything that can be lost—lose it.

If we do this on every page of the script, I promise that there is at least 20% that we can cut without losing any story.

26.

How Do We Make Our Screenplay Better?

The $1m question, literally. If we can do this well, then we can sell our screenplay for $1m, or more.

There are many books on rewriting, but the best, in my opinion, is *Your Screenplay Sucks* by William M. Akers. Each chapter is a reason that screenplays fail, and a chance to challenge whether ours stands up. Read it now, but it will be much more valuable to us after we finish our second screenplay. Even if we do read it now, we should read it again when that time comes.

To get us started, below is a set of questions that other people are going to ask of the screenplay, consciously or subconsciously, as they read it:

1) Is the protagonist interesting?

If they're not, then why should anyone invest two hours of their time reading about/watching them? Does the protagonist have a scene in the first 10 pages that shows how interesting they are? It's no good waiting till page 60 to show that they are interesting. With a dull protagonist, no one is going to make it to page 60.

Raiders of the Lost Ark (Lawrence Kasdan), wastes no time in making sure we know that Indiana Jones is the coolest, most exciting guy in the world. He's out in the jungle, searching places so scary that the locals won't approach, and then foils an attempt on his life with a whip. Sold. This is a guy I'm watching for hours with a big smile on my face.

However, "interesting" does not necessarily mean "exciting." Many protagonists are underachievers at the start of their story. The story will help them achieve whatever it is they've been avoiding; be it love or success. That's why we are watching them. But we still need to show that they have something that sets them apart from the crowd, or at least the potential to be special.

In *Romancing the Stone* (Diane Thomas), Joan Wilder is a romance novelist who lives an almost downtrodden life in New York. She is successful, but she fears her fame, is uncomfortable in crowds and unwilling to seek out love. She is the stark opposite of her literary heroines, and to all intents and purposes she is boring. To solve this, Diane Thomas makes some very smart choices.

First, the story opens as we watch one of her romance novels play out, so we see how exciting Joan's imagination is—even if her life is quite the opposite. Second, after a brief introduction to Joan, we jump to Colombia—a world away from New York—and the world that Joan is going to be thrown into. The juxtaposition of these two worlds is what interests us. How is Joan going to survive there? If we met this boring novelist, and then found out her challenge was to get to Brooklyn and deliver a book to her sister, then we wouldn't care at all. That would just be the boring journey of a boring person, but put her in Colombia, and we become excited to see how she survives.

2) Is the protagonist empathetic?

This is not the same as likeable. There is a myth that producers and studio execs want all protagonists to be likeable, that they all have to be people who are charming and nice to everyone all the time. Not true. Screenplays with all sorts of protagonists are bought and put into production, but all those protagonists are empathetic in the sense that the audience can understand why they do what they do. They want the protagonist to succeed.

We have to show in those opening pages that our hero is someone we can root for, no matter what world they come from, or what flaws they have.

The wonderful book *Save the Cat* by Blake Snyder, is titled to explain exactly this phenomenon. I'm paraphrasing, so go and read the full book yourself when you get the chance, but in essence, he argues that we need to include a scene early on where our hero saves the cat; i.e. they do something that means the audience sides with them and wants them to succeed.

Goodfellas (Nicholas Pileggi & Martin Scorsese), is a perfect example. The protagonist is Henry Hill, a kid with very loose morals who is desperate to be a wise guy. He drops out of school, gets a mailman beaten up and partakes in all sorts of crime. But when he's arrested, he keeps his mouth shut. We now know that he's loyal and honorable to those around him.

Whether we want to be a wise guy or be friends with this guy in real life is irrelevant, we now want this guy to succeed.

In *Happy Gilmore*, Happy is a loser. He can't keep a job, can't make it as a pro hockey player, and can't keep his girlfriend. Plus, he's coarse and borderline cruel, BUT he loves his grandma! And it's totally genuine. He will give up anything for his grandma; his money, his house, anything. So, when the chance arises for him to become an unlikely golf superstar, we want him to succeed.

As we established, Indiana Jones is the coolest guy on the planet, but it's still not enough. Coolness will only get us so far; we still need to have empathy for what he does—especially since his methods seem so nefarious. How does Kasdan do that? Well, after he steals the idol from its cultural home, it is stolen from Indiana by Belloq. When Indy gets back to the university, he discusses with Marcus the money he needs to get to Marrakesh to steal it once more from Belloq so that it can be placed in the museum—and there it is. Unlike Belloq, *everything* Indy does is to give these pieces to the people and put them in a museum. Now, we know his motives are pure, and we can support his choices—no matter how questionable they may be.

3) Does every scene move the story forward?

If not, then what's it doing there? This is the moment when we need to be brutal on our own work. We may have written the scene in good faith, but the development of the story may have made the scene redundant. If so, we must lose it, even if we love it. If it doesn't move the story forward, then it's not necessary and it must go.

This is not unlike the work of an editor once the footage reaches postproduction. On nearly every movie, a huge amount of footage is shot that never makes the final edit. Sometimes because the performances just didn't work that day, but mostly because the line, or scene, or sequence is deemed unnecessary to the final story.

I'm sure many of us have spent hours watching the "deleted scenes" on DVDs (remember those?). In my whole life I have only ever seen one deleted scene that I honestly felt would have improved the film if left in the final edit. It was a scene from the wonderful *Galaxy Quest* (David Howard and Robert Gordon). Other than that, all those deleted scenes prove is that editors are very, very good at their jobs. They can take the objective view of the footage that the writer and director find it nearly impossible to do.

However, to have a shot at getting our script bought and anywhere near production we must be our own editor, and we must be ruthless.

4) Are the obstacles, and the solutions to those obstacles, unexpected?

This is our first draft remember, so we have a lot of rewriting to do, but after finishing any draft if we look at something and think, "Meh, that just feels a bit predictable," then change it now. Why wait for everyone else to tell us that it was, indeed, predictable?

Martial arts films are an interesting tutorial in this topic. There is a legitimate market for martial arts movies that do nothing unexpected, with plot moves so predictable that cliché is an understatement.

Kickboxer (Glen A Bruce, from a story by Mark DiSalle and Jean-Claude Van Damme), is about Kurt Sloane whose brother is an American kickboxing champ. Together they travel to Thailand to fight the local champion, Tong Po. During the fight, Tong Po fights dirty and after beating the brother, deliberately paralyses him. Driven by vengeance, Kurt finds a local recluse who is the best Muay Thai teacher and begs to be trained to be good enough to beat Tong Po. They train in his mountain shack and Kurt falls for the old man's niece. We have many montages of his improving progress. Eventually they line up the fight with Tong Po, but not in the fancy main arena but in an underground illegal arena where the fighters will now have broken glass glued to their hands. The fight is hard, but Kurt is victorious and avenges his brother.

That plot could be used to describe upwards of a hundred or so martial arts movies, with only very slight changes to the plot details, but *Kickboxer* was a huge success, making ten times its budget at the American box office alone. Why? Because it's fantastic. However, there is not one moment of the film that surprises you. It simply delivers exactly what 14-year-old boys want.

I'm not arguing that there is not a market for such films, I'm just arguing that we aren't going to break in by writing one. Look who wrote the story for *Kickboxer*—Jean-Claude himself. He was already a star, and raising $1.5M (the film's budget) was not hard with his star power attached. We don't have that luxury.

Our plot twists must surprise and excite. If people don't know us then they have no reason to keep turning the pages other than the story they are reading. Every page must make them think, "That's nice, I've never seen that before." The first time they think, "Oh, that's just like in (insert movie name)." Or, "Yup, that's exactly what I expected to happen," that's it, our script is tossed aside

5) Does the resolution close off all the stories?

If the reader has made it this far then great, we've done something right, but we want them to finish the last page, close the script, pick up the phone to their boss and say, "I've just found a script we have to buy right now." Remember, the chances of this script ever making it to production are slim, but when people find a truly great script, they will buy it, if no other reason than to stop somebody else owning it, and that sale could be all we need to get things rolling.

We do that by giving them a resolution that is truly satisfying. If they close the script, stop for a moment, and think, "Hang on, what happened to the guy with the dog? And why didn't the waitress move with them to LA?" Again, we're done.

There was a time in American movies, predominantly the 60's and 70's, when enigmatic endings were not only okay but were the trend. Stories were deliberately left open for viewers to make up their own version of what might have happened once the cameras stopped rolling. Those days are gone, and I, for one, hope they're not coming back. I want closure.

Closing the final page of a screenplay should feel like the end of a good sneeze as all the tension that has been built up just flows out from every extremity leaving us all gooey and borderline euphoric. We can't do that if we're worrying about what happened to the guy with the dog.

Track back on all the stories you've set up. Every one of them must have a definite ending. That way the reader can stamp "Recommend" on the end of our script and go to sleep happy.

27.

How Do We Get Feedback?

Now that we have corrected all the spelling errors, fixed the story problems, cut it down by 20%, and made it as good as possible, we are ready to send it out into the world for feedback. This is not to try and sell it, this is just to get feedback from a few people we trust to tell us the truth about the script as they see it.

Before we start, we are going to register our script, to protect it. Any script can be registered with the Writers Guild of America for a fee of about $20. It's a useful way to give you some legal recourse if you feel that your work is plagiarized in any way. In that sense, it's $20 well spent. Just type "WGA script registration" into google.

Did you register it? Good. Let's get some feedback.

A big note of warning here—the time, the energy, the dedication and passion that we poured into our writing will make us strangely defensive of our work. Here is a (slightly) fictional recreation of an actual conversation I had with a young writer who had come to me for help with his screenplay.

```
INT. OFFICE — NIGHT

Hywel works at his computer. His phone RINGS.

                    HYWEL
          Hello?

                    WRITER (O.S.)
          Hi. It's me. I wondered if you
          had a chance to read it yet.

                    HYWEL
          I did.

                              INTERCUT WITH:
```

INT. WRITER'S BEDROOM — NIGHT

The young writer's room is adorned with movie posters. He looks like he hasn't slept in days.

> WRITER
>
> It still doesn't work does it? I knew it. I just can't get the logic right. He has to become her pimp at some point, but if he really loved her then he wouldn't be her pimp, would he? But if he's not her pimp then there's no story.

> HYWEL
>
> I think you're right. There's still some work to do on the logic.

> WRITER
>
> What's wrong with the logic?

> HYWEL
>
> Well, what you just described. The two choices seem to work at odds with each other. He's becoming her pimp because you want him to, not because it makes sense.

> WRITER
>
> Of course it makes sense. He needs to work, doesn't he? Even pimps need money. Why, do pimps work for free where you live?

> HYWEL
>
> Err... I think we're getting off track.

> WRITER
>
> What are you, some pimp guru now?

> HYWEL
>
> No.

```
                    WRITER
          Exactly. So, what do I need you
          for?
```

The line goes dead. Hywel waits for a moment, hangs
up and goes back to his own work.

The writer in question rang back the next night to apologize and tell me his
solution to the problem, but this exchange will become very familiar to you.

Even when we solicit advice, we hate to be told that what we have written
doesn't work, because what we hear is, "This writing sucks, you're a bad
writer, you're wasting your time. Give up!" But what people are actually
saying is, "Something here didn't work for me. I think it could be
improved."

So, here is *The Screenwriter's Journey* guide for soliciting feedback. It is very
simple. It is just once sentence and one facial expression. And here is it:

```
                    YOU
                 (smiling)
          Thank you. That's a very
          interesting insight.
```

That's it. That's all we need. No matter whom we ask, and no matter what
they say about our screenplay, we will simply smile and say, "Thank you.
That's a very interesting insight."

We can vary it slightly so as to not look looney tunes crazy, but we will stick
to this as closely as possible.

We will not defend our screenplay. We will not argue about their idea, their
suggestion or their motives. We will not tell them that they clearly didn't
"get it" or mustn't have read it properly. We will not go into lengthy
explanations about how, if they understood screenwriting, they wouldn't
mention that part of the screenplay. We will not stop them mid-sentence
explaining that we, "didn't want feedback about that character at that stage,
but just whether the story is working." We will simply smile and say, "Thank
you. That's a very interesting insight."

Later, once all the anger and hurt we felt as they spewed out their stupid,
ill-informed nonsense has subsided, we can sit down and sift through it to
work out what is useful and what isn't, but here is a little secret: It's *all*
useful. I'm not saying we should adopt every suggestion they made, but they
said it for some reason. Something confused them or didn't work for them
or didn't ring true. If it had, they wouldn't have mentioned it.

We will not and *cannot* get 100% positive comments on our work. Go and look at imdb.com. As of the writing of this book, there are 33,611 one-star ratings for *The Shawshank Redemption*. There are 36,232 for *The Godfather*. *The Godfather!* You'd think *The Godfather* would be bulletproof, wouldn't you? However, only 52% of people gave it 10/10; that means 48% of people (over 600,000 of them) have taken time out of their lives to go online to make it clear that *The Godfather* was not entirely perfect. If Mario Puzo had sent his screenplay to them for feedback, he'd have given up writing in an instant and gone to live in a hole somewhere to avoid burdening society with his talentless schlock.

The same is also true of positive feedback. When someone tells us they love a scene, or a character, or a line, what we hear is, "I knew I was a genius." But remember, this is the same idiot who two seconds ago told you that your lead character wasn't funny. What makes him more correct now? Nothing.

Plus, I have a dirty secret to share with you. People who care about you will want to find something nice to say about your screenplay even if it's not there. I can guarantee you that between 40-95% of the nice things they say are only there to balance out the myriad of things they found to bitch about. If we really want to weed out the lies, they will sound extraordinarily vague compared to the criticism. Such as, "Loved all the stuff with the parrot," or, "It flows really nicely," whereas they had a good five minutes on why the boy shouting at his dad felt forced and clichéd.

Remember, either way, good or bad, we get feedback to *choose* the ideas that can help us improve our work. The key word here is *choose*, and the only way to get all the choices we can is to smile and say, "Thank you. That's a very interesting insight."

So, to whom do we give our screenplay in order to get this wonderful feedback? This is more difficult than you'd think. The perfect feedback agent is a balance of four things:

1) Our access to them, and the chances of them reading it quickly.
2) Their ability to tell us the truth about our work.
3) Their ability to read and visualize a screenplay.
4) Their ability to understand the good and bad in our screenplay and vocalize it in a way that is useful and positive.

The perfect feedback agent would be a childhood friend who drifted out of our life ever so slightly but has since become a world-class screenwriter and who recently reached out to us on Facebook to become friends again. If you have any of them in your life, then you're all set. Unfortunately, that's a specific set of qualities. Most of us will end up using:

- Spouse/partner
- Friends
- Work colleagues we like
- Other writers we may know (who may also be friends)
- Our one industry contact

I'm going to suggest excluding any industry contacts we have at this stage. If they truly have a route into the industry, then we don't want them to read our work until it's as good as it can be, and it's not there yet. We will come back to such contacts later.

All the others are just fine, but each one carries its own challenge. Some spouses/partners are great at telling us the truth, others will be scared about hurting our feelings. Friends are usually better about being honest, but there's no reason that they've ever read a screenplay in their lives and will end up comparing it to films they've seen, instead of screenplays they've read.

Other writers will be more adept at understanding the craft but can sometimes be so desperate to show off their own knowledge and brilliance at writing that they overwhelm us with feedback that is confusing, irrelevant or unnecessarily harsh.

On the other hand, we might find someone who is unfailingly positive about everything. I had a feedback agent like this. He was a smart guy who was also a writer and a good friend of mine. We even collaborated on some TV projects. Every time I gave him a screenplay, he would call me up and tell me that I'd just written *Citizen Kane* (Herman J. Mankiewicz & Orson Welles). In fact, it was better than *Citizen Kane*. And he wasn't just blowing smoke up my ass, he truly believed it, and he had all sorts of evidence to back it up. It was wonderful to chat to him as it made me feel so good about myself and all the work that I'd put in. There was just one problem; he was wrong, and I knew it. The best I could figure was that he just genuinely enjoyed reading screenplays. He would be the worst development executive in the world. He would want to buy every script he read.

However, such feedback is just as useful as feedback from people who are relentlessly negative, and of course much nicer to listen to.

There is no such thing as perfect feedback, or the perfect person to give it to us. Find four or five people you believe will tell you the truth and give them each a *printed* copy. It's hard enough to read a screenplay; don't make them do it on the computer.

Then give them the advice that I gave you earlier; ask them to read through it and write in the margin their honest notes.

Let them know that we want the script back at the end. Their verbal notes will be great, but they will forget a lot after they have read it. Seeing their notes as they went though will be invaluable to us.

Each person is going to give us a completely different experience in terms of what they take away from it and how they communicate that to us. In each case, take from it what we can, and remember:

```
                YOU
            (smiling)
        Thank you. That's a very
        interesting insight.
```

28.

Our Third Draft

Now that we have our feedback, we are going to create a new draft. Go back to your file and resave it as: "Screenplay Name—Draft 3".

We are also going to watch out for one pitfall at this stage. We are going to refrain from *drastically* changing the basic setup.

Sometimes, when we get this first round of feedback, it can feel so overwhelming and negative that we decide that we've picked completely the wrong idea.

Well-meaning people will say things like, "I really enjoyed the stuff between the sister and the newspaper editor. That's the story I was interested in. I'd rather watch a film about those two." And so, we start thinking, "Shit, I've written the wrong film. Here I am writing a film about an investigative journalist and they want to watch a film about his sister having an affair with his editor. Should I write that film instead?"

No, we shouldn't. What they mean is those characters and their side story are working well, and elements of our main plot *aren't* working yet, so they ended up enjoying the supporting characters more. It means we've got work to do, but it does *not* mean we should give up on this story. Remember what we discussed. If we *did* go off and write that story, it would simply encounter its own problems.

I'll give you an example from my own life. My first completed screenplay (finished in 1995) was about a single father who moves into a new house that turns out to be haunted. His young son, however, is not scared and befriends the ghosts, helping them sort out their issues that are left in the living world. Looking back, it could have been a combination of what was to become *The Sixth Sense* and *Ghost Town* (David Koepp & John Kamps). The thing that I started with, the key element that excited me, was the idea that the kid didn't wasn't scared and just wanted to be their friend.

I finished the first draft and sent it out to my feedback readers. There were some positive comments, but it was mostly negative. Hurt and dismayed I decided the idea was elementally flawed and went back to the drawing board. By the time I had finished the next draft it was the story of an executive at a toy company who wakes up one morning in the world of the medieval action figures he created. It was a completely different story. The screenplay was much better because I had got better by writing them both, but I never gave myself the chance to improve my first screenplay. I never found out how good I could have made that idea had I given it the chance.

Think of it this way; what is the key element that got you excited about this story? If that remains, then you are still writing the same story and you must make any changes you feel necessary to get the best version of that story.

However, dumping that key element and starting again is not rewriting; it is starting another screenplay. We *will* start another screenplay but only when the time is right. Our job right now is to make *this* story and *this* screenplay as good as possible. All those other stories will still be there when we finish this one. If we really feel they are still worth writing, then we can do so when the time comes.

However, outside of *drastic* changes to the basic setup, we need to be ready to make any changes that are necessary.

To do this, we are going to collate all the feedback we received into three buckets:

1) Ideas we totally agree with and are going to change
2) Ideas we understand and appreciate, but don't necessarily agree with or want to change
3) Ideas we completely disagree with

Anything that elementally changes the idea will be put into bucket 3.

First, go to bucket 1. We might be surprised by just how much stuff we are dying to change, even if it's a big change and entails a lot of work. If we agree with it, and we truly feel it will improve the script then make the change.

For now, we are going to ignore bucket 3. This means we are just left with bucket 2, which is the hardest to work with. What do we do with these ideas? Implement them? Ignore them? I wish I had a definitive answer, but I don't. This is the essence of re-writing. What choices do we make? With the plethora of avenues available, how do we choose the right ones?

What I suggest is to look at each idea and ask one question: Could it make the screenplay better?

That's all we're trying to do here—to make the screenplay better. We're not trying to shorten it at this stage. We already did that. We just want to make it a better screenplay and that might mean losing some stuff that we love, as well as adding some stuff that we don't immediately agree with.

For instance, let's say we wrote a script about a fast-talking, maverick cop. He's the human version of Bugs Bunny. He is prepared for any eventuality and can talk his way out of any situation.

He's a detective in Detroit who has to investigate a murder. It's a balls-out comedy with lots of scenes of the cop breaking department rules and shaking down his sources and talking his way out of problems as he travels Detroit investigating the crime.

We send this out for feedback and people enjoy it, but the general feeling is that it's a bit like other cop films and doesn't have anything in the story that sets it apart, but everyone loves the lead character and sees it being a real star-making role. Someone suggests that maybe we change the location. He is from Detroit but what if he has to go somewhere else to investigate the murder. Somewhere he is not so familiar with.

Where's different to Detroit? Beverly Hills!

Suddenly, alarm bells go off in our mind. Of course, he should have to go to Beverly Hills, where all the rules are different, and he is a fish out of water. Why didn't we think of that the first time? That is a huge change and requires a complete Page 1 rewrite, but we can see just how much this character will be improved with that extra layer of conflict added; his fast-talking, maverick ways are going to *really* shine.

So, we rewrite the whole thing, but we haven't lost the element that set the film apart, the smart, funny lead character.

Now we send out draft two and the feedback is great. Everyone loves it. The conflict is fantastic, the story of the art dealer/ smuggler works great, but people still feel something is missing. It all feels a little cheap. It's funny but it feels almost like a kids' film with an adult plot.

Someone suggests we need to add a more serious undertone. We think about it and realize maybe it could really add something if, rather than a random murder, it was all about the murder of his friend. We could start out with humor, but then have a quite serious and tender moment between the detective and his friend, before the friend is killed in the detective's own apartment in a scene that is quite shocking and not at all funny. Now, the detective has a much stronger personal goal to investigate and catch the killer, which *adds* a layer of story.

So, we go back and change the whole script from an outright comedy to a quite serious detective plot but with some very funny scenes of the detective tricking his way through the investigation and clashing with the Beverly Hills Police.

Again, does this fundamentally change why we started writing the movie? No, but it *does* fundamentally change the movie for the better. It gives the script a chance to be more layered. It's now not *just* a comedy or *just* a detective story, and so we should do that rewrite—no matter how hard it is or how long it takes.

But what if someone said, "I love the lead character, but the cop thing has been done to death. He should be a private detective, hired by the dead man's family. But everything else should stay the same."

What does this add? Nothing. It just *changes* it for the sake of changing it. In fact, we lose a lot of the conflict from our main character being a cop who shouldn't break the rules. Plus, we lose his personal motivation to find the killer. Now, his only motivation is money. It would be changing it for the sake of changing it.

If it doesn't add conflict or made the story more layered, then it's not a change we should be making.

That leaves bucket three. Let's go back to it and just read every suggestion once more. Does anything jump out at us this second time? If not, don't worry. It's not our job to give every idea equal weight and to try them all. But if something does catch our eye, stop and think about it for a moment.

I'll give you another example from my own writing. A screenplay of mine called *Santa Claus Inc.*, was based on the idea that Santa's grotto was run like any other big corporation, with frustrated middle managers and disgruntled minimum wage elves. The big joke was that Santa decides to move the grotto to New York City and recruits a human CFO to try and turn a profit by charging the kids for the toys.

After a couple of rewrites a friend and fellow writer told me that he just didn't buy the New York thing. I was spending huge amounts of the script explaining and justifying the logic of how these elves and Santa now live and work in New York without getting discovered.

As he gave his feedback I did exactly what I've tried to help you avoid. I got angry and upset and argued with him and told him he was an idiot and that he didn't understand what I was trying to do. After all, that was the whole point of the film.

However, the more I thought about it the more I realized that this wasn't the point of the film. The New York thing wasn't what excited me at the beginning. What hooked me in to write this script was the idea that Santa ran his business like a multinational corporation instead of the colorful, fun-packed wonderland that we have seen so many times before. Therefore, the grotto didn't need to be in New York. In fact, maybe it made much more sense to bring the CFO from New York to the North Pole and make him the fish out of water. So that's what I tried, and it worked much better. It required a lot less explanation to make the setup believable and to get on with the real story.

Consider every idea you received and really think about whether it could make the script better.

We should spend a few weeks, maybe a month, re-writing this third draft. Make the changes that we believe make it better without getting bogged down in the myriad of different ways that we can tweak and re-tweak a script. Make it as good as we possibly can in a reasonable time and then we're done.

29.

Our Sale Draft

Finished all your editing? An even bigger congratulation. Let's look at what we've accomplished so far. We sat down and wrote a screenplay. We made it as good as we could. We sent it out into the world for feedback, and now we have a fully re-written and improved draft. That is a lot of work and a real accomplishment, but we're not done yet.

First, resave the file as "Screenplay Name—Draft 4." Once again, that retains Draft 3 and the new material we created in its purest form for us to use in the future if we want to.

Now we need to run back through and tighten up the writing one last time. This is the same as the exercise that we did after finishing our first draft. Go back and lose all extraneous description, get rid of unnecessary dialogue etc. You will even find yourself losing stuff that you have already edited because you will be better and even stricter this time through. Our goal this time is to lose 10-20% of the pages. It may be more, it may be less, but we are now trying to get down to our target page number of 100-110 pages, give or take the genre.

Done? Good. Well done.

We now have a sale draft of our script. To us it is Draft 4, but to the outside world this is the first draft. However, we never reference that anywhere.

The title page of our script should look like the example on the next page:

```
┌─────────────────────────────────────────────┐
│                                               │
│                                               │
│                                               │
│                                               │
│            SCREENPLAY NAME                    │
│                  By                           │
│                                               │
│             A. Writer                         │
│                                               │
│                                               │
│                                               │
│                                               │
│                                               │
│                    Tel: 333-333-3333          │
│              Email: email@gmail.com           │
│                                               │
└─────────────────────────────────────────────┘
```

Nothing fancier that that is needed. Again, trying to make our title page stand out with great big fancy fonts or graphics will achieve just that, but not in a good way. Anything other than the above and readers will immediately know that we are an amateur. No © signs, no WGA numbers. None of that is necessary. They all know it's copyrighted and protected.

And the script will not say "Draft 1" or anything similar. No one else cares what draft it is, they just want a good script. They don't care if it's Draft 1 or Draft 20. We certainly will not write "Final Draft" on it. This annoys readers for many reasons. Mainly because the presumption of anyone that their script is perfect and will never be changed is enough to put anyone off picking it up.

It will have contact details on it. We want anyone who picks it up to have everything they need get in touch with us immediately to make us a million-dollar offer. If you live in Los Angeles, put your address, otherwise phone and email are fine. If you can, get an L.A. phone number. Anything else is a dead giveaway that we don't live in LA. The bulk of the industry is out there, and so anyone not there is perceived, fairly or unfairly, as not really being serious. Get someone who lives there to buy you a pre-pay phone and mail it to you. Or try and get a skype number with an L.A. area code.

However, we are not sending this to out to the industry just yet. We are also not going to give it to any industry contacts we have. Contacts like this are gold. Whether it's a lawyer that went to school with your dad who now represents an A-list star, or a friend of a friend who was the third assistant Director on Bryan Singer's latest film. However grand or tenuous their connection to the industry may be, we only get one shot with them. If we send them a script that is anything less than fantastic only one of two things can happen:

1) They read it, hate it, and refuse to pass it on to anyone.
2) They do pass it on to people but are embarrassed when the feedback is atrocious.

Either way, we have now lost that avenue forever. That chance will never come up again and we have thrown away one of the best opportunities we had to get our work read by people who matter.

Even if we don't have such contacts, we will never send out a substandard script to production companies and agencies. Again, they will hate it and they may remember us forever, refusing to ever read our future scripts. We need to know how good our script really is.

30.

How Do We Know if Our Screenplay is Any Good?

As useful as our initial readers were, they are not much use to us now. If they love it, we don't know if they're right, and if they hate it we will justify it because they are not "industry" people.

Instead, we are going to get an objective, external critique of our work that will give us a realistic view of how our script will be viewed by the filmmaking community.

Fortunately, numerous services exist to help us do just that. There is a small cost attached, but the investment is worth it to truly understand where we are on our journey.

There are others, but the services I would recommend for this are:

1) The Black List: www.blcklst.com
2) Selling Your Screenplay: www.sellingyourscreenplay.com (which is also a very interesting podcast hosted by the site's founder Ashley Scott Myers, in which he interview screenwriters about their career journey and work).
3) Inktip: www.inktip.com

They each offer analysis by industry readers who have either worked/ or currently work as readers for major production companies/ studios or agencies.

I would get two reports to make sure we get a fair and balanced viewpoint on our script. Only one person and they may simply have taken against our work for no reason. Three or more can start to get expensive. Only get a third if the first two are wildly different from one another, but that is very rare. However, get the two reports from different places. Some companies offer the opportunity for feedback from multiple readers. I trust their professionalism, but people are still people, and maybe if their colleague has already given very low scores, they may be inclined to either think similarly or scan the work a little rather than giving it the care and attention they may have done.

Each one is also a repository for scripts that can be then read by real readers and executives at major studios and agencies. If we receive a "Recommend" they may even do some marketing on our behalf to their contacts and partners in the industry, although the details of this vary on each site.

And now we must stop and talk seriously for a moment. Wherever we send this draft, we must prepare for the reality that most of us are going to get overwhelmingly negative feedback. I don't mean that the feedback will be nothing but criticism, these are professional script evaluators and they will do everything they can to point out some positives for us to develop, but we will not receive the report we are hoping for.

This is the report we are hoping for:

***

Title: Deadbeat Dad
Author: A. New Writer

Logline: An alcoholic, on the verge of committing suicide, finds out he has a daughter and decides he wants to meet her before he dies.

Analysis: From page 1 this script jumped out at this reader as the best I have seen all year, maybe ever. Any writer that can make a hardened reader laugh and cry within 96 pages has a long and lucrative career ahead of them.

The lead character of JOE has Oscar winner written all over it and it will be easy to secure an A-List actor for the role. The twists and turns of the script are as surprising as they are perfectly structured.

Characters are honest and realistic, but each one has their own sense of humor that injects just the right balance of comedy into scenes that could otherwise feel quite overwhelming.

The development of Joe from schlubby barfly to a loving father was one of the most moving transformations I have ever read, without ever feeling contrived or clichéd.

Script: RECOMMEND

Writer: RECOMMEND

***

That's what we expect, right? Total confirmation that we are indeed the most talented screenwriter this side of the Mississippi.

Here is the report we are going to get:

***

Title: Deadbeat Dad

Author: A. New Writer

Logline: An alcoholic, on the verge of committing suicide, finds out he has a daughter and decides he wants to meet her before he dies.

Analysis: There are some moments within the script that show just how talented this writer could be with the right material, but unfortunately too many flaws in the structure and characters mean that this script has a lot of work still needed before it could be production ready.

JOE is an interesting character but the barfly that becomes a devoted dad is a cliché that needs more dimension to attract a star actor. The third Act is dependent on his decision not to kill himself at the waterfall, but this feels like it needs more motivation than just seeing his daughter's name on his phone.

There is some nice humor in scenes that might otherwise have been overwhelmingly dark, but at times it feels like characters are being funny for the sake of being funny.

It is also never fully explained as to why Joe's daughter wants him in her life or why she fights so hard to keep him considering the way he has treated her. The writer needs to look back at each character's motivation. A "happy ending" may not be necessary for this story.

Script: PASS

Writer: PASS

***

We will feel crushed when we get this report. What happened? Where is the glowing report we were expecting?

Here are the thoughts that will flash through our mind about the evaluator:

1) They are stupid
2) They didn't read it properly
3) They don't get my genre
4) They just like criticizing other writers
5) They are just plain wrong

How do I know all this? Because this is exactly how I, and countless others, felt when we sent our early scripts out into the real world and got decked by the reviews that came back. I know of only one writer whose very first script received truly positive reviews. And even that wasn't really his first script as he had been writing short films for years before that.

We will go through a tough couple of days/weeks after getting these reports back. This was months of our life. This script was supposed to be our ticket to success and riches beyond our wildest dreams.

I said right at the beginning of the book that everyone's first script is average-to-poor, but when you read that, you figured I meant everyone *else's* first script. *Your* first script was going to be Oscar-worthy. What went wrong?

Nothing went wrong.

I can't repeat this enough. Nothing went wrong. This is what every successful writer has gone through. The difference between a successful writer and an "also-ran" is their acceptance that it takes time to become a great writer, along with their ability to get up from a fall and keep writing.

Also, it never stops. There is not one successful screenwriter working today who will not experience a flop movie at some time. Having a bad script is one thing; we feel crappy and we hate it, but no one knows about our failure. Imagine having that failure discussed on literally thousands of websites, newspapers, TV shows, and discussion boards. Remember, when a movie is a success, *everyone* credits the director, but when a film bombs, you can be damn sure everyone blames the writer and their crappy script. You have done it yourself numerous times.

However bad we feel right after we receive this report it's not a patch on how bad we will feel further along our journey, even if we become successful. It is because of this feeling of rejection and failure that staggering amounts of people who write one script never write a second. Don't be one of those people.

We are not a bad writer; we are just a *new* writer. Are we really going to let the failure of the *first script we ever wrote* be the reason we give up? I really, really hope not. It's like a painter giving up because the *first painting he ever did* wasn't displayed in the Louvre. It is the same in terms of the level we are working at and the volume of competition we face.

We need to learn to use these feelings of rejection and failure as motivation to get better, not justification to give up. If we can develop that skill, then we have the chance to be a working screenwriter.

31.

What Do We Do With This Screenplay?

Even with the feedback we have received we still believe that somewhere there is a producer smart enough to recognize our genius, buy our script and put us on the fast track to success. And I can't categorically say that that isn't true. What I can say is that it is staggeringly unlikely that it's true.

Let's look at some realistic potential scenarios and decide what we are going to do with this script.

1) "You're wrong, everybody loved my script."

If this is really true, if professional readers and evaluators all go nuts over your script and are falling over each other to "Recommend" it, and you, or they want to buy your script for hundreds of thousands of dollars, then grab their offer, bank the money, move to L.A. tomorrow and please feel free to throw this book away and never pick it up again.

The horrible reality is that the numbers of us for whom that is true will be miniscule. The rest of us, who live in the real world, and have to fight for success, will struggle on without you.

2) "They kind of liked it."

A small portion of us will have received slightly more positive reviews than I presented above, and if that's true, I couldn't be happier for you, but that doesn't change our journey that much.

Even if evaluators, friends, and other writers *like* our script, it's not enough. We need them to *love* it. We need them to say, "Stay by your phone; I'm sending this to my boss to read right now."

It is certainly a viable option to rewrite it, fix the issues that are stopping people from buying it, and send it out again, but in my experience, and that of many, many writers with whom I've worked, potential buyers just find new and increasingly absurd reasons as to why it's still "not quite there yet."

Forcing us to try again, and again, and again, until no one likes the script anymore at all. Why? Because we are no longer writing what we think is a great story. We are now writing the story and the script that we believe people want.

This is something we will have to do if we are ever lucky enough to get hired by a studio. If the producer wants changes, then we will probably have to make them, but that producer has already paid us. They're not asking for those changes to decide whether to put their money into it; they've already stumped up the cash. It's very easy for well-meaning people to *imply* certain changes to our script might make it valuable, but that doesn't mean they ever intend to buy it.

Don't fall into this trap. We can waste years—literally—rewriting and rewriting a script to find the elusive buyer that is always just one rewrite away.

If this was our fifth script, I'd tell you to take the ideas, rewrite it, and try again, but for our first script, there are just too many potential issues to fix. We don't know what our mistakes are yet, so we can't fix them. We're basing our rewriting choices on what other people are saying, and that isn't enough.

Take and enjoy the positive feedback. It means that we can go into our next screenplay with a bigger smile than those people who got punched in the stomach by their reviews, but all of us still want and need to be better, and we still have development ahead of us.

3) "They hated it."

This is *by far* the biggest group. 95% or more of first screenplays are reviewed in overwhelmingly negative terms, and that includes scripts from writers who went to film school, studied screenwriting at university, or enjoyed success in other disciplines, such as novelists, TV writers, and journalists.

Our first inclination will be to send it somewhere else for another evaluation and spend more money to find someone who does get it and will give us a glowing review. Don't! After a couple of evaluations, any more is just throwing good money after bad. They will not be any different anywhere else, I promise. And even if they are different, they will not be as different as we want them to be. It may go from "hated it" to "meh," but that's as big a difference as we can realistically hope for.

Our next inclination will be to do an extensive re-write and then send it out again. Don't!

And to explain why, I want us to play a game. Grab a piece of paper and draw a dog. Any dog you want in any position you choose. You can edit the drawing, but you can't start a new drawing. When you're finished, come back.

How does your dog look? Like a dog? Good, well done.

Now imagine that an advertising agency is looking for a drawing of a dog to use in a commercial. They are paying $1000 for it. We hear about this and send our dog drawing in. A professional artist, who has been drawing since childhood, and has been perfecting his craft through years of repetition and rejection, also sends his own version in. It looks like this:

Which one is the agency going to choose?

In screenwriting terms, that's how far we are from the best in the industry. Because screenplays are all just words on a page, ours *looks* the same as those written by the best screenwriters in the world, but they are *not* the same.

So why not re-write our script to make it as good? Because we could edit our dog drawing for years and it would never be as good as the one above. The fundamentals are just not strong enough. The same is true of our script. This was our first attempt. We didn't know what we didn't know.

If we send the script out to agents, managers, and production companies, we will simply receive the same overwhelmingly negative feedback from everyone who is gracious enough to read it. This leads to two very undesirable outcomes. First, it is horrendous to keep being told our script sucks. If you hated it the first time, wait until the fourth or fifth—or twentieth—similar reply. Second, anyone who takes the time to read it and respond is significantly less likely to read our next script. We have closed off that avenue—and we need every avenue we can get.

Instead, here's what I want you to do. Draw another dog. Use the first one (and the one above) as reference and draw another one, again editing it as much as you like.

It's way better, right? Because we learned from our first effort by repeating what we did right and changing what we did wrong, as well as emulating the best of what we learned from other artists.

This is exactly what we're going to do with our writing.

And so, back to our chapter heading, what do we do with this script? As much as this is going to kill you, take any printed copies of this script and put them in a drawer. Save the file in Final Draft one last time and shut it down. That is the end of the journey for our first script.

You are either thinking, or saying aloud: "Are you kidding me, Hywel?"

I know it hurts, but this journey was never about one script. We need to get a "Recommend" from many readers to get onto the desks of decision makers and our first script was never going to be as good as the best scripts floating around the industry.

But from our second script onwards we have a real shot at creating something great. Therefore, we have to start our second script; the script when we start to become a real writer.

Stage 4:
Our 2nd/3rd/4th/5th Screenplays

32.

Starting Our 2nd/3rd/4th/5th Screenplay

This is the stage in our journey where we become good, maybe even great.

It is not necessarily the stage when we start making money. We may make *some* money. We may even get an agent, but for most of us, that stage is still way off.

What is more important during the writing of these screenplays is that we take everything we learned during the creation of our first screenplay and we improve upon it. That's the very simple goal of this stage of our journey. To go from new–to good.

Our writing will improve at an exponential rate each time we complete a screenplay. Looking back at my own journey I would score the first five screenplays I wrote in terms of craft and story success as follows:

1st Screenplay—3/10. Not as bad as some first screenplays, but close to unreadable for huge chunks of it. It bores me to tears reading it now. God knows how other people made it through.

2nd Screenplay—5/10. Some genuinely good moments, if still a little muddled in its structure and characters.

3rd Screenplay—6/10. People finally started to compliment the script and me as a writer, and justifiably so. This was a good script, but not good enough to break me out of the pack of "newbie" writers. This looked and read like a movie. Not a great movie, but a movie all the same.

4th Screenplay—7/10. A small improvement but an improvement, nonetheless. Feedback was now primarily suggestions that could improve the story, rather than feedback about how to write a screenplay.

5th Screenplay—7.5/10. No one assumed I was a new writer anymore, or that this was an early script. People spoke to me like a writer. They read the script and asked about my career and who I had worked with, rather than asking how much writing I had done. It didn't get me an agent, but it got agents talking to me.

To gauge this overall, we need at least a 9/10 to stand out from the crowd and expect any kind of real success, such as placing highly in a screenplay competition, or being optioned by a production company or producer.

After finishing each one of those scripts I believed them to be 9/10 (I actually believed them to be 10/10 but I wanted to sound slightly humble). It's only with years of hindsight and subsequent screenplays that I can see them for what they were; the development of a writer with a certain degree of natural talent who needed to learn his craft.

If we go into this stage expecting financial or industry success, we will most likely be disappointed, but if we go in expecting to get *a lot better,* then we will succeed.

I have kept everything deliberately simple up till now for a good reason. Screenwriting is not simple, and anyone who thinks it is has missed the point, but the best way to achieve success in our journey is to understand the basics before filling in the blanks with complexity. Everything from here on out relies on the knowledge we gained from starting and finishing at least one script.

By starting our 2nd, 3rd, 4th or 5th scripts we are a big jump along our journey. Most people are hit hard by the rejection and criticism of their first script and they give up. I understand that, but I'm glad that you didn't fall into that trap.

We are taking the most important step we can take in our journey; to work hard, get criticized, and keep going. That's not just a difficult step for writers, it's difficult for all humans in all jobs. Well done for getting up, dusting yourself off and continuing your journey. Failure is not failure if we see it as a step to success. To paraphrase Edison about his failed attempts to invent the light bulb, "I didn't fail, I just discovered 1000 ways not to create a light bulb."

The reason that I am blocking these four scripts together is that our experience of writing each one is quite similar. We will get better each time, but the biggest learning jump is from our first to our second screenplay.

In terms of timelines, we should be starting our second screenplay about six months after we started our first. After that, we should be starting a new screenplay approximately every four to six months, so if we are starting script four we would aim to be about 12 to 24 months into our screenwriting journey. That is just a guideline of course, but if it's taken us

six years to write our first three scripts then we need to pick up the pace—
a lot. We don't learn any more by taking longer to write them. The writing
and finishing of scripts is the important element in these early stages of our
journey, so get on with it.

I was very driven at this stage of my career and finished my first three
screenplays in less than 18 months. I lived up to my own advice of writing
every day, sometimes as much as five thousand words. My fourth
screenplay was when things started to break down. Despite my improving
reviews I was being affected by the negative reception to my work and lack
of monetary success. I had to take a full-time job to pay the bills. I was 24
years old and I enjoyed hanging out with my friends. There were suddenly
many things competing for my time and attention and writing became a
lower priority.

If you are aware that finding time to write, and the writing itself, is
becoming more and more difficult, then do yourself a favor and reset your
thinking right now.

Five screenplays is only 100K-140K words before rewrites. That's less than
the average mystery novel. With rewrites (which get more extensive with
each subsequent screenplay), we are looking at maybe 200K-300K words.
Not a huge amount for something we are hoping to do as a living for the
rest of our lives. That's the equivalent of a golfer playing a hundred rounds
of golf and deciding it's more than enough practice to turn pro, or a chef
cooking 10 good meals and deciding to open his own restaurant.

Go back and remind yourself why you are doing this. Then, put this book
down, call out to the person nearest to you, be it your spouse, partner,
roommate or friend (by phone if necessary) and say to them, "All I want in
life is to be a screenwriter and I'm letting it slip away. I need you to push
me a lot harder to write. Whenever I look like I'm not doing anything, I
want you to say to me, "Why aren't you writing?""

Done it? Good.

Let's have some good news, then. Unlike our first screenplay, it is perfectly
possible to see some real success from one of these scripts, be it critical or
monetary. However, *most* of us don't. Most of us must write many more
than five scripts before the world sees our genius. Wonderful writers, with
long and successful careers, have written 10 or 20 screenplays before
anyone really noticed them.

There is no right time to produce our best work. There is no correct number
of scripts we need to write before it all comes together the way we want.

Our journey is our journey. It does not have to be the same, faster or better than anyone else's journey.

The experience of our 2nd/3rd/4th/5th script is very different from our first screenplay—even if the format is similar: First draft; tighten up; get feedback; third draft; tighten up; sale draft.

The experience is different because we are starting this one with a finished script behind us, which means we are no longer a newbie. We are a writer, who has a product, even if we are not totally happy with the quality of that product.

What doesn't change for our 2nd/3rd/4th/5th screenplay is we need to find an idea that excites us, and we will enjoy writing. At this stage, we can be prone to trying to become too clever for our own good by wanting to produce something more mature and "worthy," rather than just creating a good story that works. Maturity is a consequence of developing our own talent and craft. It's not something we can force. In fact, the more we try, the more we end up taking a step back.

I've read first scripts from writers that, although rough and ultimately unsuccessful, showed moments of brilliance where the writer was truly writing from the heart on a topic and story they loved. Then I've read their second scripts only to feel that every word, every character, every situation is being forced out by the writer to try and fit some model of what they think "good" writers write.

Forget everyone else. Our journey is not to try and be them—or even *like* them. Our journey is to become the best version of ourselves.

When Tarantino wrote and directed *Reservoir Dogs,* he completely changed the crime genre and drove a generation of writers to try and emulate his "gangsters' chit chat," but in 1992, a single-location, gangster-heist movie would have been considered cheap and destined for straight-to-video. Tarantino didn't care. He knew he could write something exceptional. *That's* the confidence we need in ourselves. We must write what we love and what excites us.

One of the primary factors in how quickly our scripts will improve is our innate ability as a writer and storyteller. Huge natural ability doesn't mean that our first script is perfect, but it does mean that we may get better faster than other people. However, it does not mean that we will stay ahead. Drive and determination to get better will soon catch up with innate ability if someone wants it enough, works hard enough, and writes enough.

We are going to go into our second screenplay, not with the heavy heart of someone who feels their first screenplay was a waste of time, but with the exuberant bounce of someone who knows they can do better.

33.

How is Our 2nd/3rd/4th/5th Screenplay Different?

There are some noticeable changes that we should make for the writing, rewriting and selling of these successive scripts.

1) Learning and studying the craft

I suggested earlier on that we shouldn't spend too much time reading screenwriting manuals before our first screenplay.

All the books that might have confused us before our first script will make much more sense now.

Let's jump in with the big guns. We should now read *Story*, by Robert McKee and *Screenplay*, by Syd Field; the two most famous books on screenwriting by the two most famous screenwriting teachers. Settle in though, *Story* is not an easy read. Robert McKee is not here to make our life easy. He takes the business of story very seriously and wants us to do the same.

Screenplay is the grandfather of screenwriting books. Originally written in the 70's, its principles still survive because storytelling hasn't changed in thousands of years, so the few decades since it first came out aren't going to make that much difference.

I would also suggest reading *Writing Movies for Fun and Profit* by Robert Ben Garant & Thomas Lennon. It's fun to read and offers a much more pragmatic view on movies and the writing of them, by two guys who have been vastly successful and made a lot of money in the process. It also offers some very practical tips on structure and the business of movies.

Whatever books you did read before your first script, go back and read them again. You will gain many new insights.

You might even want to go back and read the story chapters of this book again. They will also read very differently this time around.

We may find ourselves disagreeing with these books (including mine). Good. Disagreeing and understanding *why* we disagree is the greatest indicator of learning.

As humans, we are prone to something called "anchoring." We give disproportionate credence to the first piece of information we are given. For instance, a coworker you trust tells you the new guy in marketing is a dick. The next day, 10 people tell you the new guy in marketing is a good guy. Be honest: You still kind of think he's a dick, don't you? Why would the first person lie?

When learning something new, the first source of information becomes disproportionately trustworthy in our mind. We will disagree with future books or opinions if they contradict the first.

The truth is that they are all simultaneously right and wrong, being written by people who arrived at their opinions through practice and experience. Our job is to take from each book what works for us, our journey, and our style of writing.

2) Research

The other change to our 2nd/3rd/4th/5th scripts is research. I argued we should not spend long researching our first screenplay. The writing fundamentals were most likely not strong enough for the script to find success—no matter how much research we did. That's not true anymore. Our second script, and all that come after, have the chance to be truly great in a way that our first script did not.

I still wouldn't go nuts on it. We hear stories of writers spending a year of their life immersed in a world before they wrote a single word of their story. That's a great idea if we are a writer with a track record of success and relationships with numerous studios and producers who are dying to buy our work when it's available. We're not there yet. No one buys a script or hires a writer because they felt their script to be "well-researched." They bought the script or hired the writer because the story gripped them from page 1, and good research will aid us in achieving that, but with the wonders of the internet, books and interviews with friends/family/friends of friends, we can be economical on the time we spend researching while still getting on with the much more important job of finishing screenplays and honing our craft.

Gauge how important knowledge of the topic is to the foundation of the screenplay. If we are writing a script about a boxer, and we've never set foot in a gym in our life then some solid, first-hand research of boxers and boxing is imperative. On the other hand, if we are writing a screenplay set in an advertising agency, but the action is all about an affair between two co-workers, then spending three months observing an ad agency sounds like ludicrous overkill. But an anonymous conversation with a couple of people who have had an affair sometime in their lives would be time well spent.

I'll give you an example. I was once hired to adapt a novel that took place, in part, in a retirement home. A friend of my roommate was staying with us at the time and it turned out he had worked as an orderly in a retirement home for a few years in his youth. We chatted for an hour or so one night and he gave me some fantastic little observations about life in such a home. Things that I may not have even got had I spent some time visiting one. For instance, he told me that he could instantly tell which residents have family that visit regularly based on how nice their television is. When relatives visit they want a nice TV to watch while making idle chitchat with their grandma and will therefore buy one as a "gift" for said elderly relative.

It was a very informative discussion, and it made me feel much more comfortable writing material for a location in which I had almost no experience. But it didn't fundamentally change the way I wrote those scenes, and a further three months of research of other retirement homes and their employees would have most likely yielded little more.

We must start to build in research as a part of our process, but do it in a way that doesn't overtake the actual writing. We can't let it get in the way of finishing scripts.

3) Rewriting

The process of rewriting will be very different now. First, we will be better at it. Second, we will enjoy it much more, as we will feel the script getting better in a way that we didn't understand the first time. Third, we will do a lot more of it.

I argued there was little point to rewriting our first screenplay more than once, as the fundamentals were just not strong enough. That is not true for these scripts. Heavy and continued rewrites of our 2nd/3rd/4th/5th scripts *may* be very valuable and successful. It also *may not*. We need to make a valued judgment of the feedback we get from our own readers and our independent script coverage. Is there a star screenplay in there, trying to get out, or are we painting over huge cracks in the foundation with watercolors?

Another reason I have grouped these four scripts together is they are really one unit in our journey. If we spend two years working on a single script, then it could take us 6-7 years to get through this stage of our journey, and *most* of us need to get through this stage of our journey before we will be recognized or enjoy any success. Slowing down this stage unnecessarily with long and protracted rewrites is still not in our best interest.

We should be rewriting one script while we are planning out another. That way we are running two valuable processes in tandem. Every subsequent script will be better than our last, but by learning to rewrite properly we are putting ourselves in the best place to turn a good script into a great script when the chance arrives.

4) Feedback

Our scripts are getting better each time. You know that yourself just from reading through them.

The question really is, how much better are they, and are they good enough to sell or get us signed by an agent? Script coverage services are still very useful, and you will be amazed at how much their coverage improves with each script. That's not accidental. Amazingly, feedback from coverage and analysis improves as our writing improves.

The combination of our own gut feeling, plus feedback from friends and associates, as well as external coverage analysis will give us a much more realistic feel for the quality of our work at this stage.

However, we are prone to being too harsh on ourselves during this stage. When we didn't get "excellent" or "Recommend" on our first script we figured they were idiots. When we still don't get it on our fourth or fifth script we start to feel that we are failing. It's just not true. The important element is that we are improving every time. If that is true, then the exact feedback is much less important.

Great screenwriters, with billion-dollar franchises behind them, do not sell every script or pitch that they create. That's not the game of screenwriting. The game is to get to a point where we can create great ideas, well told and not need 18 months to get it down on paper.

Writing *good* scripts at this stage means we are well within the parameters of our journey. I cannot say enough times; there is no correct timeline for this journey. There is only one question we need to answer right now:

Are our scripts improving?

If they are, then we must keep going on our journey.

5) Selling.

We should try to sell one, or all, of these scripts. Be prepared for a "no sale," but remember that a lack of a sale is not failure. The problem with sending out our first script was that the feedback could have been so awful as to burn the bridge with that potential contact.

With our 2nd/3rd/4th/5th scripts, we are much more likely to send out work of quality that inspires a more favorable response—even if that response is, "Thanks, but no thanks."

Remember, we only need one person to say yes to the script, or one person to be interested in hiring us for a gig, so hiding our work until we believe it is "perfect" is counterproductive. We have to get it out there to be read, and be ready to deal with the consequences, both good and bad.

A great response to one of these scripts would be, "Not for us, but I enjoyed the writing. Feel free to send me your next script." Be it from agents, or producers, or managers or even assistants, because remember, today's assistant is tomorrow's junior exec.

If we build up a network of people ready and willing to read our work as it is created, then half the battle is over. We need to keep the quality up each time so that the offer is never rescinded, but with a network like this then the day we send out a masterpiece we can create a legitimate bidding war. Or perhaps be on their mind when someone says, "Yeah, I like the idea. Do we know a cheap writer who can bash out a draft?"

Yes! They will know *us*, and we are cheap and ready to work.

34.

How Do We Improve Our Story?

By writing and rewriting our first screenplay, we gave ourselves a foundational understanding of how to create a story, but with our 2nd/3rd/4th/5th screenplay, we want to flesh that out—and frankly, get better.

When we are ready, we are going to start our 2nd/3rd/4th/5th script the same way we started our first: By finding an idea that excites us enough to dedicate another 3-6 months to writing it.

Let's go back to our story questions once more.

1) Who is the story about? (Our protagonist)
2) What is their flaw or flaws? (What needs fixing?)
3) What happens to them that changes their life for better or worse?
4) What must they now achieve? (Their goal)
5) What could get in the way of that goal? (Write down as many things as you can think of.)
6) What's the worst thing that will happen to the protagonist?
7) How must this story end?
8) What must the protagonist do to achieve that ending?

I'm going to bet that we are already feeling more confident with this process than we did with our first script. Now we know a lot of what we didn't know before, and we have a much greater knowledge of how a story comes together plus the pitfalls we will encounter.

Our 2nd/3rd/4th/5th screenplay is all about making more deliberate choices regarding our characters and story. However, we are also going to add in one question we didn't include the first time around, and this question has a bearing on all others.

9) What is my theme?

We didn't discuss theme for our first screenplay because it is challenging enough to get a basic story down on paper, but an honest and consistent theme is what will ultimately lift a story from good to great. I don't think I personally concentrated on theme until my fourth script, which was the one that people started to really compliment.

The story is what happens, but the theme is what the story is really *about*.

The Wizard of Oz is the story of a young girl whisked to a magical world by a twister, but what it's *about* is a young girl learning two important lessons. First, there is no such thing as magic; we all have what we need to succeed already inside us. The second lesson is when Dorothy clicks her heels together and literally states the theme of the movie: "There is no place like home." She even states it *three times*, just in case we missed it the first two.

The Godfather is the story of the New York mafia, and a power struggle following the attempted assassination of Don Corleone, but what it's *about* is family and loyalty. *School of Rock* is *about* discovering our true calling in life. *The Princess Bride* is *about* true love: "This is true love; you think this happens every day?" *Jurassic Park* (David Koepp, based on the novel by Michael Crichton) is *about* the arrogance and greed of humans. *The Hunger Games* is *about* economic inequality in modern America. *The Shining* can be *about* almost anything you want to read into it. (Watch the wonderful documentary *Room 237* to see what I mean.) *Frozen* is *about* not being scared to be yourself and embracing your differences—no matter what those differences may be.

Every truly great film is *about* something, and when it's done well, we don't even notice it. No one walked out of *Frozen* saying, "What a great film about accepting and enjoying our differences." Instead, literally millions of kids all around the world walked out of that movie and said, "What a fantastic film about a talking snowman." However, the next time they met someone different than them—someone with a disability, or a different race or gender than everyone else in the room—they reacted to them more positively because of *Frozen*, whether they realized it or not. That is the power of a great theme.

As you can see from all the examples I have given, themes are big: True love, friendship, betrayal, success, failure, good & evil, childhood, adulthood, individuality, aging, responsibility, equality, loyalty, survival, appreciating what you have, family, revenge, redemption, and any subset of these themes.

There are also many ways to portray the same theme. True love has been portrayed many thousands of different ways in many thousands of movies. Our theme could be "true love is unstoppable" as in *The Princess Bride*. Or "true love will destroy you" as in *Chasing Amy* or *Cruel Intentions* (Roger Kumble, based on the novel by Choderlos de Laclos).

Our theme does not need to be unique. In fact it's almost impossible to create a unique theme. There are umpteen movies about good & evil. The important thing is not that the theme is unique, but that our presentation of it through our story choices is unique.

Many sequels or remakes of successful films misunderstand how important the theme was for the success of the original film, and not necessarily the characters or action. *Die Hard* is an action movie that was *about* family and atoning for our mistakes. The more recent sequels in this franchise, such as *Live Free or Die Hard* and *A Good Day to Die Hard,* are just movies about a guy running around shooting people. Similarly, the 1988 version of *Robocop* (Edward Neumier & Michael Miner) was a deceptively complex movie *about* corporate greed and the disintegration of the middle class. The 2014 remake was about a robot cop, and that was about it.

(You'll notice I haven't included the names of the writers of the sequels or remake. That is because when a studio movie doesn't work, the people least likely to be responsible for its failure are the writers. I stand by my opinion of the movies, but I do not want to imply that the writers themselves were responsible).

When we walk out of a movie feeling empty inside, and we don't know why, it's most likely because the movie wasn't *about* anything. Sure, it had loads of action, and beautiful people, and CGI up the wazoo, but when it's not *about* anything, it is ultimately a shallow and ephemeral experience. On the other hand, a small movie made on a shoestring budget can stay with us for years if its theme forces us to ask questions about ourselves and the world around us.

As a quick exercise, go back and think about your first screenplay. Does it have a theme? Did you think about it when you wrote, it or did it just happen naturally? If it happened naturally, think just how good we could make our script if we planned it out properly.

We may start with the theme, or we may come back to this question and be more aware of the answer once we have created the rest of the story. It's perfectly legitimate to say, "I want to write a story about True Love." That gives us over 100 billion potential stories to tell. If that is the theme that is burning within us to get out then it gives us a direction to head with the rest of the questions.

Alternatively, we may come up with the idea first. E.g. What if an 18-year-old kid gets elected to public office? In that case, what is the theme? Is it corporate greed? Corruption? Honesty? Truth? Does the kid see the corruption of the system and try to break it open, or does he get seduced by the money and the power? Do we live with a system that can't be fixed no matter what, or is the theme that one person truly can make a difference?

The characters we create and the obstacles they face can build on the theme to elevate our story into something that could possibly stand the test of time and be remembered by people for generations to come.

35.

How Do We Improve Our Protagonist?

We still need a protagonist of course, but this time we are going to pay much more attention to that protagonist(s), their qualities, and their characteristics.

Everything about the protagonist must now feed into the main story and the overall theme of the film.

Let's look at a high concept idea and see how it affects our choices. In *Liar Liar*, the lead character's son makes a birthday wish that his father can't tell a lie for 24 hours. If we had that idea, then we would need to decide who our protagonist should be. What occupation or life situation should that person have? They could be anything at all, we are bound by nothing, but we are looking for something that ties into the story itself. If they were a bus driver would that have anything to do with the story? Not really. We might have some funny scenes but their life and the challenges they now face are not particularly linked. What if they were an advertising executive? They are viewed by society as people who lie for a living. That could work. What about a cop, a job title thought of as traditionally trustworthy and honest? If we examined that we might realize just how many lies even honest, trustworthy people really tell.

Maybe it's not linked primarily to their job, but the situation they are in at that moment. Maybe it's someone hosting a family event, and they are usually the person who mediates by lying about their own and everyone else's true feelings, or perhaps, it is a witness in a trial, and the *absolute* truth would get a friend or family member convicted.

The writers of *Liar Liar* (Paul Guay and Stephen Mazur) chose a lawyer who does not live up to promises he makes to his son and who is currently in the middle of a big case. To do his job and get the partnership he craves, he must bend the truth to win. In this case, the job *and* situation are intrinsically linked to the dramatic event that starts the story.

In *Being John Malkovich,* (by the quite extraordinary Charlie Kaufman) Craig Schwartz is an unemployed puppeteer who is forced to take a monotonous office job, only to find a secret door that allows him to go inside the mind of the actor John Malkovich and control him for a few hours, before being spit out onto the side of the New Jersey turnpike. Just go back and look at Craig's job. He is a puppeteer! The movie is all about control, both physically and emotionally, and so a man who controls puppets now controls John Malkovich, while other people control him.

We should explain every choice we make about our protagonist's character and how it links to the story and theme.

Second, we want to create a more detailed vision of this character. The more we know about them, the easier they are to write.

Imagine you were writing a movie where the lead character was someone very close to you, such as your mother, spouse or best friend. Let's say that they get arrested for something they didn't do. You would find writing that person into that scenario quite easy because you know that person very well, so you know how they would react. When the police turn up at your mother's door you know whether she would be angry or upset. Whether she would invite them in for coffee or start crying when they handcuff her? Who she would call first and why? You could write it more easily because of how well you know her.

We should know our protagonist just as well. If someone asks questions about them we should answer relatively quickly and easily. Even if it's not something we have thought about, we should know our character and their world closely enough to come up with an answer that fits in a realistic way.

You may have read or heard elsewhere that when we achieve this level of familiarity with our protagonist, a strange thing happens: The character starts speaking for themselves. As we write, we realize we no longer have to think about what the character *should* say, or what we *want* them to say; instead, they start saying their own lines. All we must do is write them down.

If we were writing the film about our mother, we would find her using sayings and catchphrases that our mother uses in real life. It's the same here; the characters start creating their own catchphrases and sayings.

The sooner it starts happening, the sooner we start writing characters that no one has ever seen before, because until then we are creating them from elements of other characters that we love. Most of my early male protagonists were a none too subtle version of Harry Burns from *When Harry Met Sally.*

163

It wasn't until my third screenplay that I really understood what people meant by "characters speaking for themselves." I'd heard the phrase. I even told people how wonderful it was that my characters were speaking for themselves—but they weren't. It doesn't mean they were terrible characters. Some were very good. Villains especially. I wrote villains way more easily than heroes. Many still stand up when I go back and read my early scripts. But when my characters really did start speaking for themselves, they took a big leap forward.

Some books and teachers will argue that the way to do this is to build up a detailed character biography of our protagonist before we start writing. Personally, I find this very difficult to do. Sure, I can write down some biographical information about them. Where they were born, who their parents were etc. but it doesn't feel like I'm getting to know them, it just feels that I'm making up information for the sake of it. I find it much easier and more productive to start writing and learn the character as I write them. By the time I've finished my first draft (or sometimes earlier) I really know who they are. The goal of the rewrite is then to make changes based on the character that they have become. This is what can make that first re-write quite extensive for me.

This is one of the areas where there is no right way to do something. We need to find the way that works best for us. If we have no answers, then sitting, staring at a piece of paper trying to answer biographical questions of someone we don't know yet is pointless. Similarly, we might find it very hard to write a word of our script before we feel that we know our character inside out.. Anything is fine. What is important is that by the time we get to our sale draft we can talk about our protagonist (and other major characters) as if they're friends of ours. If someone overheard us talking about him or her it should feel as real as if we were describing our wife, or boss, or best friend.

Here is an exchange I have had all too often with writers:

> HYWEL
> So, what is the story?
>
> WRITER
> Okay, so it's about a priest.
>
> HYWEL
> Great.

> WRITER

But the priest's brother is a
gangster and a druggie.

> HYWEL

Where did they grow up? What city
is this?

> WRITER

I don't know. That's never
mentioned in the script. Let's
say Chicago.

> HYWEL

Okay. Then why did they end up so
different?

> WRITER

That's not the important bit
either. They were just very
different. And he wanted to be a
priest.

> HYWEL

Okay.

> WRITER

But then the brother dies of an
overdose.

> HYWEL

Oh wow. Was it a suicide?

> WRITER

Er, yeah, maybe. So now the
priest really hates drug dealers,
right? Because of his brother.

> HYWEL

Okay.

> WRITER

But then, get this, the dealer
who sold his brother the drugs
comes into confession and tells
the priest that he was the one

> that sold his brother the drugs.
> And that he knew it was a bad
> batch of drugs.

> HYWEL
> So, it wasn't a deliberate
> overdose?

> WRITER
> Oh, right, no. It was bad drugs.
> But it was in confession, get it?
> So, the priest can't tell anyone.
> Instead he decides that he's
> going to track the guy down and
> kill him.

> HYWEL
> The priest is going to kill the
> guy? Why would he decide on such
> an extreme course of action?

> WRITER
> Because of his brother.

Such conversations prove that the writer has made no choices about their character at all, even with a finished draft in hand. It shows no thought as to how the character choices fit into the broader themes and story, and obviously no real creation of this character's background.

Let's look at how that conversation should play out.

> HYWEL
> So, what is the story?

> WRITER
> It's about a priest.

> HYWEL
> Great.

> WRITER
> He grew up in a poor section of
> Detroit with his older brother.
> The two of them were inseparable.
> Their mother died when they were
> young and then their father

abandoned them before they were
teenagers.

                    HYWEL

Wow. Okay.

                    WRITER

No matter what, they stuck
together. When he had a chance to
get adopted, he refused to go
unless they could go together and
that meant that they both stayed
in the orphanage.

                    HYWEL

Jeez.

                    WRITER

But as they get older his brother
blames himself and gets wilder
and wilder. Starts drinking,
doing drugs, stealing. But our
guy goes totally the other way.
He needs to protect his brother
and wants to do everything he can
to look after him. He's always
there for his brother no matter
what.

                    HYWEL

Okay.

                    WRITER

Always the protector, our guy
enters the seminary and vows to
devote his life to his brother and
others like him. Meanwhile his
brother gets in with a local gang.
Theft builds to armed robbery,
then to murder. And all the time,
the drugs.

                    HYWEL

Wow.

                              WRITER
                 The film opens as he's finishing
                 a service. He's met by the
                 police. They tell him his brother
                 has died. An overdose from a
                 batch of bad drugs. He's
                 devastated. Puts everything he
                 has into his brother's funeral.
                 Then the next day he's in
                 confessional and a guy comes in
                 and admits that he is the dealer
                 that has been selling bad drugs
                 around the neighborhood. And he
                 knew they were bad. He knew they
                 might kill. The guy has just
                 confessed to killing the priest's
                 brother. But it's in confessional
                 and the Priest can't tell anyone
                 about it. He has a complete
                 crisis of faith until he believes
                 that God speaks to him and tells
                 him that it must be an eye for an
                 eye. He must seek retribution for
                 his brother.

That's a script I want to read.

That is a real person with a real life and real problems. I want to know more about them and believe that the choices they make come from somewhere honest.

That's what every reader wants—a real person, with a life that started long before the cameras started rolling and will keep going after the cameras stop.

Note: As I finished writing this chapter, I checked my word count and it was 52,982. Therefore, I wrote 18 words of my next chapter before going to bed because I had set myself a target of 53,000 words.

Set your own goals and stick to them.

36.

How Do We Improve Our Characters' Flaws?

The necessity for a flaw(s) doesn't change, but we want to be more deliberate (and hopefully subtle) about that flaw, and how it links to the theme.

We hear a lot of people talking about "three-dimensional characters." What they are talking about is whether the character feels realistic or not, and a character is instantly more human when they have a clear flaw. The flaw means they are not *just* one thing. No human in the world is *just* one thing, and when they are portrayed as such, they are boring and trite.

Our characters' flaws should be tied to every aspect of their life and to the wider theme of the story. Let's look at some examples and the breadth of flaws we can encounter.

In *The Sixth Sense*, Dr. Malcolm Crowe misdiagnosed a past patient and didn't help him. That's not a flaw. It is the unfortunate consequence of being a doctor. The flaw is he didn't really care that much about it. He didn't even remember it but still accepted awards for his brilliance. That is what he must atone for. Second, to make up for this past mistake, he begins putting his work ahead of his marriage and lets his wife slip away (or so he thinks). His third flaw, of course, is that he is a ghost, but he, and we, don't learn that until the last page.

In *School of Rock*, Dewey is *mostly* flaws. In this sense, he is an antihero, someone who possesses few qualities we think of as heroic, and yet, someone we care about and root for. He is lazy. He is a dreamer. He is naïve. He is coarse. He mooches off those around him. He is not even very good onstage. He is overbearing and unprofessional. He refuses to get a job. When forced to take one, he steals his roommate's identity, and then turns up hungover. *However,* he is inspiring. He believes completely that dreams can come true. He believes people should not be kept down by "the man," and once he starts working in the school, he comes to care for the children. As an outsider in his own world, he can support them through their own fears and worries of being outsiders.

In *Iron Man*, Tony Stark is brilliant and gifted, but he is self-absorbed. He is indulgent in all the excesses that wealth and fame bring him. He manipulates those around him for his own ends. He doesn't know or care about the moral and societal implications of his work.

Tony is then kidnapped and kept in the desert. After he escapes many of these flaws are fixed in one go. He returns to America with a new purpose and a new moral compass. But he is still self-absorbed. He still doesn't see the sacrifice and love that Pepper bestows on him. He doesn't see (or want to see) the reality of his company and what Jedadiah has been doing with it. He doesn't see the moral ambiguity of his new project because he believes that it comes from a place of right and wants to only see the positives. Is he still just the killer he always was but in a new mechanical suit?

So, this time around, we are going to think more deeply about the flaws of our protagonist *and* our supporting characters.

I mentioned earlier that *Die Hard* is a film *about* family and atoning for our sins. Let's see why.

First, we have John McClane, our protagonist, a morally-good cop who puts his life on the line again and again to save the hostages. Except he's not doing it for the hostages; he's doing it all for one hostage—his wife. John's major flaw is he put his job before his marriage. When his wife was promoted and had to move to Los Angeles, he stayed in New York because he had a "six-month backlog of New York scumbags" he was "still trying to put behind bars." The whole film is about John atoning for this mistake, putting it right, and finally realizing that family is more important than anything else.

However, we also have his wife, Holly. Is she blame free here? No, not at all. When John checks in at the party he can't find his wife's name, because she is registered under her maiden name "Holly Gennero." She justifies it because of the culture of the Japanese owned company, but she too has put work before her family and must atone—and she does. At the end of the movie when John and Gus finally meet in person, John introduces his wife as Holly Gennero, which she quickly corrects to "Holly McClane." She is absolved.

Then we have Gus; the cop on the beat who supports John when his superiors don't. What is Gus's flaw? He accidentally shot a kid who was

170

holding a toy gun. Since then he cannot draw his weapon. How does he atone? Right at the end, when we think we are safe, Karl reappears and draws his automatic weapon, but before he can fire, he is shot and killed. As the crowd parts we see Gus, gun smoking. He has set his karma straight and atoned for his earlier mistake.

Lastly we have Hans Gruber, John's antagonist. What is his flaw? His flaw is that he is overconfident and lacks humility. Also, as John's opposite, he will never atone for his actions or understand the value of family.

It would be a bit crass to show this by shoehorning Hans's own family into the story, so Steven E. de Souza and Jeb Stuart make a perfect choice and exhibit both his flaws in one perfect piece of story.

Instead of Gruber's family, we have two brothers on Gruber's squad. When one of them is killed, his brother, Karl, is informed and is furious, but Hans orders him not to do anything until the detonators are planted and the police have been called. Until then "…we do not alter the plan." 1) Work before family and 2) Overconfidence that the plan is perfect and should not be changed. Big mistake. Now we know that John is going to win.

Every major character in the movie has at least one flaw that ties into the main theme. Minor characters can also have a flaw that ties in, but it's much less important and will eventually get far too confusing and complex.

As we create our own major characters, look again at the flaws of our key 3-5 players. Do they have one or more flaws, and does it tie into the theme and the dramatic premise of the script?

37.

Writing our 2nd/3rd/4th/5th screenplay

You may find this goes more quickly than the last script, but in my experience, and that of many writers I have worked with, the process of writing gets slower the more experienced and knowledgeable we become.

Early on, we are working on pure instinct and talent. Annoyingly, the more we know, the more we are aware of higher caliber writing, and the more difficult we find it to leave a first draft scene or sequence at anything below that standard.

That is why I implore you to think of all the ideas in the upcoming "How to improve…" chapters as things that we are primarily going to achieve in rewrites—*not necessarily in the first draft.*

Our first draft is never supposed to be perfect. It is supposed to be a sound foundation for us to use as a springboard for brilliance. Remember how much the first draft of our first screenplay changed? This one will change even more. The more our first draft is altered in rewrites, the more we are improving as a screenwriter. It means that we have learned the key lesson:

A screenplay is not a document to write,
but a document to rewrite.

Just because this is our 2nd/3rd/4th/5th script doesn't mean we will sidestep any of the problems we encountered while writing our first script. Let's remember the key challenges:

1) Getting stuck
2) We are on page 30 and we've only just got to the inciting incident
3) We've been writing for 3 months and we're nowhere near finished
4) Did we pick the wrong story?

All will still rear their ugly head I'm afraid, but we may even encounter a few more. Such as:

5) This is worse than our last script

2nd/3rd/4th/5th screenplay

6) Why are we bothering to write another script that everyone is going to turn down?

7) I've just watched *Knives Out*. Maybe that's the type of film I should be writing.

8) I've just watched *The Grand Budapest Hotel*. Maybe that's the type of film I should be writing.

9) I've just watched *The Godfather* again. Maybe I should pack this in altogether

And many, many more.

Ignore them all!

They are all just our inner critic popping up to make us feel bad. Our inner critic is a wonderful fellow. Without him we would never edit anything, and we'd think that any old tripe we write is perfect. We need him, but we must control him.

When he pops up to speak during the first draft, we must say, "No, not yet. I know you don't think this is any good, that's because it isn't. It's just the first draft. Go away! Come back when I'm rewriting."

Watching other fantastic films is a killer. When we are stuck and struggling and beating ourselves up, seeing someone who emerged from all that with perfection is the ultimate kick in the teeth.

If you do stumble onto an unexpected gem of a movie, just remember the screenwriter in question had the same feelings while they were writing it.

When Charlie Kaufman was writing *Being John Malkovich*, at some point he stopped writing, put his head in his hands and thought, "What am I doing? A movie about getting inside John Malkovich's head? This is gibberish. Why don't I just write a good action movie?"

Kaufman's next movie, *Adaptation*, was all about the fear, dread and self-loathing we experience when we get blocked writing.

Push on! Push on! Push on! And finish that first draft.

I envy anyone who can naturally sail through the first draft without stopping. If you can, you have a massive advantage over every other writer. True genius will only come from rewriting, so the faster we get through the first draft and into rewriting, the faster we can find that genius.

Stage 5:
Advanced Rewriting

38.

How Do We Improve Our Feedback?

Never underestimate what an achievement it is to finish a screenplay. It is a lot of work and it is hard to do. Many PHD theses are no longer than a screenplay, and they are both just as hard to write successfully. But when a PHD candidate finishes everyone calls them a genius and they get to call themselves "Doctor." When we finish, no one cares about it, and they certainly don't call us "Doctor."

Each time we finish a script I am going to bet that we are instantly aware of how much better it is than our last script. The first draft of our latest screenplay is regularly better than the best version of our last screenplay. With each script we understand so much more about every aspect of the craft.

This also means we can look back critically (both positively and developmentally) on our previous scripts and realize just where we succeeded and failed. We don't have to. I found it very difficult to read my old scripts once I finished a new one. Partly, I was embarrassed by how unreadable they now felt, but mostly, I just wanted to move forward and concentrate on my latest script.

We are now starting the journey of re-writing our latest script and there are some extra elements and ideas that we can add in to get the best results.

First, follow the exact same rules as before and save your file as "Screenplay name—Draft 2" to preserve your first draft for future reference.

Then, tidy up the spelling and grammar. Make it as readable as possible. This time, we are going to send it straight out to readers we trust. We want them to read the purest form of the story, as it just poured out of us. We made our first screenplay "better" before we got feedback, because the first draft of a first screenplay can be truly awful, but the first draft of our 2nd/3rd/4th/5th screenplay won't be awful at all and will be much more readable in terms of story, characters, and dialogue.

There will still be lots of criticism, but we will notice a difference in the feedback, and if they are the same readers as our first screenplay we will undoubtedly get a lot of praise about just how much better it is than our first script. This is a nice ego boost to kick off the feedback session.

The same rules apply though. We are there to smile and thank them for their feedback no matter what it is.

The first time however, that was all we did. I suggested not asking any questions because we don't really know what to ask, and we are very prone to getting emotional about the answers.

We will still get emotional about feedback!

But we are more experienced, so we can ask a few questions this time. These questions should be directly linked to what we are trying to achieve with the script. Not, "Did you like the scene in the park?" but questions that really allow us to make choices. Even choices we might not like.

Examples could be:

1) "What would you say is the theme of the movie?"
2) "How did you feel about the protagonist at the start of the movie and had that changed at the end?"
3) "Was there anything you didn't believe or felt was forced or unrealistic?"
4) "If you were asked to put your own money into buying or financing this script, what would stop you saying "yes"?

Don't start off with questions. Let your readers give their feedback unfiltered at first. The questions can then direct their feedback to areas we know will be of use to us. Once we have all the feedback we need, we are going into a substantial rewrite.

39.

How Do We Rewrite Our 2nd/3rd/4th/5th Screenplay?

This is going to be a lot of work I'm afraid. And know now that rewriting suffers from the law of diminishing returns.

Let's say there was a magic robot that could objectively grade our script against the best in the world. And the robot scored our first draft as 5/10. The expectation for our first extensive rewrite should be to take that up to 7/10. However, the next rewrite will rarely take it to 9/10 or 10/10. More likely we will see it go up another 0.25 or 0.5 of a point each time for the next two or three rewrites.

At some point, frustratingly, the quality of the script will plateau. We can keep rewriting it, but eventually, each rewrite will simply *change* it, rather than *improve* it.

Truth be told, the more we keep rewriting it, the greater the chance of reducing the quality of the script. This is one of the reasons we should save our real first draft, untouched. I have read numerous screenplays from writers where each subsequent draft moves further and further away from their initial vision as they try to rewrite the script to suit the vision of a potential buyer until the script is simply a hodge podge of different people's ideas. It is the spec script equivalent of "development hell." We don't have anyone forcing us to make these changes, instead we ruin the script all on our own.

Many times, when I read a draft like this, I tell the writer to go and get their untouched first draft and read it through from beginning to end right here and now. Then I watch them as they enjoy the reading of their own material, remembering once more what it was about this story that they loved so much before they destroyed it in rewrites.

Understanding that, we are still following the three key elements of rewriting.

1) Fixing story problems

2) Make it shorter
3) Make it better

Go back to *Your Screenplay Sucks*, by William M. Akers. You will notice many additional tips this time around. Another book to read at this stage is *Making a Good Script Great* by Linda Seger. Both books understand perfectly that the challenge is not to get everything right the first time, but to get everything right *eventually*.

A wonderful ally to have on this new journey, if we can find one, is a single trusted advisor. What we ideally need is one person who has some understanding of screenwriting and a desire to help us. It could be a teacher, or a fellow writer, or a friend who is smart enough to understand screenplays even though they may not write them, but it must be someone who can spend a decent amount of time with us and understand what we are trying to achieve beyond, "Yeah, I like that script."

This is the reason that writing groups have existed over the years, be they a group of writers getting together in person, or an online forum. At some point, our spouse, boyfriend or best friend may just not be useful enough anymore.

There are also people who will provide this service for you, for a fee. The most famous is probably Lee Jessup, author of *Getting it Write: An Insider's Guide to a Screenwriting Career*. Lee offers various services to writers at all stages of their careers and has many working writers who credit her entirely with their success.

However, I would not advise investing money into such a person until we are quite far along our journey. I would suggest no less than five finished screenplays before we look to make this a paid-for relationship. By that time, we will be much clearer on our skills, our weak areas and our expectations.

Until then, you can do it for free. I implore you to try and make a friend who is a fellow screenwriter, ideally at a similar place in their own journey to yourself. Someone who has yet to start their first script will seem like a naïve newbie to us now, while someone with an agent selling their work all over town may give advice that feels patronizing or over our head.

The reason a partner in this process can be so useful is that staring at the screen is not good enough. We must discuss our ideas and problems aloud. By doing so, we stand a very good chance of "saying" the answer without realizing it. It's not that the other person gave us the answer, it's that by having the other person there to act as a foil we created the answer for ourselves.

We also start saying answers to problems that we didn't realize we had. I have had many conversations like the following:

INT. LIVING ROOM — DAY

Hywel and a writer sit with glasses of wine.

                    HYWEL
          Maybe he doesn't even go to the
          party.

                    WRITER
          Exactly. He only goes because he
          lied. *That's* why he needs to stop
          lying. OH, MY GOD! The whole
          film's about lying. That's the
          theme of the movie. Everyone
          keeps lying to each other and...
          OOH, OOH! It's all about lying!
          Now, I know what's wrong with my
          antagonist. She lies but gets
          away with it.

The writer pulls out her laptop and starts typing.

                    HYWEL
          Maybe he could...

                    WRITER
          Go away, I need to write!

Hywel gets up, picks up his glass of wine and leaves sheepishly.

It's perfectly possible to rewrite on our own of course, but I am keen that we don't think of this journey to screenwriting success as a solo endeavor. Just like learning to speak another language, or improving at a sport, we want and need other people involved. They may take on a formal "teacher" or "coach" role, or they may simply act as a partner for our development. Either way, the longer we try and do all this by ourselves the harder it is to improve.

When rewriting our first script, I suggested any major change to the story was the equivalent of starting a new script, and, as such, should be avoided. Now that we are more knowledgeable about the quality of our work, there is more validity in making major changes to the script in rewrites. However, we still don't want to move too far away from our original inspiration or get lost in substantial rewrites that *change* but do not necessarily *improve* the script.

Here's an interesting example from the real world of high-profile screenplays. In the mid 90's Matt Damon and Ben Affleck were both up and coming actors. Damon was making more of a splash, but they were both working. They had both worked as actors for Kevin Smith. Telling Smith about a screenplay they had written, he used his connections to help get it read by studio players. That screenplay was of course *Good Will Hunting*, the film that would go on to win Affleck and Damon the Oscar for Best Screenplay.

It was bought by *Castle Rock Entertainment* (Rob Reiner's company) for $300K—a lot more than they had been making as actors at that point— and the two of them went through the development process. The script they bought was about the FBI chasing down Will Hunting because he was a threat to national security. Rob Reiner didn't like that direction and encouraged them to concentrate on the core story of the boy genius coming of age—but a full draft exists with the original spin on the story. Who knows whether it would have been a better film or not? Probably not, but sometimes, a draft like this is useful—even if just to realize the *wrong* direction for our script when pointed out by someone knowledgeable.

However, we are not writing to order. We have the freedom right now to change the direction of the story quite dramatically and not piss off anyone other than ourselves, so if we truly believe that it will produce a better, more unique script, then do it.

Remember, our first draft is usually an immature incarnation of our idea. To mature and grow into a deeper, more fully formed story we may want to change it considerably. The key element is still that we hold onto the thing that we believe sets this script and story apart.

Look at all the feedback again and ask yourself, "Does it add conflict or make my story more layered?" If it does, then we should make the change, or we should at least *try* it and see what happens. As with the *Good Will Hunting* story, it may add a layer that is simply not necessary or confuses the story, in which case, we'll have to take it out, but at least we'll know.

Rewriting at this stage is frustrating and time consuming. We are still developing as a writer, so our first drafts are not as succinct and structured as they could be. Meanwhile, we are desperately keen to get our career moving and so every script we start and finish without a sale feels like a wasted opportunity.

I know it's frustrating but there is a very positive outcome to all this work that will not become obvious until much later down the line.

Analyzing problems within scripts and fixing them through rewriting will be one of our major sources of income when we are lucky enough to get a real career going. It would be great if our career was primarily creating and writing scripts from scratch, but most of the money paid to writers by studios is for rewriting. They bought a pitch from a writer who was then hired and paid to write the first draft. After that draft is turned in they feel that it doesn't realize the idea they fell in love with in the way they hoped and so they turn to a "fresh pair of eyes"; i.e., another writer(s) to come in and fix/punch up or simply improve the draft in their hands.

The first stage of this is to choose a writer they trust/are excited about/can afford and send them the current draft. Our job as the writer in question will then be to read the script and develop our own take on the material. What are the problems? What works? What can be improved? What should be changed completely?

We will then be invited to pitch our take on the script. To get the gig, we need to verbalize all the problems *and* solutions. Therefore, learning to assess a script—including our own—for problems and potential solutions is not just a means to an end to improve our own work, but also an independent skill necessary to maintain our career as a screenwriter when we are lucky enough to break in.

It is also why it is so beneficial to build up a network of writers around us. Each of them can read and assess each other's work and provide guidance and ideas for how to fix and improve the scripts.

When we read their scripts, we will see glaring errors in structure and plot that we can't believe they missed themselves. Similarly, they will read our work and be baffled as to why we can't see the issues with our characters and setting.

After reading enough scripts we will become much more adept at seeing problems in our own work. And when we see an improvement we can make—make it. To guide us a little, the next few chapters look at the key questions we should ask of our script.

40.

How Do We Improve Our Scenes?

It is almost guaranteed that in our first draft our scenes are too long, too expositional and not enough happens. We are going to improve that.

A scene may pass the test of whether we learned something, but if all we get are facts and information then it's frankly a bit dull and lacking in conflict.

Remember, we're not recreating real life, we are writing drama. And in drama there has to be conflict.

For instance, let's say our protagonist is a detective. She meets up with her colleague who has been investigating a suspect in a murder. The protagonist (and the audience) need to know what the colleague has found out.

INT. OFFICE — DAY

Dana walks in. Jeffrey sees her and gets up.

> JEFFREY
> Great. You're here. I've got the information you requested on Bob Shay.

> DANA
> What did you find out?

> JEFFREY
> You were right. He had a record a mile long, including a four-year stint for armed robbery.

> DANA
> I knew it.

> JEFFREY
> That's not all. He knew the victim.

>   DANA
> He said he'd never met her.
>
>   JEFFREY
> He worked in the same office for a
> whole summer three years ago.
> Colleagues say they were friends.
>
>   DANA
> His alibi is still solid though.
>
>   JEFFREY
> Or is it?

Jeffrey pulls out some photos.

>   JEFFREY
> I ran his license plate. This is a
> tollbooth in Connecticut on the
> same day, 30 miles from the
> victim's summer home, and that's
> Shay's car.
>
>   DANA
> Great work Jeffrey.

That is a data dump, and that's fine in episodic television, which is completely different to movie writing. The drama in a show like *CSI* or *Law & Order* is not based around character development. The characters barely change episode to episode. In many cases they barely change season to season. The drama is built around the volume of turns and revelations in the story and how the detectives (or doctors) discover and act on those revelations. A good data dump scene is perfectly useful in episodic TV, and single interior locations are cheap and easy to shoot, but the really good shows will still find something extra to add into the scene to make it more dramatic.

Movie writing, however, is all about character development and conflict and the scene needs more. Yes, we want the information, but it must be given out in a more dramatic way.

Understanding this, we can make scenes more dramatic in a couple of ways:

1) Give the scene more than one thing to achieve.
2) Add some extra action that makes it more interesting.

3) Add some character development. Let us learn something new about our characters.

Let's try that scene again.

INT. CAR — NIGHT

Dana sits in the car staring at a diner through binoculars watching Bob Shay. The passenger door opens, and Jeffrey gets in.

Dana never looks away from the binoculars.

> DANA
> What did you find out?

Jeffrey opens his folder.

> JEFFREY
> Well, you were right. He had a record, including a four-year stint for armed robbery.

Through the binoculars Dana sees Bob get up.

> DANA
> He's on the move. Come on!

She jumps out of the car.

> JEFFREY
> Oh, here we go.

He follows her.

EXT. STREET — CONTINUOUS

Jeffrey scurries down the street after Dana, scrabbling around in his folder.

Dana keeps her eyes fixed on Bob across the street.

> JEFFREY
> That's not all. He knew the victim. They worked in the same office for a whole summer. Colleagues say they were friends.

Dana watches as Bob stops at a door. She stops. Jeffrey stops behind her.

Bob turns to see if anyone is following him.

Quick as a flash, Dana turns and grabs Jeffrey and kisses him passionately.

Jeffrey drops his folder in shock and embraces the moment and the kiss.

A moment later she pulls away, dispassionate, and turns around just enough to see Bob going into the building.

> DANA
>
> Got you!

She notices photos on the floor that have spilled from Jeffrey's folder.

> DANA
>
> What are those?

Jeffrey has to compose himself as he picks them up.

> JEFFREY
>
> Oh, er... His toll booth. Ha! Not
> his toll booth. I mean, his plates.
> His license plates. I ran his
> plates and they showed up at this
> toll booth, 20 miles from the
> victim's house on the night of the
> murder.

> DANA
>
> Great. Come on, let's get in there.

She runs off across the street as Jeffrey tries to regain his composure.

What's different in the second version?

1) We gave the scene more than one thing to achieve. A scene of Dana and Jeffrey following Bob to his hideout could have been a legitimate separate scene, but now we've combined them into one, making this scene more interesting in the process.

2)   We added some action. We are now following a suspect, which is way more interesting than sitting in an office.

3)   We added character development. We now know that Jeffrey is in love with Dana and that she does not feel the same about him. At least for now.

It's not a magical scene. I don't see it being quoted alongside the final scene of *Casablanca*, but it is much improved, and that was the point of this exercise.

I'll give you an example from my own life. My third spec script was about a young boy who finds a dragon's egg. (A page of this script was included earlier). The boy brings his female neighbor into his confidence and together they raise the dragon, almost like their own child.

I wrote a scene where the dragon had to learn to fish to feed himself. The two kids take the baby dragon to a river and as he tentatively explores the water the two kids begin splashing each other and laughing until one of them looks over and discovers that the dragon has caught a fish all on his own. They run over together to cuddle and congratulate the dragon.

It was a nice scene but didn't strike any more of a chord with me as I wrote it. I gave the script to a writing teacher I had at the time for some feedback, and this was the only scene out of the whole script that he wanted to talk about. He kept going on and on about how wonderful it was, and it took me a while to understand why. Finally, I got it.

It was because I achieved two *massive* elements of the story in one scene. The dragon had become independent and no longer needed the kids with him constantly—which opened the story greatly and allowed him to grow as a character—*and* the two kids bonded and solidified their friendship, making them partners in this journey—and I did it in a charming and funny scene about a dragon learning to fish that was a page-and-a-half long. *That's* screenwriting. I'd love to say it was deliberate. It wasn't.

Thanks to the fact that my teacher would not shut up about this scene it became the biggest learning of my screenwriting journey. A scene doesn't have to be huge to achieve huge things in our story.

There was also a negative consequence to this. I started to compare every scene I wrote to this stupid dragon fishing scene. It became my barometer of a "good scene" and anything that didn't achieve just as much, just as effortlessly suddenly seemed like a bad scene.

This wasn't true, and even if it was, every scene can't be equal. The best screenplays in the world have better scenes and less good scenes. That's why great scenes stand out and get remembered. We can't throw something away just because it's not up to the standard of the best scene in our screenplay. If we can improve the scene, great, do that, but if it moves the story forward, has conflict, reveals character, or all three, then it's still a good scene and worth keeping.

41.

How Do We Improve Our Subplots?

Subplots are there to support and build on the main plot. For our first screenplay we listed all the people that the protagonist encountered and whether they were a help or hindrance to his goal. Each one of those people is a subplot.

Some subplots are very small, while others run through the entire script in conjunction with the main plot. There is usually one key subplot, bigger than all the others, which will act as a primary role in the development of the protagonist. In many cases this is a romantic subplot but could be any other type of relationship.

Here are some movies that are not primarily romantic in genre but have a character as the key subplot that offers a romantic element to the story.

Speed: Annie, the substitute bus driver.

The Bourne Identity: Marie, his accidental savior from the embassy.

Miss Congeniality, Eric Matthews, her FBI colleague.

The Fighter: Charlene Fleming, the woman who gets him away from his oppressive family.

Ghostbusters: Dana Barrett, their first client.

The Hunger Games: There's two here, of course, but it's really Peeta Mallark for this first story, the boy from the bakery.

The Sixth Sense: Anna Crowe, his wife. As he attempts to regain the romance.

The character within this key subplot should have their own beginning, middle and end which should be as clearly defined and nearly as complex as the main plot.

In the remake of *The Italian Job* (Donna Powers & Wayne Powers, based on the film written by Troy Kennedy-Martin), Charlie Croker is a thief who pulls off the job of a lifetime by stealing $30m of gold in Italy. He is double crossed by one of his gang, Steve, who shoots Charlie's mentor and leaves the rest of the gang for dead in a freezing lake in the mountains.

189

We pick up the action a year later as Charlie tracks Steve down to Los Angeles and tries to recruit Stella Bridger, the daughter of his murdered mentor, to help him steal the gold back.

Let's remind ourselves of the key structural story elements:

1) Meeting our protagonist and discovering their flaw(s) that needs to be fixed.
2) The inciting incident. The thing that starts the story.
3) Refusal to act.
4) The end of Act One: When the protagonist chooses to act or is forced to act to achieve their new goal.
5) The first major obstacle.
6) The second major obstacle.
7) Midpoint.
8) The third major obstacle.
9) The fourth major obstacle.
10) The end of Act Two: The worst moment the protagonist faces.
11) How the protagonist turns it around and solves their problem.
12) The resolution.

Stella is a supporting character, but let's see which elements of story structure Stella's story has in *The Italian Job*:

1) **Meeting our protagonist and discovering their flaw(s) that needs to be fixed.** Stella is a safe cracker just like her dad, but she works for the police cracking safes under a warrant. She is cool, can drive a mini very fast and is very good at her job. Her flaw? She is too honest and "safe." Usually a good quality, but we can see that she needs a little excitement and a little of her father's spirit.

2) **The inciting incident. The thing that starts the story.** Charlie visits her and asks her to join the gang to steal the gold and beat Steve.

3) **Refusal to act.** She sends him away. She wants nothing to do with it. Her father missed her childhood because he was in prison and she is different.

4) **The end of Act One: When the protagonist chooses to act or is forced to act to achieve their new goal.** She changes her mind and joins the gang. It's not about the money, it's about avenging her father, who deep down she loved very much.

5) **The first major obstacle.** Stella has to fit in with the gang. She is not a criminal. She has to win them over, and relearn how to crack Steve's Worthington 1000 under the pressure of illegality.

6) **The second major obstacle.** Stella has to visit Steve to get the layout of his home. She must face her father's murderer. And she must go on a date with him and be charming.

7) **Midpoint.** On their date he works out who she is and mocks the death of her father. None of this is fun now.

8) **The third major obstacle.** The plan is changed. Now she has to crack the safe underground from the back of an armored car. The risks are much higher.

9) **The fourth major obstacle.** Steve has switched the safe. It's not the Worthington 1000.

10) **The end of Act Two: The worst moment the protagonist faces.** She is not familiar with the safe and does it wrong, nearly blowing the whole plan. She tries to do it without her tools – by touch, just like her father, but she can't. She gives up.

11) **How the protagonist turns it around and solves their problem.** Charlie convinces her to try again. She relaxes and channels her father. And she succeeds. The safe is open and they have the gold. In one fell swoop she has turned around her own story and the main plot. She has also fixed her major flaw – her anger at her father.

12) **The resolution.** She gets to hit Steve in the face before she and Charlie go off into the sunset and enjoy each other—not the money—*and*, by living the life of a criminal, she now understands and can forgive her father for neglecting her. She has let go of her dad's death and moved on. She and Charlie have changed and grown.

Stella is a major ally of Charlie's to complete his goal, but she also has her own story arc that runs the entire length of the film with as much depth as Charlie's.

Another example of a smaller but wonderfully effective subplot would be Brooks Hatlen in the *The Shawshank Redemption*. Brooks is the kindly, elder statesman of the prison and is friendly to Andy when he arrives. Brooks is then paroled and scared to take up his life on the outside. Finally, lost and alone in this new world, he takes his own life, reminding Andy and the others what will happen to them if they stay there and become institutionalized.

Let's look at his subplot and which structural elements exist in his story.

1) **Meeting our protagonist and discovering their flaw(s) that needs to be fixed.** We meet Brooks early on. He is a fixture of the prison and friendly and helpful to Andy, especially when Andy joins him in the prison library. He even tells us when he arrived and cites the date 40 years earlier so that we know how long he has been around. His flaw? He no longer sees Shawshank as a prison. It is simply his home. He goes about his life quite cheerfully. His bird and the other men are his adopted family.

2) **The inciting incident. The thing that starts the story.** When he is paroled. This is what changes his life. Otherwise, he would have happily stayed at Shawshank forever. This happens quite late, on page 46.

3) **Refusal to act.** He doesn't want to leave. He's institutionalized. So much so that he holds a knife to Heywood's throat, threatening to kill him so that he can stay in prison.

4) **The end of Act One: When the protagonist chooses to act or is forced to act to achieve their new goal**. This happens just two pages later, when Brooks walks out of prison, a free man for the first time in 40 years.

5) **4 major obstacles to overcome.** Not 4. Just 1, which is fine for a subplot. In this case, it is living life on the outside. He can't get used to cars, or his job or the realization that the life he was accustomed to has gone.

6) **The end of Act Two: The worst moment the protagonist faces.** He says in his letter back to the prison, "I'm tired of being afraid all the time. I've decided not to stay. I doubt they'll kick up a fuss. Not for an old crook like me."

7) **How the protagonist turns it around and solves their problem.** Unfortunately, his suicide solves his problem on page 50.

8) **The resolution.** None beyond his suicide.

From Brooks' inciting incident onwards, his entire story is one sequence and five pages long, but this subplot and this character aid Andy in his main story in many ways. It gives him a purpose in the prison; to create the best prison library in America and dedicate it to Brooks. And it gives Andy the impetus to make sure that he does not become institutionalized in the same way. He has to get out while he still can. (Although we don't know how until later.)

Just like these examples, every subplot must aid/ hinder the main character and the main story. If it doesn't, what is it doing there?

We also see from these examples that subplots and their structure are not bound by the same limits and page number parameters as the main plot. They may not include all the key structural elements, and those elements can appear on any page, but each major character must have his or her own story arc. Maybe their story has two of the eight key structural elements, maybe they have five, maybe they have all eight, it depends on how much time we spend with them and how much they help or hinder the protagonist.

When someone is introduced who has no purpose beyond a superficial interaction with our protagonist, we immediately know it is false.

To understand how *not* to do it, we go back to *Austin Powers: International Man of Mystery,* and the brilliant character, Basil Exposition. Basil is a spoof of characters in spy movies (and almost any other genre) who turn up with no other purpose than to deliver key information to the protagonist (i.e., exposition), and then disappear. No development, no story, just exposition. Don't do that!

The last point to make on subplots is that we also need to open the subplot in a way that creates the correct expectation for that character.

If our protagonist is a spy and he or she goes into a diner, and the waitress hands them a coffee as they wait for their target, we have just had a very small subplot. The protagonist had an obstacle; he was thirsty and had time to kill. The waitress was the agent in fixing the protagonist's time/coffee problem. Job done. We would not expect to ever see the waitress again for the rest of the story.

However, if we got this:

INT. DINER — DAY

Joe walks to the counter.

                    JOE
          Coffee please. To go.

The WAITRESS hands him his coffee. As she does so she also slips him a note. Joe feels the note and looks up. She makes eye contact for a split second before walking away.

Joe takes the coffee and surreptitiously pockets the note.

JOE

    Thanks.

He throws some money onto the counter and walks out.

EXT. DINER — CONTINUOUS

Joe walks around the corner and looks back to check that no one is following. Then he retrieves the note.

It reads: "I know who is trying to kill you."

We had better meet that waitress again. If we don't, we're going to spend the rest of the film wondering who she was and how she knew this information. But one more scene may be enough. This doesn't necessarily imply that she will become a huge character, it just means that we will see her again in some form. What if we get this:

INT. DINER — DAY

Joe walks to the counter.

JOE

    Coffee please. 4 sugars.

The waitress, SHELLY (26), hands him his coffee. Her uniform is stained and frayed but she has an easy-going manner and manages to keep smiling all the way through her shift.

SHELLY

    Sweet tooth huh?

JOE

    When I had teeth. The sugar rotted them all.

SHELLY

    You should have listened to your mother.

> JOE
>
> You kidding? It was my mother who gave me all the sugar.

He throws a $20 note down on the counter.

> JOE
>
> Keep the change.

Joe winks at her and leaves. As the door closes, Shelly's FRIEND comes over.

> FRIEND
>
> $17 tip? You should have given him your number.

> SHELLY
>
> Him? Not my type.

She looks out of the window at Joe.

I think we all know she *is* going to see him again. How do we know that? For two reasons. First, because she got a name and a character description. She wasn't just "WAITRESS". That means she is a medium-to-large-sized character. Second, because we stayed with her after Joe left. If Joe is our protagonist, then we are following his story, which means if we break away from his story to meet someone else when he's not there, then this person must be important because we are now starting a new story with Shelly as the protagonist.

This is how we open up subplots in a way that lets the reader know what to expect of that subplot later. If, in this scenario, Joe and the waitress were to meet again but only to get more coffee, then the whole piece after he left was pointless and idiotic. It confused the reader as to the significance of the encounter. But if Joe and the waitress end up sleeping together, or going into business together, or solving a crime together, then that small moment with the coffee fits with what we expect to happen later. She doesn't need to be in 60% of the screen time, but she needs to figure prominently.

The last thing to look at with our subplots is whether we have multiple characters achieving the same thing. If two characters interact with the protagonist but they both offer the same help/hindrance, and both change the protagonist in the same way, then do we need both? Can we conglomerate them into one character? Remember, no more characters than are absolutely necessary.

42.

How Do We Improve Our Dialogue?

We didn't go into any real detail about dialogue at all for our first draft because it is something that is best learned by doing.

In many ways, dialogue appears to be easiest part of the screenplay to write but is arguably the hardest element to do well because it's difficult to put our finger on the difference between good and great dialogue.

The core tools that we are going to use to improve our dialogue are:

1) Making it true to the character
2) Show don't tell
3) Avoid being "on the nose"
4) Creating subtext

1) Making it true to the character

Easy as it sounds, dialogue needs to sound distinct to this, and only *this* character. One way to check if we are succeeding is to give a section of the script to a reader and delete the names and character descriptions, replacing them with character #1, character #2 etc.

At the end, ask them to describe those characters from their dialogue. How close are they to the way we wrote them? In my own experience, people ended up describing someone very similar to me. On one occasion I was writing an old man of 60 and one my readers described them as "a young girl, maybe 18." I had to rewrite a lot of his lines.

Every line can be said in so many ways. Are you writing it the way *you* would say it, or the way *this character* would say it?

Let's try an example. A car loses control and careens into the front of a movie theater. Our character runs into a police precinct across the street to alert the police to what is going on outside. That's the setup. Now let's see how different characters might get to the same goal through their choice of dialogue. Here is a list of potential characters.

1) You. What would you say?

2) A 10-year-old child.
3) Another Policeman.
4) A criminal, in on the crash, who is trying to clear the precinct to break out someone inside.
5) A tourist who speaks only a little English.
6) An illegal immigrant who speaks a lot of English but fears deportation.
7) The Mayor of the city.

Try it out.

Because we are now concentrating so hard we may find it more difficult than we usually would to put the words into our characters' mouths. That's because most of the time we are really giving them a slightly amended version of our own words, but by writing that down first, we drive ourselves to create something different.

Acting, or acting classes of any sort, can be very useful to writers when creating characters. If you haven't done any then I suggest you enroll yourself as soon as possible.

Good actors can get into the mind of a character so much that they can truly start to speak for that character, especially when they get up and start improvising. A technique that some actors swear by and others hate.

We want to do this, but we may not be natural actors. The more palatable version is to simply to say the lines aloud as we write them, with as much character gusto as we can manage. If you're writing on a plane or other public place, then at least say them in your head.

When we finish a scene, we should go back and read through the whole piece in each of the character's voices. Does it sound correct? Does it sound like what that character would say? If they have an accent, put it on. Every word can sound totally different with an accent and the emphasis of an accent can dramatically change the flow of the line.

I do this without thinking sometimes and have found myself in a public place saying the lines of my characters (in character) quite loudly, only to turn around and realize that everyone is staring at me.

The second part of "true" dialogue is making sure it is honest. This sounds easy and *is* easy—until we write a line we really like. Oh, the dread of writing a great line. Why is it so terrible? Because we will fall in love with the line and want to hold onto it no matter how little it fits the character, scene or story.

If it is truly honest to the character, scene and story then we've written a line that might be quoted for many years to come. Here are some great movie lines that were honest to the character, scene and story:

"Louis, I think this is the beginning of a beautiful friendship."

"Frankly my dear, I don't give a damn."

"A boy's best friend is his mother."

"You've got to ask yourself one question, "Do I feel lucky?" Well do you, punk?"

"I love the smell of napalm in the morning."

"Say hello to my little friend."

"Nobody puts Baby in the corner."

"You can't handle the truth!"

"Sixty percent of the time, it works every time."

"Acca-scuse me?"

There's a reason we remember these moments and quote them for generations. They are moments when everything came together perfectly. In many cases I bet the writer themselves never imagined they would have quite the effect they did. I bet many of them weren't even the writer's favorite line in the script.

But when we do write something we truly love, we want to keep it, at all costs. We can't. We have to lose lines we love if they are not honest to the character.

I have written a line I thought was truly great but knowing that it didn't fit the character at that moment, I've then tried to rewrite the whole scene around that line. In some cases, making heroes into villains and shifting entire structural elements around so that the line can stay.

It doesn't work.

If the line is not honest to the character, then no amount of rewriting is going to change that. The line must go. Don't delete it forever. Keep it somewhere, perhaps in a word document of truly great lines. You never know, it might fit somewhere else, or it may never appear in any script ever. At least we wrote a great line. Better to have undiscovered gems than never come up with any gems at all.

This idea of dishonest dialogue links to our discussion about logic problems in our first screenplay. It is the same issue. It's making characters say things we want them to say, rather than what that character *would* say in that moment.

2) Show don't tell

Frankly, does the line need to be there at all?

Film is a visual medium, and, as such, we want to *show* our audience what is going on. If a daughter is angry at her mom and says, "I'm very angry with you," then we are *telling* our audience what is going on—but what if the daughter comes home, and the mom tries to hug her? The daughter pushes her away, stomps upstairs, and slams her bedroom door. Now, we are *showing* the situation through actions and images, rather than words.

To take it to its epitome, we can *show* the audience a *huge* amount without *saying* anything at all.

A good example of this is: "I love you." Lots of characters will fall in love during the writing of our many screenplays, but we almost never want them to say, "I love you." Think back over the myriad of wonderful movies about love and romance. How many times does a character actually say, "I love you,"? Great writers find many ways of showing characters falling in love without any words at all.

Amy dances with the Knicks cheerleaders (*Trainwreck*); Vivian kisses Edward *on the mouth* (*Pretty Woman*); Becca watches *The Breakfast Club* (*Pitch Perfect*); Mark buys Bridget a new diary (*Bridget Jones's Diary*). These are all moments that say, "I love you," and express it deeper than the actual words ever could.

A scene that does this impeccably is from the wonderful teen comedy *Bring it On* (Jessica Bendinger). Head cheerleader, Torrance, is staying at the house of a friend. The friend's brother, Cliff, and Torrance have a crush on each other that has so far been noticeably unspoken.

Torrance goes to the bathroom to brush her teeth in her pajamas. Cliff is already there doing the same. The two of them awkwardly brush their teeth, with Torrance trying to remain as ladylike as possible. However, as the teeth brushing progresses Torrance gives up on remaining polite and the two of them try to outdo each other with how much spit they can create until they are both spitting at Olympic level.

It is the most sexual scene you will ever see. The attraction between them that was so far unspoken is now loud and clear, but no one gets naked and not one word was spoken. Instead, it's about brushing your teeth. It is a masterclass of "show don't tell."

3) Avoid being "on the nose"

You may have heard this phrase elsewhere. What it means is dialogue that is too honest, too blunt. For instance:

>   WIFE
>   I'm so angry with you. You really
>   embarrassed me in there. I really
>   thought we had a better
>   relationship than that. I don't
>   think I want to speak to you for
>   the rest of the day.

No one ever says stuff this honestly and directly. Not in movies, and not in real life. We very rarely say exactly what we are thinking—even to the ones closest to us. "On-the-nose" dialogue is when people say what they should be *thinking* but not *saying*.

The wife above would be *thinking* this as she leaves the place with her husband, but the *dialogue* may go as follows:

>   HUSBAND
>   What's wrong?
>
>   WIFE
>   (staring straight ahead)
>   Nothing. I'm fine.

We need our characters to say a huge amount in as few words as possible. So, instead of:

>   SHERIFF BRODY
>   Oh shit! I just saw the shark and
>   it's HUGE. Way bigger than we
>   thought it was. Jeez, there's no
>   way we're gonna catch that thing.
>   We should just go home and forget
>   it. We're all as good as dead if
>   we keep going.

We get:

>   SHERIFF BRODY
>   You're gonna need a bigger boat.

Instead of:

<pre>
            TERMINATOR
      That's a mistake. I'm much
      stronger than you think, plus I'm
      a cyborg, so I wouldn't
      disrespect me if I were you. This
      is not the last you'll see of me,
      I promise, and when I return, I'm
      gonna be pissed!
</pre>

We get:

<pre>
            TERMINATOR
      I'll be back!
</pre>

These are two of the most memorable, most quoted lines in movie history so let's not put the pressure on ourselves to be that good all the time, but let's go back through our first draft and look at every line. Is there a more subtle, less blunt and maybe shorter way of saying it?

4) Creating subtext

Great dialogue is all about the subtext, or hidden meaning, of what our characters are saying.

Back to "I love you" for a moment. Even if they do use words, great writers find *different* words to say it.

Rose tells Jack, "I want you to draw me like your French girl, wearing this. Wearing *only* this." We know at that moment it's true love, and neither one of them comes close to saying it. Westley says, "As you wish." (*The Princess Bride*); Sam says "Ditto." (*Ghost*) Dorothy Boyd says, "You had me at 'Hello'." (*Jerry Maguire*); Melvin Udall says, "You make me want to be a better man." (*As Good as it Gets*)

The subtext is what we learn behind the words. It's what they're saying without really saying it.

Sometimes this comes out as a conversation about one thing, when they are really *talking* about something else. A wonderful example of this comes from *Pretty Woman*.

Vivian has left, never to see Edward again. Edward is leaving the hotel to return to New York. He stops by the front desk to check out and asks Barnard Thompson, the hotel manager, to return the diamond necklace that he borrowed for their date to the opera.

                    MR THOMPSON
              (indicating the necklace)
        May I sir?

                      EDWARD
        Of course, please.

Mr. Thompson opens the box.

                    MR THOMPSON
        It must be difficult to let go of
        something so beautiful.

He closes the box.

They are not talking about the necklace. But if the Hotel Manager simply walked up to Edward Lewis and said the exact same thing about Vivian it would be crass and "on the nose". By using the necklace as a metaphor, they can say out loud what Edward, and the audience, are all thinking.

The paradox of dialogue therefore is that some of the best dialogue is cut and never put back, because we find a more visual, more honest way to express what the person is thinking.

Go back and look at all your dialogue and ask the following questions:

- Is it necessary?
- Is there a more visual way of saying the same thing?
- If it is necessary, is there a more subtle, interesting or sub textual way of saying it?

43.

How Do We Improve Our First 15 Pages?

We talked about the importance of the first 15 pages, but now we are going to delve into the details of why they are so important and what we can do to make them as perfect as possible.

If you have been reading professional and amateur screenplays, then you will now be acutely aware of just how much you have made up your mind about a script by page 15. You will also have experienced the sinking feeling in your stomach when you start another screenplay and realize by page 5 that the rest of the script is going to be a slog to get through, and you are already wondering how many pages you'll read before giving up.

Just because a script was put into production and became a great film doesn't necessarily mean those first 15 pages were dynamite. Some films truly come to life as they play out. We are indifferent in the first 30 minutes, we enjoy the next 30 minutes, and we are blown away by the last 30 minutes. This is a wonderful experience to have in a dark movie theater but again, *we do not have that luxury*. Our spec script is there to sell us as a writer, and it needs to start on Page 1. If it doesn't, the brilliance of our last 30 pages may never be read.

The first 15 is about showing the reader that they have an enjoyable, professional, well written script ahead of them.

Think of it like a job interview. Most interviewers will admit that they have already made their decision about a candidate before they even get to the room. Based on what? First impressions. Which, in the case of a job interview, is based on their clothes, the handshake, and idle chit chat they make as they head to the room. For a screenplay, it's our first 15 pages.

Here's an exercise for us all. Let's say that Steven Spielberg himself has agreed to read our script—but only the first 15 pages. That's it. If we submit more he will stop reading at the end of page 15, even if it is mid-sentence. And based on those 15 pages he will decide whether to finance our movie.

Go and look at your script right now. Do you believe that based on those first 15 pages you would get funding?

I'm going to bet that after reading your first 15 pages we have some or all of the following thoughts going through our mind:

1) "Well, the story doesn't really start till page 18."
2) "The moment that really brings my main character to life is at the end of Act One on Page 30."
3) "A lot of those first 15 pages are setup and it's all necessary, but they're not really the most exciting 15 pages. The best 15 pages are later."
4) "I love all this dialogue, but I'd have to lose a lot of it to get the inciting incident in before page 15."

The reality is as far as we're concerned, *anyone* who picks up our script is Steven Spielberg. We must impress every one of them as if they have the power to greenlight the movie, because without their recommendation, it can't possibly get to the next person in line.

Plus, every one of them will have a strong feeling by Page 15 whether this is a script they are going to "Recommend" or "Pass." It can change as they keep reading. They could think it's a "Recommend" at Page 15 and a "Pass" by the end, and they *could* move from a "Pass" to a "Recommend," but that is much more difficult to achieve.

Each script we complete will be much better than the last, and each first 15 will be noticeably more readable and enticing than our previous efforts.

However, there are areas on which we can concentrate, to make the most of these first 15.

1) Get to the inciting incident

It should happen in our first 15. We are not Sorkin. We do not have the luxury of knowing that the reader will finish the script. Don't let them think that we don't know what we are doing. They don't know us, and they don't know our work. The one thing we can do is excite them. And the way to do that is to get to the story as soon as possible and show them what a brilliant idea it is. If it grabs them then they will keep reading.

How do we do make this possible? With our second tip:

2) In late; out early

This is a famous screenwriting credo. What this means is that we should join the story as late as possible and leave it as early as possible. It can also be applied to any single scene, but let's think about here it in terms of our story.

The script we are writing is a snapshot of the life that our protagonist has been living for many years before we meet them, and will continue to live for many years after we leave. The question, therefore, is how late can we join them and still understand everything we need for this part of their life to make sense?

In *The Bourne Identity*, the story we watch is the chapter in Jason Bourne's life when he must rediscover who he is. That's an interesting chunk of his life. But he's Jason Bourne. He's also had a very interesting life up until the moment that the fishing boat hoists him out of the sea.

Tony Gilroy and William Blake Herron could have included years of Jason Bourne's life at the beginning of the film. We could have seen him joining Treadstone, his training, some missions, and finally, the failed mission when he got shot—all of which would have been very exciting, but none of which were necessary to depict *this* slice of his life.

This slice of his life is about his discovering all that stuff, and the life he was leading, and whether that is the life he now wants for himself. They entered the story as late as possible: Just as an unconscious Jason Bourne is pulled out of the sea. We will learn everything relevant that has happened before as we watch the story unfold in real time or in flashback.

Give the reader no more setup than they need. The quicker we get into the story the more the reader will thank us for it and assume us to be a skilled writer.

3) Open on an earlier story

We must set up our characters for the inciting incident to mean anything. Therefore, we want to set them up without boring the reader.

To achieve this, we can give the reader a story to watch and enjoy while the bigger story develops to its inciting incident. A mini story, as it were, that introduces all sorts of information about the protagonist and the other characters that we need to know. By putting it into its own story, it dramatizes that information in way that keeps the reader engrossed until the real story starts.

The opening of *Raiders of the Lost Ark* is an obvious example of this. Indy's theft (or rescue?) of the golden idol has nothing to do whatsoever with the search for the lost Ark. But it is a near perfect way to introduce everything we need to know about Indiana Jones. That whole sequence is also a wonderful little story to itself. We want to know how on earth he's going to overcome all these obstacles and whether he's going to get away with the idol. We are overjoyed when he outruns the boulder and appears to have succeeded, only to have Belloq take it from him.

However, the rule is that if we open on a mini story, that story must link to the main plot later to justify its existence.

That sequence in *Raiders* ends up at 12 pages, so it would be frivolous writing if that sequence had literally nothing to do with the rest of the film. Fortunately, Kasdan is a genius, and he makes sure that it ties in later when Indy discovers that Belloq is working with the Nazis to recover the Ark and culminates in the repetition of the near perfect line, "Dr. Jones. Again, we see there is nothing you can possess that I cannot take away."

The sequence introduces everything we need to know about Indy *and* links to the bigger story.

Toy Story could have opened with Woody and the toys in his bedroom. We could have spent a few minutes with the toys, getting to know them by seeing them interacting with each other. We'd get some basic information, and then Andy could burst in carrying a Buzz Lightyear Doll. That opening wouldn't be dreadful. We would still enjoy our time with the toys.

But Pixar are way better than that. They open with the birthday party. It turns out that birthday parties are the worst things in the world for toys. Instead of just seeing the toys chatting to each other, we see them reacting to a dramatic situation. Each of their reactions and roles in the birthday party tells us everything we need to know about them.

The birthday party is the story we are watching that keeps us entertained at the beginning of the film. Not only does it dramatize the characters, but it links to the main story when one of the gifts that Andy receives is his Buzz Lightyear, and that is the inciting incident for the main plot.

Enter the story as late as possible, but potentially on the end of the protagonist's last story if it dramatizes things we need to know about the protagonist, or ties to the main story, or both. It can be the perfect way to build character, set up the story, and make the reader instantly interested.

4) Avoid gimmicks.

Don't get clever. We are trying to show that we can create a professional, well told story. Readers will give us 15 pages to prove just that.

Therefore, we are not going to open our screenplay with a fantastical scene that ends with a flashback. Such as:

```
                                          FADE IN:


EXT. THE WHITE HOUSE — DAY

Crowds outside cheer as the main gates open.

JOE, (24) rides out on a camel. He is naked, but
covered head to toe in honey and has the PRESIDENT
sitting behind him.

                    JOE (V.O.)
          I bet you're wondering how I
          ended up on the back of a camel,
          smothered in honey, with the
          President of the United States.
          Well, let me tell you.

                                          CUT TO:


INT. BASEMENT — NIGHT

Joe sits playing on his X-box.

                    JOE (V.O.)
          It all started 6 months earlier.
```

Such openings are a clear indicator of an unconfident (and new) writer who has realized that the first act of their script is turgid rubbish. To try and offset this they show something from a much better scene later in the vain hope that the hook of this tantalizing tidbit will make the reader trudge through 70 pages of rubbish to get there.

It doesn't work. Readers will get bored just as quickly as they would have without the confusing opening scene. I can only think of a handful of produced films where this device truly works, such as *Maverick* or *Goodfellas*, but I see it used in upwards of 20% of scripts from new writers because they lack the confidence in their writing. Show interesting characters in well-structured scenes that build an intriguing and surprising story. That's what will keep them reading, not cheap tricks.

5) Keep cutting

Be ruthless. Keep cutting your first 15 pages until it is as tight as it can possibly be. Once a reader is hooked by the story, they will forgive a little bit of fluff later, but they will roll their eyes at any line or moment (or scene) that feels superfluous in the first 15 pages. Show them how adept you are at brevity. And show it right up front.

✳✳✳

When our first 15 pages are built on craft, confidence and a captivating inciting incident we are giving ourselves the best foundation to win over readers that are new to us and our work.

44.

How Do We Improve Our Second Act?

Second Acts are where good stories go to die.

The first Act pulls in the reader, and a great third Act can help get the script bought, but a terrific second Act is the mark of a truly great writer. Not only will we create a script worth buying, but it proves to a producer that they can rely on us to write scripts that keep investors and stars reading right until the end.

When we try to improve our second Act, we are talking about story. Witty dialogue and exciting set pieces are all great, but if the reader has lost interest in the story, then they will start skimming.

So, what does a great Act Two need?

It needs change and revelation.

Change is where we see the characters develop as people. Revelation is where we learn new things about the plot, the characters and the world in which they inhabit.

If we don't have either of these things, then all we have is "stuff" happening. Think of how many times you have been bored in CGI heavy action movies. Things may blow up. Monsters may crush cities, and robots may smash each other to bits, but if we are learning nothing new, or seeing no genuine change in our characters then we will lose interest.

If we have built our second Act around increasingly difficult obstacles and surprising solutions, then we have given ourselves the solid structural foundation we need to build on, but if that's all we have, then it will ultimately be quite shallow. We need every scene to reveal something new to the audience or show our characters changing, learning, and growing.

You may have heard people talk about "plot-driven" and "character-driven" stories. When they say "plot-driven," they are referring to stories that are balanced more towards revelation, whereas "character-driven" stories rely more heavily on character change. Neither one is right nor wrong. The ratio of revelation-to-change in our second Act is determined by the genre and story, but it must have a balance of both.

The balance of the two elements can be thought of like this:

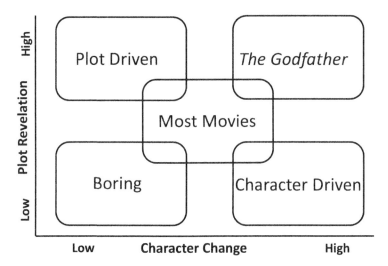

Other than the "Boring" bracket, we can have a truly great movie in any other place on the board, but it is very hard to create massive amounts of plot revelation AND character change in the same script. When it happens, such as *The Godfather*, you may have lightning in a bottle. Other movies I would argue achieve this are *Star Wars Episode V: The Empire Strikes Back*, *Citizen Kane*, *The Shining*, *Terminator 2: Judgment Day*, and *Toy Story*, and I think their places in the annals of movie history are sealed accordingly.

However, most movies—and most *great* movies—do not need this. They simply need the correct balance of revelation and change, and the correct balance is determined by the genre and story.

Plot Revelation

Great episodic TV drama is built almost exclusively on revelation to drive the story, especially in the crime genre. Never start watching an episode of *Law & Order* or *NCIS* when you are supposed to be going to sleep. It's impossible to turn off. Every scene unfolds a new and surprising piece of the puzzle and you are forced to keep watching, desperate to find out *who* did it and *why*, and then – *will* they get away with it? But the lead characters don't change at all.

In movies, crime stories, action-adventures, and thrillers rely more heavily on revelation in their second act. We go to new places, meet new people and constantly get new information regarding the physical journey of our protagonist.

A great example of such a movie is *National Treasure*. It is based around the simplest of goals – where is the treasure? Benjamin Franklin Gates is running around Washington DC trying to find the mythical treasure. Every obstacle is a clue that must be solved, and the solution will provide them with the next clue. Each clue and each obstacle become increasingly difficult. At every turn they are thwarted or battled by Ian Howe and his team. We are excited by the action because we want the next clue. We want to know if the treasure exists. We want to see the treasure. The set piece action sequences, such as stealing the Declaration of Independence, are great fun, but they mean so much more because we are so excited to find out what is written on the back. What clue will it provide?

Character Change

Other genres and stories rely much more heavily on character change than revelation. We see the characters change and grow because of the choices they make when faced with obstacles. We learn about new aspects of our characters that were hidden or unknown to us and them.

The Breakfast Club (John Hughes), is a wonderful example of a character driven piece, relying almost entirely on change rather than plot revelation. The setup is simple, five disparate teenagers from different cliques are brought together for a Saturday detention in the school's library where we learn more and more about each person; why they are here, their home life, their struggles, their fears, and ultimately, their similarities. They leave seeing themselves, and each other, in a totally different light. They will never be the same again, but they have gone nowhere and done nothing of importance.

Plot Revelation AND Character Change

Most screenplays need a solid mixture of both. Even when a screenplay relies primarily on revelation for their second act, they can never rely *solely* on revelation. There must still be an element of change in their characters. In *National Treasure,* we watch the transformation of Benjamin Franklin Gates from wide-eyed dreamer, intent on chasing a nonexistent treasure, to national hero and multi-millionaire, who is reunited with his estranged father.

The Bourne Identity is thought of as an action film in the vein of James Bond, but it is more of a thriller in terms of structure and design. We open on a character of whom we know nothing. Indeed, neither does the character himself. As each sequence unfolds, we learn a little more about Jason Bourne, Treadstone, and what led to him being found unconscious in the sea. Sometimes we learn information at the same time as Bourne, sometimes we learn it before Bourne and enjoy the moment when he discovers it himself. But we are always learning new things.

Therefore, the action sequences *mean* something. They are not just action for the sake of action. If Jason Bourne beats someone up with a magazine, then it's fun to watch, and we will probably want him to win the fight, but if the person has information that will fill in a piece of the puzzle and satisfy our curiosity about what happened, then we *need* Bourne to win the fight. We care so much more about it. That is why *The Bourne Identity* is an exciting and satisfying action movie, when so many other movies with massive CGI action sequences aren't. In those movies, we don't care about the action, because—win or lose; blow up or don't blow up—we don't learn anything about the story or the character we didn't know before.

Similarly, *The Breakfast Club* has a plot. It has movement around the school and interactions with the few other supporting characters that support and allow the character change that occurs.

All cinematic stories require an element of both revelation and change. Things must happen, and our protagonist must change. *How* they change is dictated by their goals.

Conscious vs. unconscious goals

As we've discussed, as soon as our protagonist has agreed to go on their quest, they will develop a conscious goal; to get back home to Kansas (*The Wizard of Oz*), to lose their virginity (*American Pie*), or to stop their children losing their virginity (*Blockers*), to find their daughter's killer (*Three Billboards Outside Ebbing, Missouri*) etc. This is the goal that drives the story forward.

They will also have one, or more, unconscious goals. These are things they must change to be a better, happier person.

The easiest way of thinking about unconscious goals is to realize that they are intrinsically linked to the character's flaws. We all have character flaws that, if fixed, would make us better people, but most of us are blissfully unaware of them. So are our characters. They think they are perfect, just as we do. These unconscious goals will become more obvious to them as the story progresses and may even overtake their conscious goals as more important.

Katniss Everdeen, in *The Hunger Games*, is an interesting example. She is essentially a "good" character. She is caring of her sister, hardworking, and resourceful. Her inciting incident comes when her sister's name is pulled from the bucket to enter the Hunger Games. Katniss does not hesitate. She immediately volunteers as tribute in her sister's place. Her conscious goal is now obvious; to survive the Hunger Games. Interestingly though, we have not really seen any flaws that need to be fixed. We have no obvious unconscious goal. Her goal really is just to survive. However, as the games progress we begin to see her flaw. Katniss does not realize how important she could be to the potential uprising against the capitol. Her unconscious goal, therefore, is to realize her inner strength and become a figurehead for the revolution. That's a hell of an unconscious goal to put on someone. Indeed, she has no idea of the revolutionary sentiment that is growing outside the arena in the districts, but by the end of the movie her unconscious goal has overtaken her conscious goal. She chooses to eat the berries and take her own life as a statement against the capitol. Survival is no longer her goal, and thus she completes her character arc from unknown survivalist to teenage martyr, and leader of a revolution.

In *Shaun of the Dead*, Shaun is a 30 something underachiever who cannot give up his childhood friends and commit to an adult relationship. When London is overrun by zombies Shaun's conscious goal is to stay alive and protect his girlfriend, his mother, and best friend. But his unconscious goal is to finally grow up and take responsibility for his adult life. By the end of the movie he has killed his mother (once she became a zombie) saved his girlfriend and himself, and he has finally committed to her by moving in with her. However, he does keep his best friend—now a zombie—in the garden shed to play video games together.

It is this need to achieve their conscious and unconscious goals that will create the revelation and change.

Act Two is where we build our protagonist's arc.

Our protagonist's arc is an imperative part of storytelling. They "arc" in the sense that they start out in one place and end up somewhere different. At the end, they are a *different person* than they were at the beginning.

This change can manifest itself in many ways. The change could be physical. It could be a change of outlook on the world, or a change in attitude to a single person. It could be a change of location, or a change in prospects. It could be major change involving many of these elements, or minor change, only slightly affecting one element. The type of change and severity of that change must be dictated by the story and characters. Let's look at some examples.

Physical Change

Never Been Kissed (Abby Cohn & Marc Silverstein), sees protagonist Josie Geller change from a dowdy, greasy haired loser to a confident, blonde, prom queen.

Dallas Buyer's Club (Craig Borten & Melissa Wallack), and *Philadelphia* (Ron Nyswaner), see their protagonists deteriorate through the ravages of HIV and AIDS.

Boyhood (Richard Linklater), is a fascinating case of physical change, literally watching Mason grow up over the seven-year shooting schedule from a small boy to a man going into adulthood.

Situational Change

While You Were Sleeping (Daniel G. Sullivan & Frederick Lebow) sees Lucy change and grow from lonely orphan to a much-loved part of an extended family.

The 40-Year-Old Virgin sees Andy change from a friendless virgin into a popular, happily married man. Plus, he loses his virginity.

Office Space (Mike Judge), sees Peter Gibbons change from a miserable, cubicle based officer worker with a cheating girlfriend, into a happy, relaxed man in a great relationship who is working outdoors and "making bucks."

Attitudinal Change

Bruce Almighty sees Bruce end the movie in the same job, in the same apartment, and with the same girlfriend, but his attitude to those things is totally different. He is now happy.

The very underrated *Ghost Town* sees Dr. Pincus remain in the same job and the same life, but he has realized that "being such a fucking prick" hasn't got him anywhere and has opened himself up to kindness, friendship and love.

Dirty Dancing (Eleanor Bergstein), (and any other coming-of-age movie) sees Baby change emotionally from a child to an adult, along with all the pain and reality that comes with it.

Location Change

Planes, Trains & Automobiles (John Hughes), is all about getting home from New York to Chicago for Thanksgiving. Del and Neal travel to many places, but the film ends, as it must, with their arrival in Chicago.

In *Working Girl* (Kevin Wade), Tess McGill undergoes other changes, but the most eloquent expression of her arc is the move of twelve feet from the secretary's desk to the private, windowed office where she sits in the final shot of the movie.

The Truman Show (Andrew Niccol), ends as Truman exits the studio; the only world he has ever known, daring to go out and enter the real world.

Major Change

Major changes are offered to characters who have the biggest problems. The epitome of this is Ebenezer Scrooge, a man so vilified by the world around him that everyone is happy when he dies. His change from cold-hearted miser to kindhearted benefactor is one of the most wonderful major changes in literature.

As Good as it Gets (Mark Andrus and James L. Brooks), sees Melvin Udall change from a bigoted, racist, obsessive-compulsive into a charming, caring savior who takes in his gay neighbor and protects his waitress/girlfriend's son.

Good Will Hunting (Ben Affleck & Matt Damon), takes Will from a prison-bound street thug to a think-tank genius who will most likely change the world.

Minor Change

Minor changes are reserved for characters in episodic movies that have many similar adventures, such as James Bond, Indiana Jones or Iron Man. Each adventure is not supposed to be isolated in their life as unique and is therefore not expected to affect major change. They are basically the same at the end of the movie as they were at the start, but we will still see minor changes in some areas. Tony Stark may be more socially aware. James Bond may have realized that he has the propensity to love, even if he then suppresses it. Indiana Jones may have reunited with an old girlfriend or bonded with his father, but essentially, they are the same characters.

***

Our character's arc will take them from "flawed" to "fixed." The character's arc is not just essential to great storytelling, it also serves a very useful secondary purpose; it is essential to attracting a star actor.

The world is full of screenplays. Most are awful. Some are good. A smaller number are very good, and a few are exceptional. But even if our screenplay is exceptional it doesn't guarantee that it will get produced. Why? Because to get made it must still raise the financing, and the single most important element in raising financing is having a star name attached.

A screenplay could be considered mediocre by everyone involved, but if Tom Hanks likes it and agrees to star in it then the next day it will be considered the best screenplay of the moment and fast-tracked through the studio to be green-lit at every level. Studios will sometimes even make movies they don't like (if it's cheap enough) to keep a major star happy and attached to other projects.

Actors aren't stupid. They know perfectly well that the key to plaudits, awards and future work is to portray the most interesting characters on screen. And interesting characters are the ones that have the most flaws and go through the most change. Those characters can be funny, or serious, or scary, or angry, or meek. There is no "right" character to attract a star actor, but a good place to start is one that has a clear and demonstrable character arc. Does their character change? Do they show range? Will they be interesting to watch as they develop?

True movie stars are inundated with scripts. They read very few of them. The one thing that their agent/ manager/ friend can pitch to them about a script is the basic story and the character arc of the character that they would be playing.

If those two things are locked in, then it is *way* easier for everybody to get excited about our script.

<pre>
                    AGENT
          So, you're a plastic space toy
          that comes to life when no one is
          watching, but you *think* you're a
          real space ranger. You don't
          realize you're just a toy, and
</pre>

when you get lost with another
toy — a cowboy, I think — you use
all your tools, as if they're
real — like a laser, and your
wings. — but then, you discover
the truth: You're just a toy, a
nothing, and you're devastated,
ready to give up, but then, you
discover being a toy is the
greatest thing in the world. Way
better than being a space ranger.
There is a kid who thinks you're
the greatest, and you have to get
back to him, and at the end, you
even fly — for real. Kids are
going to be watching this thing
for a hundred years. You'll be
immortal!

Before we start writing, let's make a plan of our character's arc. Don't worry if it's not perfect, it will most likely change in rewrites anyway, but we should have a clear vision of who and where they are at the beginning, and who and where we want them to be at the end.

Then, for each obstacle, we must ask ourselves:

1) How will our protagonist overcome this obstacle?
2) What will they learn/fix by overcoming this obstacle?
3) How are they changed by dealing with this obstacle?

They can change a little, or a lot. They can change for the better or worse, but they must change.

Now, we have a second act filled with revelation and change. Every incident not only moves the *physical* journey forward but also moves the character's *emotional* journey forward. Now, we have a second act.

45.

How Do We Improve Our Resolution?

We want our resolution to be something special. We obviously want our reader to have enjoyed the whole script, but the last 10-15 pages should blow them away. When they turn the last page, they should be unable to pick up another script from sheer emotion and surprise at reading something so special. Their next move should not be to write coverage but instead to pick up the phone and call their boss to tell them to drop what they're doing and read this script.

How do we make that happen? By going back to one of our key story principals. Give people the ending they always wanted on a route they couldn't possibly have imagined.

People want all the satisfaction and comfort of the ending they expected, but they want it in a way that they have never seen before.

Back to the Future has one of the greatest resolutions in movie history, and here's why: Marty hits the lightning bolt just in time and gets back to 1985, and even though he arrives too late to save the Doc from being gunned down the Doc survives because of Marty's letter from 1955.

It's wonderful. Everything is fixed and there are no loose ends. This would be a perfectly satisfying ending to a wonderful movie, but what makes *Back to the Future* so special, and why I think it struck such a chord with people, is that we now have an additional, and completely unexpected, resolution sequence.

Marty wakes up back in his bed and walks through for breakfast where he encounters a beautiful, up market house. Not the shabby shithole he lived in at the beginning.

His brother, Dave, formerly a fast-food worker, is now a successful businessman. His mom and dad walk in to reveal a trim, fit, successful, and *happy* couple, instead of the slobby, overweight underachievers we met at the beginning. Plus, his parents' attitude towards his girlfriend has changed completely because of their encounter with Marty. Marty even has a brand-new 4x4 in the garage, and Biff, his father's old boss and nemesis, is now cleaning their cars.

These aren't problems that *needed* to be fixed, but this unexpected resolution makes Marty's life incomparably better. It's a wish-fulfillment fantasy we all think about. What if I woke up one day with a better house, a happier family, and a cool car outside? Plus, it's not some stupid genie or wish that does it; it is all because of Marty.

How could anyone walk out of that movie with anything other than a huge smile on their face?

Another near perfect resolution is *Tin Cup* (John Norville and Ron Shelton). Our journey with Roy McAvoy, the slobby driving range pro, to the US Open has been fun, but Roy has one major character flaw; he always lets his emotions get the better of him. He blows up in every tournament and ruins his chances for success. Therefore, we know that this has to be fixed.

As expected, the problem rears its ugly head once again in the Open when for three days in a row Roy refuses to lay up to the 18th green, instead choosing to "go for it" and putting his ball in the water each time.

The final round arrives. If Roy lays up, he has the chance to win the US Open. This is his chance for redemption—but he can't do it! He can't play it safe. He doesn't just want to win, he wants the record, so he goes for the green again, and again puts his ball in the water.

All is not lost, though; if he takes his drop and makes par, he can still force a playoff—and maybe win the tournament.

And here is where Shelton is a genius—Roy can't do it!

He can't even take a drop. He has to make the shot from the fairway. The shot he has failed to make four times now. He has to prove to himself that he's capable of making it.

And thus, sets up one of the most tense and surprising moments in sports movies. Will Roy make the shot? He's lost the competition. Now he's just battling himself.

He drops the ball on the fairway and swings. It's a perfect shot, but the ball goes into the water—again. Still, Roy won't move. He has to make the shot. Ball after ball goes into the water, and with each strike he is falling further and further down the leader board, until he has only one ball remaining. If this goes into the water, he will be disqualified.

He strikes it. The whole crowd (and the whole movie theater, by the way) is completely silent watching this ball. It not only lands on the green but drops perfectly into the hole. He made the shot. The shot that everyone said couldn't be done, and he did it with a score of twelve.

So, is it wrong that Roy's flaw isn't fixed? No. It's fantastic. It is a perfect example of a writer so skilled at their craft that they know when and how to break the rules. The ending we all needed was that Roy got the girl and was successful at the US open, and he was! More so than if he won, in fact. As Molly says to him:

> MOLLY
>
> Five years from now no one's going to remember who won, who lost, but they'll remember your twelve!

Roy McAvoy is now immortal.

Remember, I'm arguing that these resolutions are as close to perfection as it's possible to be. These resolutions stand out in a world of great resolutions so let's not beat ourselves up if ours isn't quite as good, but why not shoot for the stars?

Also, a *good* script with a *fantastic* resolution will potentially be remembered, "Recommended," and bought sooner than a *very good* script with a *good* resolution. A *great* script with a *fantastic* resolution will create a bidding war.

So, what can we do to make our resolution stand out? Go back and think about movies you have loved over the years. Movies that made you almost giddy as you walked out of the theater. What was the difference? Why did they affect you so much?

The minimum we need is to make sure that all stories are closed off in a satisfactory manner. After that it's about looking at our world and our characters and really thinking about how we can set this story apart.

A good question to ask ourselves is: "Is there anything in the last 20 pages that will truly surprise the reader?"

If we stopped a professional reader at Page 80 of our 100-page script and asked them to describe what they thought would happen between Page 80 and the end, how close would they be? With their years of story experience, if they are extremely close, then the act of reading those last 20 pages is nothing more than confirmation. The resolution may be professionally written, but the reader's brain will start skimming—even if they are enjoying it—because we are only giving them a correctly-presented version of what they expect.

There must be something that holds their full attention. There are two ways to do this:

1) Present the story in a way that makes it genuinely difficult for the reader to be 100% sure of the resolution.
2) Present the story in a way that the reader will *assume* they know the resolution, only to surprise them with what happens.

I'll give you an example of the first option. *13 Going on 30* (Cathy Yuspa & Josh Goldsmith) is about a 13-year-old girl who makes a wish of sorts at her birthday party that she could be 30. (An age she believes is the best thanks to a magazine article she read).

She then wakes up in a New York apartment as a beautiful 30-year-old woman with a hockey player boyfriend and a dream job editing a fashion magazine. However, she quickly realizes that this life is not all it's cracked up to be. Specifically, she has lost touch with the boy who was her best friend when they were kids.

Interestingly, although some fairy dust is involved, the movie appears to quite deliberately never tell us whether she has really jumped 17 years or whether she has simply woken up with amnesia and remembered herself as the 13-year-old she would perhaps like to be again.

I watched this with a friend who was also a writer and very story savvy. We stopped the movie at about 45 minutes, turned to each other and genuinely could not say with confidence how this movie was going to end. We knew she would end up happy and with the man she loved – somehow. But we genuinely couldn't tell whether she would go back and wake up as her 13-year-old self once more, or whether she would get her memory back, stay the grown woman she now was, but realize the terrible choices she had made and try to do better?

We made a bet and chose one each. I was wrong, but I was fine with being wrong. It is a body swap comedy that was made primarily for quite a young audience, but I was genuinely forced to wait and find out what the resolution would be.

As an example of the second option, let's turn back to *Se7en*.

20 minutes before the end of the movie, Mills and Somerset are investigating the "pride" killing. They have encountered John Doe, but he got away. We have two more of the seven deadly sins to go. If we stopped

the film at this point and asked what would happen between now and the end, we would all have a solid expectation. Mills and Somerset will keep getting closer to John Doe. He may or may not get away with another killing, but the detectives will eventually outsmart him and catch him, just before—or just after—the last deadly-sin killing. It's been so good up until now that even if that happened, I'm sure it would all be very exciting and interesting until the end, but that's close to what will happen.

Okay, let's start the movie again and see what happens:

Mills and Somerset walk into their precinct and a man shouts at them from below the stairs. Mills turns around as somebody shouts, "It's him!" And it is! John Doe has just walked into the precinct and handed himself in.

The police surround him and draw their weapons, but we in the audience are all going, "What? Hang on, that's not right! What the hell is the rest of the film if he's just handed himself in?"

What is the rest of the film? Sheer brilliance, that's what. Not one thing that happens from now until the end of the film is anticipated or expected— even as each section develops—and yet, it all makes *perfect* sense within the story and characters that were set up. It closes off every story in a way that we expected but by taking a route not one single person in history could have expected. I won't detail it here, but if you still haven't seen the film or read the script, then go and do both immediately.

It cannot be a cheap surprise though. It can't be surprise for the sake of a surprise. You will know by now what a fan I am of the script for *The Sixth Sense*. Unfortunately, this admiration does not extend to all of Shyamalan's work. In stark contrast, an example of a cheap surprise for the sake of a surprise is exhibited in his script for *The Village*.

The Village is a film about an 18th century village where the town elders keep order through the threat of monsters that live in the woods surrounding the village.

It's a nicely dark and creepy movie. I enjoyed it. Until the end, when the lead character finally escapes through the woods to search for help and arrives in modern day America. It turns out, you see, that it's been 2006 all along. And the village elders just wanted to keep everyone trapped in a nostalgic past.

This "twist" has nothing to do with the rest of the film. In no way does it link to the characters, theme, or plot. It's just a surprise for the sake of a surprise. At best, it's annoying; at worst, it belittles the whole film we've just watched. Everything we have enjoyed has been based on the sensibility of a different time. We accepted the actions and reactions of the characters because they were not modern-day people. When it turns out they *are* modern-day people, then it just makes everything that happened seem stupid. The struggle against mystical forest beasts is quite fun in the 1700s. It's risible and idiotic in 2006.

So, let's recap:

1) Present the story in a way that makes it genuinely difficult for the reader to be 100% sure of the resolution.
2) Present the main story in a way that the reader will *assume* they know the resolution, only to surprise them with what happens.

That is one way to make our spec script stand out in the pile of scripts they have to read that day.

Stage 6:

The Business of Movies

46.

Hollywood vs. Independent Movies

This book is designed to help us understand the journey to becoming a working screenwriter, the pinnacle of which is still seen by most as being hired to write for a major Hollywood studio.

However, the indie movie scene has always existed in some form. For those of you who never made the connection, "indie" stands for "independent" (i.e., independent from the big Hollywood studios). If your movie is funded by anyone other than the major Hollywood studios, then you are making an indie movie of some sort, but the distinction between Hollywood and independent movies is not as clear as you may think.

The current major Hollywood studios, in order of market share, are: Disney, Warner Brothers, Universal, Sony, 20th Century Fox (although recently merged with Disney), Paramount. Nowadays, they primarily make their money from a relatively small slate of movies (usually 10-20 per year). These movies run from high to super-high budgets, safe in the knowledge that the studio has the marketing and distribution network to all but guarantee a return on investment. Most of their movies are produced in-house, meaning they were purchased and funded by the studio throughout the life of their production. However, they may buy movies for distribution that were produced by other production entities if they are sure of a substantial return on their investment to warrant the marketing outlay.

Then, there are the mini-majors, which are still considered studios by most when it comes to independent filmmaking. Current stars are such names as Lionsgate or STX Entertainment, but many have come and gone over the years, such as: Summit Entertainment, New Line Cinema, as well as Miramax, and the Weinstein Company. Their revenue model is not that much different from the majors. They may get funding through more circuitous routes, but they make their money through distribution and back-end profit share on the movie. As their description suggests, they are just smaller versions of the major studios—although they can be more amenable to original material, and they usually produce a slate of movies that has a greater range of budgets, from very small to quite large. In general, they stay away from super-high-budget movies because just one true flop can kill such a small studio completely—as happened to United Artists with the *Heaven's Gate* fiasco, or New Line Cinema with *The Golden Compass*. Like the majors, they will produce movies from beginning to end, but they are also regulars at festivals and film markets to pick up movies that are being talked about and have already found a following.

Bypassing both of these, a producer will need an independent distributor to get their movie into theaters. There are numerous companies that include distribution as part of their business model, to which these producers can turn.

More recently, Netflix has become a major producer and distributor of feature motion pictures (along with their massive TV division), and it seems like HBO is going to move more in that direction to compete. Both entities are very interesting because, in many ways, they operate and finance similar to a studio, but unlike a studio, box office returns are not the sole factor when choosing which films to greenlight. In fact, there are no real revenues to speak of. Instead, publicity, audience desire, and internet chatter appear to be the criteria for which movies to finance or buy.

Along with their high-profile deals with people such as Adam Sandler, Netflix have also been the winning bidder for movies that were originally intended for a theatrical release, and most people involved seem very happy about this. In addition, they plan to release upwards of 100 original movies in 2019, and unlike studio slates (which are much smaller), these movies run the gamut in terms of tone, story, budget, cast, and intended audience. Again, without the burden of box office revenues (specifically, opening weekend) to justify their purchase, they can let a film build in popularity slowly and become a truly "talked-about" movie—similar to the way studios ran up until the '70s, when *Jaws* and *Star Wars* changed the movie landscape.

As of the writing of this book, they have produced a few movies that have definitely become popular with audiences and well-received by critics, such as *The Irishman* (Screenplay by Steven Zaillian, based on the book by Charles Brandt), *Roma* (Alfonso Cuaron) *Bird Box* (Screenplay by Eric Heisserer, Novel by Josh Malerman), *Okja* (Joon-Ho Bong & Jon Ronson), and *The Meyerowitz Stories* (Noah Baumbach), but so far, nothing that has truly affected the pop culture landscape in a way that looks set to keep 16-25-year-olds away from the movie theaters anytime in the near future. Maybe if they ever stumble upon their own real franchise, then we may see a truly seismic shift in the way movies are made and distributed.

However, at minimum, in terms of sheer volume, Netflix has opened a new landscape for writers, the likes of which has not existed in a while. Plus, they definitely appear more willing to take a gamble on original and different material, as well as material from new(er) writers.

Beyond those big-name entities, indie filmmaking can run the gamut from international film financiers (enjoying enormous tax breaks), to Kickstarter, to raising money from friends and family.

Importantly, indie success is also a perfectly viable route to get noticed by the major studios as a writer or director of quality. A lot of chapters in this book are about how to get your script noticed by the right people. Well, one way of getting noticed is to get a script *made*—even if it's made cheaply. A finished film is still a much rarer commodity than a screenplay—even if the film is not everything we hoped for, or as slick as we would like. Agents, managers, and producers will find it much easier to watch a finished film and assess the writer than by another script on the pile.

For many writers, the goal is not to get to Hollywood at all but to work regularly and successfully in indie movies, where there is more freedom, less regulation, and a much greater chance for a writer to see their original vision realized in the final film.

Go and look at the credits of writers you admire on IMDB. Very few of them jumped straight into $100M movies. Many of them worked their way through budgets and opportunities to finally arrive at the blockbuster movie offer. Later in their careers, many moved back to lower-budget independent movies. Some of these moves may have been through necessity, if the phone stopped ringing from studios, but in many cases, these writers chose to go back to a place where the pay was less, but the respect was greater.

We must understand going into this journey that writers can be replaced at any time. Once a producer, production company, or studio has bought our original screenplay or hired us to write a script, they can do whatever they want with it. A studio's favorite pastime is replacing writers. When a project stalls, an easy way for a producer to look like they are doing whatever is necessary to keep it going to is to replace the writers. "Look," they say, "it stalled because the last writer didn't get it. But, don't worry, I've got [insert Hot New Writer X] on it now, so we're all good."

This can also happen on indie movies, but budgets are much stricter, and bringing on a new writer costs money the production probably doesn't have, so producers and directors are much more likely to work with the original writer to iron out any problems they see.

Indie movies can be made anywhere, by anybody, especially in a modern world, where the expense and hassle of film and film developing is no longer needed. Indie movies can cost as little as a $1K, or upwards of $100M.

Indie filmmaking also allows relatively unrestricted choices in terms of subject matter, characters, or potential audience. What a wonderful world indie filmmaking sounds like, right? Why don't we all do that? Because *most* indie films lose money (or at least, take a very long time to see any return). *Making* the movie is the easiest part. Finding an audience—and, therefore, any hope of making your money back—is the real challenge. Go and look at Apple's "Trailers" app one day. Loads of interesting films—many of them festival-award winners—which you will never see again because they will not find large-scale distribution. Some just weren't very good, but some *were* good and never even made their money back, let alone turned a profit. That's why most investors won't spend a dollar without a big-name star to set it apart, or a clear route to distribution.

As such, the money we will make from indie films as writers is limited. Up-front fees can be very low, and back-end profits are usually nonexistent, but it can still take just as long to get the movie made—meaning we need many projects on the go to keep money coming in.

You can be involved in independent films anywhere. Use social media to find film-minded communities in your area. Offer your services to people whenever possible. Find a group of filmmakers who share your vision and start shooting.

Even if you are self-funding, an amazing array of channels now exist for the distribution of indie features, such as Vimeo, Amazon Instant Video, and Netflix. Realistically, don't expect to make much money from these channels as a new filmmaker with no track record or big-name stars, but until recently, the only way to even get a movie seen by real people was through festivals or a very expensive theatrical release. That's not true anymore, so why not take advantage of it?

Whatever type of films we want to make, or whatever world of filmmaking we see ourselves working within, the principles of great storytelling don't change. We still need to master the craft, whether we expect our film to cost $1K, $1M, or $100M, but being a "Hollywood" writer is not the be-all and end-all of screenwriting.

47.

How Do Studios Make Money?

Independent films can be made entirely separate from the big studios, but even the most independent film can end up needing or using the power and reach of a studio at some point. So whatever career we see ourselves creating it is useful to know how studios work.

What films do studios want to make? Simple: They want to make films that make money. If they believe there is a strong chance a film can make money, then it would be stupid not to invest in the production and distribution of it. That is how their business works.

However, William Goldman wrote in *Adventures in the Screen Trade* what has become the most oft-quoted phrase about Hollywood: *"No one knows anything."*

This has been misquoted over the years to imply that studio executives are stupid. This is not what Goldman meant. He meant that no matter what they say, no one really knows if a film will be a hit, or why some films succeed, but others don't. Production budgets and marketing budgets are poured into movies that die in their opening weekend, never to be seen again, while sleeper hit movies from no-name directors and writers that are pushed out on ten screens go on to earn back tens or hundreds of times their production budget.

Having a runaway hit movie is a great thing, but due to the sheer gamble of movie-making, what studio heads are actually doing is trying *not* to fail. There is a big difference.

When they fail and have a noticeable flop, there is a good chance they will lose their job—even if they had a set of monster hits the year before. One huge flop can be all it takes.

Therefore, the job is not to try and decide which films are most likely to succeed, it's to decide which films *are least likely to fail*. This is an important distinction.

To give themselves the best chance of success (or the least chance of failure), decision-makers at studios will use whatever tools they have at their disposal to try and hedge their bets against failure and make the "safe" choice. Everyone in the world, in almost any job, does the same thing, but the choices the head of a studio makes are visible to the whole world, and so they are discussed and criticized by the whole world.

Two elements have always existed to help studio-heads play it safe with confidence:

1) Star actors whose popularity can (theoretically) guarantee an audience
2) Sequels to successful films

Stars have existed in some form practically since the invention of movies, and sequels always offer a safer choice than a gamble on new material. In fact, in more recent years, sequels (and potential franchises) have regularly yielded more money than their originals; therefore, they are virtually a no-brainer.

Outside of those two, literary adaptations offer a degree of pre-built audience, and in some cases, the chance at awards glory (which is not as good as box office success but can still be desirable).

Transferring stars from other successful forums, such as TV or stand-up comedy, can offer an expectation of success. "Saturday Night Live" has been one of the most lucrative proving grounds for comedians-turned-movie-stars for some 40 years.

Since 2001, comic book adaptations—and the potential franchises they provide—have been incredibly lucrative for almost every studio.

Let's look at the 10 top-grossing movies from each of the last few decades, and their U.S. domestic gross:

1980s:

1) *E.T. the Extra-Terrestrial* ($435M)
2) *Star Wars Episode VI: Return of the Jedi* ($309M)
3) *Star Wars Episode V: The Empire Strikes Back* ($290M)
4) *Batman* ($251M)
5) *Raiders of the Lost Ark* ($248M)
6) *Ghostbusters* ($242M)
7) *Beverly Hills Cop* ($234M)
8) *Back to the Future* ($210M)
9) *Indiana Jones and the Last Crusade* ($197M)
10) *Indiana Jones and the Temple of Doom* ($179M)

A good decade for Indiana Jones, as well as Lucas & Spielberg, who were directly involved with a combined 7 of the Top 10 movies.

The top-grossing movie, and four others, were truly original screenplays, leaving four sequels, and one comic book adaptation (the one that really started it all).

1990s:

1) *Titanic* ($658M)
2) *Star Wars Episode I: The Phantom Menace* ($474M)
3) *The Lion King* ($422M)
4) *Jurassic Park* ($402M)
5) *Forrest Gump* ($330M)
6) *Independence Day* ($306M)
7) *The Sixth Sense* ($293M)
8) *Home Alone* ($285M)
9) *Men in Black* ($250M)
10) *Toy Story 2* ($245M)

Another completely original movie at #1 (though based on a famous incident). Behind that, we have four other original scripts in the Top 10, two sequels, two literary adaptations, and one comic book adaptation.

2000s:

1) *Avatar* ($760M)
2) *The Dark Knight* ($534M)
3) *Shrek 2* ($441M)
4) *Pirates of the Caribbean: Dead Man's Chest* ($423M)
5) *Spider Man* ($403M)
6) *Transformers: Revenge of the Fallen* ($402M)
7) *Finding Nemo* ($380M)
8) *Star Wars Episode III: Revenge of the Sith* ($380M)
9) *Lord of the Rings: Return of the King* ($377M)
10) *Spider Man 2* ($373M)

Another Cameron original at #1. Behind that, *Finding Nemo* (Andrew Stanton, Bob Peterson, David Reynolds) is the only other truly original movie. Otherwise, we have five sequels, three comic book adaptations, one literary adaptation, and *Pirates of the Caribbean*—whatever that is. Let's call it a "theme-park adaptation".

232

2010-2019:

1) *Star Wars Episode VII: The Force Awakens* ($936M)
2) *Avengers: Endgame* ($858M)
3) *Black Panther* ($700M)
4) *Avengers: Infinity War* ($678M)
5) *Jurassic World* ($652M)
6) *The Avengers* ($623M)
7) *Star Wars: Episode VIII—The Last Jedi* ($620M)
8) *Incredibles 2* ($608M)
9) *The Lion King* ($543M)
10) *Rogue One: A Star Wars Story* ($532M)

Not one movie here was based on absolutely original material. Therefore, we have six sequels, one live-action remake, four comic book adaptations, and one spinoff from the Star Wars universe. Plus, *Jurassic World* is the only movie on the list that is not owned by Disney.

Looking at it by decade, it is very easy to see the development of the industry over the last 30 years. Studios and executives can't be blamed for this. There have been plenty of truly original movies made over the last 30 years, but audiences have not turned out for them. If they do turn out, it's usually for the sequel—after having discovered the original on VHS/DVD/streaming/download, rather than having gone to see it at the theater.

Here is a selection of original movies, as well as their sequels, and the grosses involved:

Toy Story ($191M) / *Toy Story 2* ($245M) / *Toy Story 3* ($415M)
American Pie ($102M) / *American Pie 2* ($145M)
Die Hard ($81M) / *Die Hard 2* ($118M)
Shrek ($268M) / *Shrek 2* ($441M) / *Shrek the Third* ($321M)
Harold and Kumar Go to White Castle ($18M) / *Harold and Kumar Escape from Guantanamo Bay* ($38M)
Pitch Perfect ($65M) / *Pitch Perfect 2* ($183M) / *Pitch Perfect 3* (105m)
The Terminator ($38M) / *Terminator 2: Judgment Day* ($205M)
Lethal Weapon ($65M) / *Lethal Weapon 2* ($147M)
Bad Boys ($66M) / *Bad Boys 2* ($138M)
Austin Powers: International Man of Mystery ($54M) / *Austin Powers: The Spy Who Shagged Me* ($205M)

Obviously, there have also been a tremendous number of sequels that grossed considerably less than their originals, but all the examples above are movies that were critically well-received (at least, for their genre), had terrific word-of-mouth from the moment they were released, and yet, still could not find a substantial audience on first release. In all cases, the sequel was more about giving the studio the chance to make the money from the movie they really deserved the first time around, given how good the movie was, and how much everyone enjoyed it.

Current audiences are somewhat loath to attend an original movie—even one with fantastic word of mouth. However, they will attend the latest *Transformers* movie in droves, despite scathing reviews and poor word-of-mouth. If that is the case, why on Earth would studios do anything *but* give the audience another *Transformers* movie?

As of the writing of this book, there are only 16 movies in the Top 100 grossing of all time that are truly original stories—four of which are from Pixar, and for that reason alone we should give them an Oscar every year. Here they are, alongside their rank in the Top 100, and their domestic gross:

3) *Avatar* ($760M)
6) *Titanic* ($659M)
17) *Star Wars Episode IV: A New Hope* ($461M)
23) *E.T. the Extra-Terrestrial* ($435M)
28) *The Lion King* ($422M)
43) *Finding Nemo* ($380M)
47) *The Passion of the Christ* ($370M)
48) *The Secret Life of Pets* ($368M)
52) *Inside Out* ($356M)
58) *Zootopia* ($341M)
67) *Forrest Gump* ($330M)
83) *Independence Day* ($306M)
91) *The Sixth Sense* ($293M)
92) *Up* ($293M)
93) *Inception* ($292M)
100) *Monsters, Inc.* ($289M)

However, all-time box-office grosses are obviously heavily affected by the continuous rise in ticket prices (and, more recently, the premium price of 3D). Want to see something interesting? Here are the Top 10 grossing movies of all time, adjusted for inflation, and their U.S. gross in today's money:

1) *Gone with the Wind* (1939) ($1.8B)
2) *Star Wars Episode IV: A New Hope* (1977) ($1.6B)
3) *The Sound of Music* (1965) ($1.2B)

4) *E.T. the Extra-Terrestrial* (1982) ($1.2B)
5) *Titanic* (1997) ($1.2B)
6) *The Ten Commandments* (1956) ($1.1B)
7) *Jaws* (1975) ($1.1B)
8) *Dr. Zhivago* (1965) ($1.1B)
9) *The Exorcist* (1973) ($987M)
10) *Snow White & the Seven Dwarves* (1937) ($973M)

A few of these have made their money through multiple releases over the years, but it is still a very interesting list. Not all truly original. There are some literary adaptations in there but not one sequel, and interestingly, not one movie from the last 23 years (*Star Wars Episode VII: The Force Awakens* is at #11, with $8M less than Snow White).

In fact, the highest-ranked comic book movie adaptation, adjusted for inflation, is *Avengers: Endgame* at #16 on the all-time list.

What does this tell us about movies that get made today? It tells us we're kinda screwed because we can't write a sequel to a hit movie, or a comic book adaptation. We don't own the material. But, remember: This whole endeavor is to get us recognized, signed, and *hired* to write the next *Iron Man* (Mark Fergus & Hawk Ostby and Art Marcum & Matt Holloway), or *Night at the Museum* (Robert Ben Garant & Thomas Lennon, Based on the Book by Milan Trenc) because (like it or not) those are the movies that get made and will continue to be made for the foreseeable future.

To look desirable to studios, should we be writing films that are similar to their output? *Absolutely not!* Creating cheap knock-offs of successful movies is a dead giveaway that we have no idea how the business works.

However, we should be writing material that shows we understand the business, their choices, and the realities of distribution.

It's easy to look at modern box office grosses (and the news stories that surround them) and assume every movie made is adapted from a comic book. Obviously, this isn't true. Most studios still create a "slate" of pictures from different genres, suited to different audiences, hoping to attract different people and find an elusive hit movie.

Let's compare the theatrical release schedule of two studio distribution slates from 2019:

Walt Disney Studios Motion Pictures:

1) *Frozen II*

2) *Aladdin (2019)*
3) *Dumbo (2019)*
4) *Captain Marvel*
5) *Star Wars: Episode IX – The Rise of Skywalker*
6) *Maleficent – Mistress of Evil*
7) *The Lion King (2019)*
8) *Toy Story 4*

This discounts everything that came onto their slate from the recent merger with Fox. As such, it is only 8 theatrical releases, and all of them ultra-high budget. Thanks to some savvy purchasing, Disney now owns the two powerhouse franchises of Marvel and the *Star Wars* Universe. Along with Pixar, and their own in-house animation department, they have almost no use whatsoever for spec scripts from new writers. Writers get invited in once they have a successful track record elsewhere.

Universal Pictures:

1) *1917*
2) *Cats*
3) *Black Christmas*
4) *Queen and Slim*
5) *Waves*
6) *Last Christmas*
7) *The Adams Family (2019)*
8) *Abominable*
9) *Don't Let Go*
10) *Good Boys*
11) *The Art of Racing in the Rain*
12) *Fast & Furious Presents: Hobbs & Shaw*
13) *Yesterday*
14) *The Secret Life of Pets 2*
15) *Ma*
16) *A Dog's Journey*
17) *Little*
18) *Us*
19) *How to Train Your Dragon: The Hidden World*
20) *Happy Death Day 2U*
21) *Glass*

This is a pretty broad palette of movies, from kids' animation to horror to flat-out comedy. Some films based on previous properties or sequels but lots of original films in there.

Studios know that not every movie is going to gross $1B worldwide and budgets are allocated accordingly, but genre and audience expectation must fit the budget. A movie with a small potential audience is not necessarily ruled out as long as its production budget is so small that even a moderate audience can return its budget, plus a profit. Equally, a film can cost $250M, but it needs a built-in audience to recoup that money, and then some.

Writing a small, family drama set in a summer house in Nantucket is fine. But if that script ends with a meteor hitting the Earth and a 20-minute CGI sequence of disaster that is going to cost $60M to make, we will look like an asshole, no matter how well-written it is.

Audiences are (simplistically) broken down by studios into four different potential markets:

1) Males under 25
2) Females under 25
3) Males over 25
4) Females over 25

It is absolutely fine for writers to create their script to be attractive to only one or two of these groups, but box office potential will drop accordingly, and thus, budget must drop accordingly. The holy grail is the "four-quadrant picture," a movie that is attractive to all four quadrants. These include animated movies, to which kids will be taken by their parents, or family comedies, such as *Night at the Museum* or *Home Alone,* (John Hughes), which broke out of its kid movie roots to be watched and loved by people of all ages. It also includes comic book movies—hence the love of these projects by studios over the past 30 years, after *Batman* proved that, along with 15-year-old boys, the movie would also be attended by their parents *without* them.

Remember, the production budget of the movie is not the studio's only expense. They must also pay for marketing and distribution, which includes all the trailers and TV spots, internet ads, newspaper ads, and then the actual physical distribution of the picture to theaters across the whole world. Such distribution costs have reduced ever so slightly in recent years with the advent of digital distribution. A physical print of a movie used to cost roughly $3K. Therefore, to open on 3,000 screens, you needed 3,000 prints of the movie. That's nearly $10M right there. It's one of the reasons movies opened in different territories at different times so that prints could be recycled and sent on to different states and countries.

Marketing and distribution on big, blockbuster movies can easily double the budget. Therefore, on a $250M movie, the studio might need to make $500M just to break even. Even on a $20M movie, with marketing and distribution of $10M, they need to make $30M to break even. Remember: Studios don't get the entire ticket price. That is split with the theater 50/50 (maybe 70/30 on opening weekend, depending on the deal). Therefore, on our $20M movie, with an average ticket price of $9, they need over 6.5 million people to go out to the theater and stump up their $9 to make their money back. There had better something very special about this movie to warrant that.

On the $250M movie, they need roughly 110 million people to see it around the world. That means nearly 2% of the *entire* population of the world will need to go to this one movie, just so the studio can make their money back. This doesn't even make them a profit.

There's Blu-Ray, TV, and digital distribution after the fact, but if no one cared enough to see it in the theater, then those numbers can be relatively small.

It's amazing they bother making movies at all. Most corporations could stick their spare cash into government bonds and make more money. It's lucky filmmaking is the sexiest industry in the world, or we'd never get to watch movies.

"But, hang on," you say. "Studios are immensely profitable. Look at all the smash-hit movies you just listed above. They all made many, many times their budget back in pure profit."

Wrong!

The reality is most movies don't make one single penny in profit. Some of this is because the economics are more complicated than we realize, but part of it is because it is not advantageous to anyone for a movie to make a profit. If there is profit, then tax must be paid on that profit. If the film makes a loss, then there is no tax to be paid. In fact, they are able to write off that loss against profit on other endeavors.

How does this happen? Creative (but very legal) accounting. Every studio movie is set up as its own company. The movie is not technically part of the studio; it is its own entity with its own profit-and-loss statement, and its own tax returns. This is done for numerous reasons, but the most logical is for financial protection. If the movie loses huge amounts of money and can't pay for itself, no one comes knocking on the studio's door, looking for a payout. The studio is, in fact, a creditor of the movie, just like everyone else.

That movie then *pays* the studio for services performed on the movie's behalf—primarily, by way of a distribution fee of roughly 30% of revenue. Then, the movie must pay gross-participation money to producers, directors, and major stars who negotiated this as part of their deal. This is all before it must then pay back its original production budget and marketing.

Let's use *The Avengers* (Joss Whedon; Story by Zak Penn and Joss Whedon) as an example. That movie cost $220M to make, but it grossed $1.5B around the world. That is a very profitable movie, right? Wrong again.

Of the $1.5B in ticket sales, the movie only gets roughly $750M. From that $750M, they have to pay the studio a 30% distribution fee of $225M. This leaves the movie with $525M. From that, they have to pay a percentage of the remaining "gross" revenues to key creative talent. This can vary massively, depending on the talent involved, and the success of previous movies. Let's be generous and say it was only 20%. I can only assume, in reality, it was much higher than this, given the vast array of expensive talent in the movie—but let's say 20% (or $105M) between them. That leaves the movie with $420M.

However, the movie still needs to repay the studio for the initial production budget, print, and advertising, which was around $440M in total, leaving the movie with a negative balance of $20M.

Even if there is anything left at this stage, believe me when I say that something will be found to allocate that money to. Before you know it, the movie will be many millions in the red—meaning there is no profit, and no tax to pay.

But, the money had to go *somewhere*. Who gets the money? Well, the theatre chain got $750M. That's pretty good. Plus, they made money from selling comically overpriced soda and popcorn. However, running theaters is expensive. They take up *a lot* of space, need to be in prime locations to get all their theaters filled, and have to continually update their sound and projection equipment to keep up with the industry and audience expectations. They are not as profitable as you'd think.

The producer, and stars came out of it okay; that's for sure. They got paid a fair chunk up-front, and shared in the gross participation. Joss Whedon, as director and writer certainly got paid well, although writers almost never get gross points. They will usually get profit points. However, the value of these is debatable because, as we just saw, there most likely won't be any profit. That doesn't mean there isn't any residual money for the writer; on a hit film, there can be wonderful residual money in DVD sales, TV, and streaming deals, and these residuals can keep coming for many years. Sometimes, a film with a small enough budget can make so much money that it's difficult to hide all of it. Anyone with profit points on *The Blair Witch Project*, (Budget: $60k, Worldwide Gross $248M) or *Paranormal Activity* (Budget $15k, Worldwide Gross $193M) came out with a pretty penny.

The studio did come out with its distribution fee of $225M. That's a fair chunk of cash. But, remember: They had to put up the initial production budget *and* marketing costs of $440M to get their $225M back. For every massive hit like *The Avengers,* there are many more flops, or mediocre successes, for which the studio's distribution fee is meager to say the least, and they have to quickly write off the production costs they know are not coming back.

Movie-making is expensive and risky—even when you have the best accountants in the world, who utilize every financial trick in the book.

We need to go into this with our eyes open, and we need to be supportive of the many financial decisions that must be made to minimize the risk and maximize the chance of profit for the studio and other investors—be it a $250K indie or a $300M summer blockbuster.

48.

The Role of the Producer

The role of the producer has always been a confusing one. First of all, there are many different types of producers listed in the credits: *Executive producer, producer, line producer, associate producer*. What are they all doing?

I will try and give a quick explanation of what each of these roles might be, but it is the true role of *producer* we will try to make sense of.

Producer:

Important jobs on a film set will have a guild or union that regulates the employment of those people. There is the Directors' Guild of America (DGA). The Screen Actors Guild (SAG), the American Society of Cinematographers (ASC), and the American Cinema Editors (ACE). It has never been necessary to be a member of these guilds to work on a film— and non-union, indie film work is common (and necessary) to keep paychecks coming in for most people as they start out—but once you are working in the upper echelons of the industry, you are expected to be part of these groups.

Producers also have a guild—the Producers Guild of America, which has existed since 1962, but has been the vaguest concerning who is a member, and whether membership is necessary or expected to be employed and credited as producer.

In 2012, they finally created the onscreen designation of "p.g.a", assigned to the producer(s) who performed a major portion of the producing duties on a movie. Interestingly, though, it is not necessary to become a member of the guild to receive this designation onscreen.

For over 100 years of cinema, anyone could call themselves a producer without any real mechanism to disagree or prove them wrong. Therefore, it became a job title that many people claimed for themselves without actually doing anything to achieve it.

So, what does a *real* producer do? Real producers create and shepherd projects from inception to distribution and beyond. They are the first person on a project, and the last person off it. They are the people who find the project—either from books, scripts, articles, their own ideas, or any other source.

They are the people who hire everyone along the way. They buy the script or hire the screenwriter they feel is suitable for the project. They search for and hire the director they think can lead the story through production. Their relationships with agents and stars will get them the star name they need to get the film greenlit by the studio.

They will be in the background or foreground throughout the whole production, making sure no star tantrum or primadonna director will let it get off-track. They manage the ongoing relationship with the studio, through good times and bad. If problems strike, and budgets spiral, they are the person who must manage everyone and keep the production moving forward.

When the movie is finished shooting, they will hire the composer and be a voice in the edit along with the director (depending on the director's contract). They will work with the studio on the tone, style, and length of the final edit, as well as the marketing team on its trailer, posters, and plethora of other marketing products.

When the movie gets released, they will coordinate with PR and marketing teams on the interviews and articles being created. They will be coordinating awards marketing to get the film into festivals (if suitable) or noticed and remembered by Academy voters. In the old days, they even had to sit and watch every print of the movie being created to make sure the film was perfect and didn't have blotches or problems.

Directors and stars may get the most visible role when a movie is released, and people may speak of a movie as being the director's (such as "Ridley Scott's *Alien*") but when done properly, there is really no one more responsible for a movie's success than the producer—and potentially, no one more responsible for its failure.

So, if that's what the actual producer is doing, then what are all those other job titles?

Executive Producer:

This title is used for various different reasons. It could mean this person owns the original material on which the movie is based, but they are not involved in its daily travels to production. It is also used regularly for people who have put up funding for the production. That way, the financier feels important and makes sure they guarantee their back-end compensation but can then remain a silent participant through production. Or, it is used to bring somebody onto the production who everyone feels is valuable but is not actually going to do much. For instance, the producer may send the project to a very big-name director, who turns down the directing job but is keen to offer their knowledge and expertise to the writer, as well as the final director they end up hiring. Such guidance may be desirable, and their name may be useful to entice stars or studios into the project. Therefore, in general, Executive Producer means the person is important and will make some money if it's a hit, but they are rarely involved in the actual day-to-day running of the production.

Line Producer:

This is actually a defined-but-misunderstood job title. The line producer is the person who is brought on to budget the movie, as well as to manage budget and HR issues throughout the production. They are brought on early in pre-production and are usually on set every day to manage production problems, adjust shooting schedules, and take care of people issues to keep on the original budget. They do not own the movie in any way, rarely see any profit participation, and certainly won't be onstage collecting an Academy Award.

Associate Producer or Co-Producer:

These are both a bit of a catch-all job title. It could be someone who is more than an assistant to the producer but does not yet have the experience or quality to be listed as a producer. Or, it could be anyone who has done something useful for the production, and the producer or studio wants them to feel a little more important and give them a title that brings them a little more money. For instance, someone in another technical role, who is being paid less than their normal fee to work on the production. Not executive-producer money or prestige, but a little more. You will sometimes see writers also get associate producer or co-producer credits.

***

The only people whom writers are interested in is *real* producers—people who are creating and selling projects to studios and financiers.

In some cases, they are people who have a production deal in place with the studio. Such deals can be offered to independent producers, who have created a track record for success, or, in many cases, people leaving their management job with the studio, who have taken a production deal as part of their severance package. Such a production deal means the studio has offered to fund a certain number of projects through development. It may also include offices on the lot, and other perks, depending on the producer's past hits. In most cases, it does not mean they are guaranteed to make any movies—although, some very upper-end producers may have a deal that guarantees at least one or more films are produced.

The producer must still create a package of sufficient quality (e.g., star, script, director) to entice the studio to greenlight their picture. However, studios are obviously keen to work with producers on their lot to make their expenditure worthwhile and to work with people they know and trust. Any producer with a production deal is working with top-tier talent at every stage. They get A-list scripts from A-list writers through A-List agencies, and it will be almost impossible to get your new, unrepresented script to such a producer.

The second place such producers exist is at production companies. These can run the gamut from a one-man operation, running out of someone's bedroom, to a staff of hundreds with massive hits to their name, and a first-look deal at a studio. An example of a very top-tier production company would be Imagine Entertainment, owned by Brian Grazer and Ron Howard. For decades now, Grazer has been one of the most prolific and successful producers in Hollywood. As a team, the two of them have produced such monster hits as *Apollo 13* and *The DaVinci Code*. But, even without Howard as director, Imagine has produced a plethora of other hit movies—such as *8 Mile* and *American Gangster*—of which Grazer is listed as producer on nearly all of them.

Like many successful production companies, Imagine had a long-term relationship with a studio—in this case, Universal—who distributed many of their movies. However, relationships like this may change, and other studios may try to buy out that relationship by offering more lucrative terms to the production company for the projects they create.

Again, such an entity is dealing at the very pinnacle of the industry. They are not interested in finding new material from brand-new writers. That's not to say you could never get them to read it, but it'll be a struggle.

Many production companies are owned by stars and run by their producing partners to give the star more control over the projects they do. As such, they will primarily be interested in scripts with a lead role for the star, but not exclusively.

However, many producers are completely independent, and many production companies are very small, very new, or have a small group of past credits to their name. Not enough to sit with the big boys, but enough so that they have the necessary relationships to get movies made.

Ultimately, studios will buy a project they believe will make money, no matter where that project comes from. If a no-name producer manages to buy the rights to a book or script that becomes sought-after, then that producer has a chance to get their project into production.

Similarly, a relatively unknown producer may have the resources to get a script from a no-name writer into the hands of the one big star they are friends with. If that star agrees to be attached to the project, then both the producer and the writer have a chance to jump up the studio ladder quickly.

Or the producer's contacts and expertise may be with financiers, looking to independently fund movies outside the studio system. Any producer without a production deal must get out there and hustle. It's an incredibly tough job—even with a list of hits to your name.

The one thing they absolutely need, are scripts. Otherwise, they can't do anything. That's where we come in. We have the product they need, and although they will ultimately invest their time and money in very few scripts, they will be keen to work with anyone who can supply them with their lifeblood.

Never write off top-tier producers and production companies—because, hey, miracles do happen—but be realistic and work to get your scripts into the hands of producers who are willing, if not keen, to get work from new writers. A well-written introductory email or letter can win over even the most cynical producer.

Don't just blanket emails to anyone with producer in their title. Understand what sort of movies they make, and why you think your script would be suitable for them. Name-check the work they've done and explain why your project is worth their time.

No matter how hard we have to work to get our script read, a good producer has to work way harder to get a project bought by a studio. Strike out and forge these relationships whenever you can. Many will come to nothing, but you may just meet the next Scott Rudin or Brian Grazer as they are starting their own career, and that relationship could be all you need to set yourself up with work for the next 30 years.

49.

Credit and Arbitration

Getting a writing credit on the movie we write is very important. It determines the money we get paid, and the money we will subsequently make from ancillary sales to DVD, TV, Netflix, HBO, etc. Credit on a hit movie will all but guarantee us future work in some way.

You would assume that getting credit for something we wrote should be easy, but I'm afraid it's not. Not always.

Some big-budget, tent-pole pictures can have upwards of 10 or 20 writers who gave input to the script. However, they don't all get credit. Why?

When more than one person has worked on a script, final credit will be decided by a process called "arbitration." This is undertaken by the Writers Guild of America (WGA). The various scripts written by different writers fighting for credit are submitted and read by a panel of experts (other working writers), who then decide which writers contributed significantly to the final product, and which writers should get credit.

The rules are relatively simple, and if you are interested, they can be found here (as of the time of this printing):

https://www.wga.org/contracts/credits/manuals/screen-credits-manual

(I'll bet some of you reading the paper version wanted to click on that, didn't you?)

The key credits that can be allocated are:

- Story by…
- Screenplay by…
- Written by…

There are others, but let's look at these three:

"Story by…"

This is allocated when the writer contributed significantly to the overall story and structure, but not necessarily the details and dialogue within it.

Let's say, I wrote an original script about a hooker that is picked up by a millionaire. She learns from him how to want a better life, and he learns from her how to be less uptight. It is dark in tone and quite depressing, as we see the harsh realities of life as a prostitute.

However, by the time it goes into production, my entire script has been rewritten, and not one word of it has survived. In fact, it is now a frothy comedy with lots of "life-on-the-street" giggles and fun.

However, the key idea for a hooker being picked up by a millionaire, and the development of the two characters, has survived. Therefore, I would be entitled to a "Story by…" credit.

"Screenplay by…"

This is allocated when the writer has made a significant contribution to the screenplay in areas such as dramatic construction, characters and characterization, original and different scenes, or dialogue, but either the writer did not originate the story, or the story was based on previous material, such as a book, newspaper article, or original screenplay.

In this case, a "significant contribution" is determined as 33% of the final screenplay—except in cases where the source material was an original screenplay, in which case any subsequent writer or writing team must contribute more than 50% of the final screenplay.

For this reason, it is difficult for more than two writers or writing teams to receive a "Screenplay by…" credit, no matter how many writers actually worked on the script at some point.

So, let's say, I get hired to rewrite someone's depressing script about a hooker and a millionaire. I keep the basic idea, but I change their characterization a lot. I take out all the depressing stuff and I make it a comedy instead, replete with a zany hotel manager and slippery snails.

I didn't create the story, so I am not entitled to a "Story By…" credit, but almost everything that happens onscreen was written by me, so I contributed way more than 50% of the final screenplay. So, I get my "Screenplay by…" credit.

"Written by…"

This is allocated when the writer is entitled to both the "Story by…" credit and the "Screenplay by…" credit. In other words, they created or contributed to the overall story and made a significant contribution to the final screenplay.

There still might be more than one writer who is given a "Written by…" credit if two writers contributed equally to the story and the final screenplay.

So, let's say, I wrote my script about the hooker and the millionaire. Other writers came in and changed it from a dark film noir to a glitzy comedy, but none of them contributed more than 50% to the final product. Therefore, I would remain the sole credited writer on the script, and I would get my "Written by…" credit.

If you're interested, this is exactly what did happen with *Pretty Woman*. Even though other writers were brought in to rewrite the dark drama into a family-friendly comedy, JF Lawton remained the sole credited writer on the final film.

As you can imagine, not everyone is happy with the results from arbitration, but for right now, it is the fairest way to make sure the writers who made the most significant contributions get the credit.

It is also the reason there are a number of writers making a very good living who don't have many (or any) screen credits to their name.

"Script doctors" are writers who are trusted to be able to "punch up" a script in trouble. They might be brought in at the last minute to do a "polish" rewrite on a script just before it goes into production.

Such work can easily be paid $50K-$200K (or more) for a week's work, but that writer never expects—and probably, never even fights for—screen credit.

The Farrelly brothers were well-known and successful writers for many years, making a very good living writing, rewriting, and punching up comedy scripts, but none of their scripts ever made it into production, thanks to deals continually falling apart at the last minute.

Tired of always being the unknown writers, they decided to direct their next film (*Dumb and Dumber*) themselves. That way, the script and director would already be in place. All they needed was a star actor to say yes, and they could get straight into production. They found one in Jim Carrey, during his breakout year.

Go back and look at movies you have watched regularly. Take a look at the credits once more. Even those of us who are writers do not always really absorb those credits enough to understand the contribution each writer might have made to the final product.

50.

I'm Embarrassed to Tell People I'm A Screenwriter

Of course we are. If we don't live in L.A. then we seem naïve and idiotic for entertaining the idea. If we *do* live in L.A. then we are one of the nine million people in the city who claim to be a screenwriter. (L.A. has a population of roughly four million people. The other five million turned up this morning with their screenplay.)

Let me tell you a story; only once in my life did I tell someone I was a screenwriter with real, honest confidence. I was 22. A year earlier, my first play had been produced in a small theater in my hometown. The play was well-received but made very little money (as all plays do) and to support myself as a writer I decided to break into the more lucrative world of movies. I had written my first screenplay, which had recently been sent out to agents, but I had not yet received any replies. I still had the youthful exuberance of someone expecting to be eating lunch with Spielberg a few weeks later.

One morning, I bumped into a guy with whom I'd gone to high school. We had been friendly, but not exactly friends. We enjoyed a few minutes of, "Hey, how you doin'?" chit chat, before he asked the question all middle-class people ask eventually: "What are you doing for a living now?"

I said, without any hint of embarrassment or false bravado, "I'm a screenwriter."

"Oh, right," he said. "I remember you were into that stuff in school." We continued with our chat for a few minutes before wishing each other well and going on with our lives, never to see each other again.

I didn't think much of the encounter at the time, until about two years later, when I bumped into a different high school friend and was inevitably asked the same question. By now, with no Spielberg lunches to my name, I was working in a sales job to pay the bills and writing my fourth script.

I paused before answering my friend and finally realized I couldn't bring myself to say, *"I'm a screenwriter."* I mumbled something about being in sales but looking for something more permanent. We chatted for a few more minutes before wishing each other well and going on with our lives, never to see each other again.

But, this time, when I walked away, I was devastated. It was the first moment I started to believe I had failed.

Except, I *hadn't* failed. At all. I could have gotten to the point I was at much faster if I had pushed myself more, but I had actually achieved a lot. I was starting to turn out scripts of real quality. I was having real conversations with people of influence about my work. Agents were starting to reply to my inquiries and were reading my scripts. The Development Executive of the Zucker Brothers' production company had called me to tell me how much he liked my script, but they had something similar in production. He didn't have to do that. I had been hired to do some rewrites for a young producer. He wasn't paying me, but he still chose me over the many hundreds of other writers who would have done it for free.

These were all signs of success, but all I saw was failure.

This change in mindset was more responsible for the stalling and destruction of my journey than anything else. You cannot think this way.

You *are* a screenwriter!

You may not have had any films in production yet—or even sold any scripts—but you *are* a screenwriter, and you should act like it.

The reason we don't like talking about our writing is because we are worried about being asked *the question we all dread*:

> STRANGER
> Oh, you're a screenwriter? Have
> you written anything I would have
> seen?

This is the world's most terrifying question to all of us who are trying to break in. We hate it because it exposes all the worst fears we hold about ourselves. The answer we are desperate to give is:

> YOU
> Nothing! I've written nothing!
> I'm a fraud, a wannabe. Just slap
> me and leave me here to weep.

Instead, the answer we are actually going to give is:

```
YOU
Annoyingly not. It's a tough
industry. Most of us have to
write for years before we finally
get something onscreen.
```

The reason we should give that answer with confidence is: a) it's true, and b) there is no exact definition of when someone can legitimately claim to be a working screenwriter. As we discussed earlier, many writers make a very good living without ever having a script go into production. Other new writers may have representation with a very good agent but have not actually sold a script or made any money. Experienced writers may have worked on many scripts that went into production but have never received a credit. If they can all claim—without any tangible evidence—they are a working screenwriter, then why shouldn't we?

Never act like you're not good enough, or you won't get there. What would you rather: Some people think you're slightly deluded, but you end up as a working screenwriter, or no one thinks you're deluded, but you never reach your dream?

I know which one I *did* pick, and I know which one I *should* have picked. Make the right choice.

51.

Will Someone Steal My Idea?

No. They won't. It's that simple.

I'm not claiming it *never* happens. We are a planet of eight-billion people. Everything happens somewhere. But, it happens very, very rarely. Here's why: It's just not worth the hassle. To anyone. It's not worth the possibility of lawsuits. It's not worth the potential smear on their reputation as a plagiarist. It's not worth watching their greenlit project get cancelled at the last minute because of those lawsuits.

Why is it not worth the hassle? Because it's so cheap and easy to buy our idea.

Movies are an expensive business, but the cheapest part of the process is to secure the rights to a script from a new writer. The real expense doesn't occur until the movie goes into production, so there is no reason at all *not* to secure the legal rights to the movie idea by buying it from us, either as an outright purchase or in the form of an option. An "option" is a small fee paid to secure a window of time for a studio or producer to own the script and get it produced. If they do not get a deal made within that window, then the rights revert back to the writer, or the option period can be extended for another fee. Option fees can be anywhere from zero dollars to tens of thousands of dollars but are usually a few hundred to a few thousand dollars for new writers.

Let's say, a producer loves the idea of our script but hates the script itself. If they steal our idea without telling us, they still have to pay a writer they trust to actually write up the idea properly before they can go off and sell it to a studio. That writer will cost many times more than it would cost to buy the idea from us. Where's the incentive in that against the risk of future lawsuits?

New writers are cheap to indulge, and established writers are too risky to steal from, so in both cases, it makes no sense for anyone to put themselves in harm's way of a lawsuit.

Despite all this, there are always a couple of lawsuits flying around at any one time from writers claiming studios or producers stole their idea. Many are from loony-tunes people, whose original script is so far removed from the final film that such claims are rightly shot down by the courts very quickly.

I was once browsing a forum for screenwriters and became interested in a thread by a writer who claimed Marvel had stolen his idea for an intergalactic band of superheroes as the basis for the movie *Guardians of the Galaxy* (James Gunn, Story by Nicole Perlman and James Gunn). He spoke in detail about how he had sent it to various people in the industry—not Marvel, but other people connected with Marvel—and the similarities in the two scripts made it impossible to have created one without the other.

Other writers had chimed in and offered support—some even suggesting he sue—until one writer who was more knowledgeable about Marvel than me, asked the most important question: "When did you write your script?" His answer? 2010. The contributor then pointed out, politely, that the Marvel movie was based on their own comic, first produced in 1969 and updated in 2008, and that, therefore, if anyone was guilty of plagiarism, it was this writer himself.

Did this writer steal Marvel's idea? No, of course not. He just happened to write a movie about superheroes in space that, when it suited him, bore enough similarities to the Marvel movie for him to feel wronged. I wonder how many similarities he continued to argue after realizing the truth of the timeline.

In the same vein, it is not impossible for a movie that goes into production to bear some similarities to a script that already exists. Remember, there are over 50,000 scripts registered with the WGA each year. That's 50,000 movie ideas a year. How likely do you think it is that some produced movies may slightly resemble one of those ideas?

That is why these lawsuits get started. The numbers of real cases of plagiarism, or scripts being stolen, are infinitesimal. I completely understand anyone who truly feels wronged and wants to engage in such a lawsuit, but it is ultimately an endeavor that screws new writers more than anyone else, and we will learn why in the next chapter.

52.

How Do We Sell Our Screenplay?

Thanks to the existence of frivolous plagiarism lawsuits, when we want to send our script out to a studio, production company, or producer, it will take on a new description. It will now be known to anyone in the industry as "unsolicited material". In other words, they didn't ask us to send it to them.

For that reason, they will not read one word of it and will return our script unopened with a semi-curt note stating they do not read unsolicited material.

This is to protect themselves against lawsuits down the line. They can't be accused of stealing our idea if they didn't *read* our idea.

So, what scripts *will* they read? They will read scripts from legitimate sources they can trust to understand the realities of the industry and—in the very unlikely case of perceived impropriety—act in the best interest of the industry. These sources include agents, managers, producers, and entertainment lawyers, and that's about it. Anyone else, and it could open them up to a potential lawsuit.

If studios won't read our script unless it comes from an agent, will an agent read our script? No. They won't. If we send our script, unsolicited, to one of the big four agencies, we will get much the same response as we would from a studio.

The big four talent agencies are CAA, William Morris-Endeavor, UTA, and ICM. They represent all the hyper-successful and expensive talent in the industry. They take on writers as clients once they are established and are very likely to start making big commissions very soon. They are, in general, utterly uninterested in discovering new talent. It is just not worth their time.

So, if studios won't read it, and agencies won't read it, who will?

We need to find people for whom it is worth the risk because they are not getting access to A-list material from big-name writers. Smaller agencies, or new agents looking to build up their client roster, may be open to unsolicited material, as may smaller, newer production companies. They will most likely send us a disclaimer to sign, but they may read it.

Some managers consider discovering new talent to be an important part of their role and may accept scripts from new writers. Actors are a potential route, if we can get it to them personally. Going through their agency will never work for scripts from new writers.

This is where we need to be creative and learn an important lesson: This industry will never come to us. We have to go to it, and we have to be savvy and dedicated to break in. Sitting with our finished script on our desk and waiting for someone to call and say, "Hi, I'm a major film producer, and I have a few hours to kill; you don't happen to have a script I can read, do you?" isn't going to happen.

I can't tell you how many writers I've met (including myself, by the way) who piss and moan about their undiscovered genius, and how no one will give them a shot. But, when they are pushed, they are forced to admit they sent the script out to a few people, got turned down, got angry, and then stopped sending it out.

No one owes us a living in this industry.

It will only happen if *we make it happen* by trying and failing, then trying again and failing again, then trying again and again, until someone pays attention to us.

We need to get our work into the hands of many potential buyers and representatives to ensure a very small group of them recognize our genius and want to work with us.

I don't know exactly what will tip the scales in our favor and get that sale, but I do not that *not* trying hard enough is guaranteed to fail.

However, selling our script is not an activity to itself. It is something we do *at the same time* as writing our next script. Six months of trying to sell a screenplay without any writing is six months lost from our journey. Even if we do sell it, the first thing any agent or producer will ask is, "What's next?" We should already be deep into the next script when this happens.

"How to get an agent" is one of the most blogged about topics in screenwriting, so just type it into Google and read away. Steal any idea you can. Syd Field himself even wrote a book on this topic called *Selling a Screenplay*.

The historically standard way to get our script read was to send out query letters to agents, managers, or development executives at smaller production companies, detailing the logline of our script, and a small paragraph about ourselves, then politely asking if they would read it.

It didn't always work, but there was a chance.

However, in the world of email, it takes almost no effort for anyone with 120 pages stuck together with brads to email every agent in North America, asking them to read their script. So, every agent at every agency—no matter how big or small—is now inundated with query emails, and as such, that route of entry into the market is flooded. That doesn't mean we don't do it. Anything that has a small chance at success is worth trying, but don't go into it working on the principle that you will be deluged with replies (or even get *one* reply). For this route to really work anymore, our logline has to be a *very* high-concept idea that might just hook in the agent or executive's assistant enough to convince them it's worth reading the first few pages. Or, we may have some sort of hook that makes us stand out. For instance, have we already sold a script? Is something we wrote in production (even a hyper low-budget one) or available for them to watch? Did our script place highly in a well-known screenplay competition? Do we have some tenuous personal link to the agent? Anything that lifts us above the crowd.

In the modern world, we need to be much savvier, much more diverse, and much more inventive to get noticed and get our script read.

Screenplay competitions are a growing avenue for the recognition of new writers. Their worth in terms of getting us recognized or signed is debatable, as these competitions run the gamut in terms of respectability, recognition, prizes, and potential for success. The Nicholl Fellowship is the most respected of them, as it is part of the Academy of Motion Picture Arts and Sciences (the Oscars), and, as such, has a built-in channel to those in the industry with positions of power. Winning the Nicholl Fellowship would give us a strong chance of meetings with some genuinely good agents. Placing well will also open a lot of doors and will get us some meetings if we play it correctly.

However, as well as being respected, the competition is also quite highbrow. Like the Oscars, they are looking for more than a well-made family comedy.

Other famous competitions are the Sundance Screenwriting Lab, the Bluecat Screenplay Competition, the Austin Film Festival, and Scriptapolooza, which is run by a very small company (I think it might even be just one guy), but it is run effectively and professionally, and people in the know really do pay attention to it. There are also many, many more.

They mostly require some sort of fee for entry (which is how the competition makes its money), but some also offer feedback as part of that entry fee, which can be useful.

Don't go nuts and enter them all, but entering a couple that we feel suit our material can be a good way to gauge its reception and potential for success. As mentioned, placing well in any competition can be something to include on a subsequent query email that may make it stand out from the crowd.

The Black List is an interesting avenue for exposure. The Black List started out a few years ago as an informal gauge of industry personnel at studios and agencies of their favorite as-yet-unproduced screenplays. The list was distributed annually and listed the screenplays in order of popularity.

It gave a very welcome bump to screenplays from otherwise-unknown writers who were sitting on the studio backburner. Appearing on—or, indeed, *leading*—the Black List could suddenly get our script bought if unsold, or put into production if sitting in development hell, or definitely moved up the priority list for a studio.

As its popularity grew within and outside the industry ("The Black List" became a well-known phrase outside the filmmaking community), they decided to monetize the idea, and The Black List website (www.blcklst.com) now offers a repository for scripts that industry personnel can search and read.

As ever, there is a fee attached for evaluations, but these evaluations then form the success of the script on the site. High scores mean it could rank in the "Top Screenplays" section or potentially as the "Featured Script," which is emailed out to the entire mailing list. There is then a monthly fee to keep the script hosted and searchable on the site. To be blunt, if our evaluations get a crappy score, then we might as well take the script down and save ourselves any more expense, since no one is going to bother reading it, but if it scores tremendously well (8/10 or above), then a small outlay each month for a few months could be money well-spent to see who finds and reads the script. Remember, anyone who reads for a living is already inundated with scripts, so none of them are bouncing to the computer each morning to check the site, but it is certainly one of the places they may look, since some of the work of weeding out the rubbish has already been done for them.

Again, a high score or placement in featured categories on The Black List is something that, when mentioned in a query email, may make the agent or development executive pay a little more attention.

Outside of these more traditional avenues, the world is our oyster for getting noticed. A more recent development has definitely been for people to shoot their own material. Producers are often happier to watch a few minutes of footage to whet their appetite. Maybe shoot a fake trailer, or a "Funny or Die" video, or, if you're good at pitching, shoot yourself pitching the idea and email the link to anyone who will pay attention (more on pitching later).

Try contacting directors or actors directly. We'll never get close to an actual movie star—they have far too many systems in place to make sure of that—but second and third-tier actors are more accessible. Actors are vain people; they will feel flattered you have written a script "especially for them," whether that's true or not. No one outside the top 10 A-List stars has the power to get our movie made, but remember, that's not the goal here. The goal is to get people of import and influence to read our script, and anyone who can help us make that happen is a useful ally.

In all cases, the response will generally be less successful than we want it to be. The chances are we will not place very highly in our first few screenplay competitions. We will not get the 9/10 score on The Black List we hoped for. We will not get replies from any agencies. Actors will completely ignore us, and our "Funny or Die" video will get 100 views, and then disappear.

Again, I'm not trying to sound facetious when I say, don't get upset about it. None of this is failure. These are all the avenues we need to explore, until we find the one that works for us and opens the doors we need.

We only need one.

53.

Who Will Read Our Screenplay?

Once we finish our script and send it to "Hollywood"—located at 1 Hollywood Road, Hollywood—who will actually read it? With very few exceptions, our script will be read by a "reader." Sounds obvious, but the script reader is a very important, and yet elusive, job title. It is not really a job title at all; it is the description given to anyone who is the first port of call for a new script.

Senior executives have neither the time, nor the inclination, to read through the thousands of scripts flooding in to find the fantastic few, so they pass that job on to others.

Firstly, there are readers in full-time jobs with major companies, such as studios, talent agencies, and production companies. These people may be employed just as readers, but they also may be interns, assistants, and junior members of staff who are keen to move up by discovering a diamond in the rough.

Then, there are a lot of freelance readers, who make approximately $40 per script. These people can be other writers hoping to break in, post-grad students, or freelance workers in a variety of other jobs, trying to keep some sort of income coming in while they pursue their own dreams.

This person reads the whole script (in theory) and writes out "coverage." This is a 1-2-page document detailing the plot of the film, the major elements of screenplay structure (such as the concept, characters, and dialogue), and finally, a brief summation of the writer's talent, and the screenplay's potential.

It gives the higher-ups something tangible to work from. A template they can scan very quickly to find out the pertinent information about any script that has come in.

The report may offer those judgments of the writer and the screenplay separately. A sample report may look something like this:

COVERAGE REPORT

Title:	Fashion Week	Date:	12.01.2018
Type of material:	Screenplay	Author:	A. Writer
Number of pages:	95	Genre:	Comedy
Submitted By:	Author	Era:	Modern Day
Analyst:	J. Smith	Location:	New York

	Excellent	Good	Fair	Poor
Premise		X		
Plot	X			
Characters			X	
Dialogue		X		
Structure	X			
Marketability		X		

	High	Medium	Low
Budget		X	

Logline: A young, country girl runs away to New York to pursue her dreams of becoming a fashion designer but is eaten up and spit out by the Big Apple.

Synopsis: AMY CHILDS (20) lives in rural Indiana but dreams of moving to New York and making it in the fashion industry with her own show during fashion week. Her parents still see her as their naïve little girl and want her to stay close by.

After a big fight, she steals some money from them and gets on a bus to NY.

Once there, her dreams start to fall apart very quickly. Everything is so much more expensive than she thought. She is ripped off by her landlord, and her attempts to break into fashion are pitiful and ridiculed by everyone in the industry.

Very soon, she has spent all her money but is too embarrassed to call home. Sitting in a coffee shop by herself, a woman, VIV (24), at the table next to her, starts screaming when she spills coffee on herself. She has a job interview in 30 minutes and is now covered in coffee. Amy offers her a shirt—one of her own creations.

Later on, Viv calls her to let her know she got the job—as an assistant to a famous fashion designer. After being commended on her shirt, she has recommended Amy for a job as an office assistant—the most junior position in the company, but Amy jumps at the chance.

Viv takes Any under her wing and teaches her about life in the city. The two of them become fast friends, and Amy starts to make her way in NY. She is treated poorly at work, but her personality and drive start to win people over.

Out one night, she and Viv meet a man they both like. He ends up calling Amy afterwards, and this creates a rift between the two women, but at work, Viv is still friendly and helpful.

As NY fashion week approaches, the famous designer is having trouble with their collection and lets it be known they are keen on seeing ideas from others.

Amy sees her chance to present some of her own designs. One piece in particular she feels would suit the current collection. She gives it to Viv, who promises to pass it on, but later that day, Amy is fired with no reason. She discovers later that Viv told people she was stealing.

She was already struggling to make rent, but now, she will be broke. Worse, she finds out Viv has passed off Amy's design as her own. The designer liked it and has incorporated the style of the piece into the overall collection. But, Amy has a trump card: The piece was one she designed back home, and she has a picture of it in her high school yearbook.

She calls home to her best friend to get the yearbook and bring it to NY. If she can get to the designer, she can prove what Viv did and show them the work was hers.

Her friend does as she asks but also brings Amy's dad with her. He orders her to come home, but Amy refuses. When her dad sees how much Amy has changed, and how driven she is, he agrees to stay and help her.

Amy has to use all her newfound street smarts to sneak her way into the fashion show and get to the designer, but she does it and proves the provenance of her work. Viv is fired. Amy is hired as the new assistant, and her dad leaves for Indiana, proud of his little girl.

Analysis: A surprisingly funny and charming script in the vein of *Coyote Ugly*. The writer brings the world of NY fashion to life enjoyably and realistically.

It is medium-budget but has audience appeal to both males and females, and a variety of age ranges. Dialogue is funny and snappy, and at no point does the story feel labored. Some characters are a little two-dimensional, but the writer clearly understands structure and brings a simple story to life with ease.

Script: Consider
Writer: Recommend

***

The coverage will end with one of three words:

- PASS
- CONSIDER
- RECOMMEND

This is the most important part. This one word will determine whether the executive requests the script, so they can read it themselves, or simply moves on to the next coverage report.

It's funny to think some of the most successful movies of our time had such a report written about them, and they did not all get a "Recommend." There are always stories about scripts that went on to make millions—if not hundreds of millions—of dollars, that were initially turned down by various studios. If that script came from a relatively unknown writer, then its first port of call would definitely have been a lowly reader.

Even if the script is from an experienced writer, it will still pass through the reader at some point—if, for no other reason, than to get the above coverage report produced. This coverage report is the shorthand that executives throughout the studio need to keep track of the many projects running at any one time, without having to read all the scripts.

For those of us trying to break in, the script reader is God. Without their "Recommend" at the bottom, our script is dead. No one else is going to read it.

Therefore, we are writing our script *for* the script reader. If only we knew exactly who that was going to be. What we can do, though, is build up a picture of the challenges they all face, to be as aware as possible of what our script needs to get that elusive "Recommend."

Firstly, readers can be required to write coverage for anywhere from 10-30 (or maybe more) scripts a week, often on their own time, once their real work has finished. Even if they are being paid for this, they have to read the whole script *and* write the coverage for their $40. The hourly wage on that doesn't work out well in their favor.

If they're not being paid any extra, then the stack of scripts in front of them is nothing more than a barrier to getting to sleep.

However, in all my discussions with anyone who has indulged in this joyous position within the film industry, one prevailing characteristic shines through: Every time they pick up a script, they *want* it to be fantastic. Nothing would send them to bed with a bigger smile than to find a script with which they can bound into work the next day, hold it up, and say, "I've just found the next *Hunger Games.*" (Gary Ross, Suzanne Collins, and Billy Ray, Based on the Novel by Suzanne Collins)

That's why it is so depressing for them when script after script is poorly structured, illogical nonsense.

One gentleman I know worked for 6 months as a reader for Tom Cruise's Cruise/Wagner Productions, ostensibly looking for projects in which Cruise himself would star. Over that period, he read over 200 scripts, in addition to his other duties.

Of those 200 scripts he vociferously recommended just 2. Both of which did go into production, but neither of them with Cruise/Wagner. For 20 more he put them as a Recommend, and 20 Considers.

With these odds against us, we want our script to stand out for all the right reasons, and the first way to do that is to be very deliberate about the length of our script. Imagine a reader has a stack of 15 scripts to get through, and it's 11 PM, and they need to wake up at 6 AM. Which script are they going to read: The 100-page script or the 135-page script?

It doesn't have to be 11 PM. Think of how busy you are in your own life. The reader is busier; I promise. If they have three hours to get some reading done, they could potentially read three 90-page scripts, or two 120-page scripts. It's more efficient to read the shorter scripts. They're not lazy people; they're just logical.

They will get around to reading the longer scripts, obviously—they can't put it off forever—but don't underestimate how much more laborious those extra 30 pages make the whole enterprise. Therefore, the longer script needs to be exponentially better than its 90-page counterpart to stand out.

Most movies are thought of as 120 minutes—and therefore, 120 pages—but as mentioned, I am keen for you to start learning the skills of brevity and editing as soon as possible. Therefore, I will be pushing you to create screenplays around 100-110 pages. However, what determines the acceptable page length more than anything else is our genre. A simple explanation is: The funnier or scarier our script, the shorter it needs to be, and the darker and more dramatic, the longer it is allowed to be.

The actual runtimes of successful films are not our guide here. Our guide is the expectation of the reader. Anything less than 90 pages, and they will assume we simply couldn't come up with enough material. Anything over 120 pages, and they will assume we don't understand the industry. The two-hour film was developed because it allows an optimum amount of entertainment for the viewer, while allowing an acceptable number of screenings per day to maximize revenue for the theater and the distributing studio.

Before some of you start scoffing, I know two of the most successful movies of all time are *Titanic* and *Avatar,* at 194 minutes and 162 minutes respectively, but believe me when I say, we are not James Cameron. When we are, we can hand in our 300-page opus. Until then, we are going to do everything we can to get the reader on our side.

We are going to be as efficient as possible and keep the page count down. We are also going to choose a title that effectively describes the genre of the script. Readers don't have a logline to work with, so if we do have a 120-page screenplay, the only thing letting them know it's a drama script—and, as such, that it warrants a high page count—is the title. Similarly, picking up a 90-page script with a title that screams "comedy" lets them know our page count is appropriate, and they might have an easy and funny read ahead of them.

Any script around 100-110 pages can get away with being pretty much any genre, and that's why it's a useful page count to keep in mind. 100 pages could be a 90-minute film if it includes lots of dialogue, or a 120-minute film if it's predominantly action, but at 100 pages, we're not putting off any readers from wanting to pick it up.

Next, we have to make sure they keep reading. We have talked a few times about readers giving up on Page 20 and throwing the script across the room.

"How can they do that," you may ask, "if they have to write a coverage report on the whole plot?" Easier than you'd think; I promise.

Firstly, there is a big difference between reading a script and skimming a script to get enough plot details to be able to write coverage. Secondly, if their judgment is a PASS, then there is almost no reason for anyone else to ever read the script, so even if a few plot details are a little off, no one is ever going to notice.

Covering 20-30 scripts a week may seem impossible while also working a full-time job, and it would be—if they truly read every single script with the diligence we would like them to. Many readers use and teach the 10-10-10 method. You read the first 10 pages, 10 pages in the middle, and the last 10 pages. If you now feel it suitable then you may go back and read the pages in-between, but if is a clear PASS, then they have no reason to go back when they have so many other scripts to get to. Even if they do read every page they start skimming very quickly.

To keep them reading properly, it's less about our script being immediately fantastic, and more about avoiding the things that will annoy them. What the reader wants to think at the end of Page 1 is: "*Oh, thank God. A real writer.*" That means they can relax and just enjoy the writing. It doesn't mean they will love the script, but they know very quickly whether the script will be easy to read and professionally presented.

They want to enjoy the script, but certain things will make this difficult for them, including basic elements, such as spelling errors and incorrect formatting. Another problem to avoid are the tropes and clichés of new writers, such as every female character being described as "beautiful" or "attractive," no matter what role they play in the story, or great, big blocks of action text that just make the whole page look daunting. A great story can get lost if our script is simply too irritating to read.

A wonderful book that details all such problems (and many more) is *500 Ways to Beat the Hollywood Script Reader* by Jennifer Lerch. It does exactly what it says on the tin. It lists 500 tips, collated from professional readers, of things that help or hinder their job. It's a very quick, enjoyable, and useful read.

So, they've picked up the script, we've proven we know how to write, and we've kept them reading right to the end—but that's not enough. How do we get them to "Recommend" the script?

To do this, we need to surprise and excite them. This sounds easy in theory but is very difficult in practice. With the sheer volume of stories people consume these days through TV, film, and the internet, it is nearly impossible to surprise *anyone* anymore, let alone someone who reads scripts for a living—and yet, surprise and excite them, we must.

To explain what this looks like this, I am going to tell you the true story of a script. There once was a young filmmaker. To break into the industry, he borrowed money from his parents and other family, then wrote and directed a very low-budget film. That film didn't make much of a splash, but it did get him noticed by studios. After years of writing and struggling, he finally got a deal with a studio. He wrote and directed a film with a $7M budget. The studio was run by a famously difficult producer who railroaded the young filmmaker and made his experience a misery. Meanwhile, the filmmaker was getting some writing work with other studios, but nothing that made him a star writer.

Furious at the treatment he'd received from the difficult producer, the filmmaker decided to get back at him by writing a script so good that every studio would want it. The filmmaker would then make sure the difficult producer would not be allowed to buy the script.

The filmmaker went away and wrote the script. After giving it to his agent, he specified some very detailed rules. The script would be offered for sale for only one day. The minimum acceptable offer would be $1M (far more than he had so far made as a writer), and he would have to be attached as director. The last condition was that the difficult producer would be mailed—not emailed—the script, making sure he would not be able to get an offer in.

The script went out, and by the end of the day, after a furious bidding war, it was bought for $3M, with the writer attached as director for another $600K, just as specified.

That filmmaker was M. Night Shyamalan, and the script was *The Sixth Sense*.

This screenplay was on our list at the beginning of this book as one we had to read. If you haven't, I implore you to do so now. Personally, I think *The Sixth Sense* is a very good movie, made from an exceptional script.

I want you to recall how you felt when you read it. Especially the last page. That ending didn't particularly work for me in the theater. I didn't hate it, but it didn't affect me the way it affected the rest of the huge audience the film attracted.

But, when I read the script, five years after seeing the movie, that last page blew me away—and I knew it was coming! Imagine how it would have felt to readers on the day it was first sent out.

266

That is how we need to make the reader feel, and if we do, then believe me; they will not be able to write anything other than "Recommend"—or maybe get someone to give you $3M for it.

The producer was Harvey Weinstein.

54.

The Studio Hierarchy

To build our career, we must first understand where we fit into the overall hierarchy of movie making. From movie credits, it may look like writers are very important. After all, the three last credits before a movie starts are the director, producers, and writer. That must mean writers are as important as directors and producers, right? Wrong! Big wrong! Whopping wrong!

There are so many people who are *considered* to be more important on the movie, and this is a distinction we should get used to right now.

No movie can get made without a script, and no movie is going to be a hit with a terrific script, but that doesn't mean anyone in the industry considers what the writer does to be important. Instead, they feel writers are easily interchangeable and replaceable. After all, it's just typing words on a page; anyone can do that.

Writers are fired at will. Writers are replaced at every stage of production, from the first draft to the on-set rewrites. Writers are ignored, belittled, and insulted by directors, producers, and stars. Even assistants don't think it's out of line to criticize or ignore a writer.

I tried to think of an analogy to the world of filmmaking that would be understandable to people who haven't been around it, and the best I can think of is the NFL. Here's how their jobs compare to those on a film set:

The Team Owner is the **studio**. Usually invisible, but ultimately, all-powerful. Has the power to fire anyone and shut the whole caboodle down if they so wish. Gets most of the money.

The General Manager is the **producer**. Ultimately, in charge, but not the most visible person on game day. The person who hires (and could fire) everyone else on the field if they wanted, but usually lets their team get on with it once the game has begun.

The Coach is the **director**. In charge on game day. The public face in charge of the team. Ultimately responsible for any success or failure. Only fired once there is catastrophic (or prolonged) failure of some kind.

The Offensive Coordinator is the **director of photography**. Hugely well paid. Absolutely instrumental to the team. Ultimately fireable but hired for their singular expertise and mostly left alone to do their job.

The Quarterback is the **movie star**. Handsome, chiseled, athletic, famous, and shouldering a huge amount of the burden of any success or failure, but paid massively well for the trouble. Probably the highest-paid person on the field, even though they technically answer to a few other people.

Other well-known actors are the equivalent of your **wide receivers** and **star running backs**. Handsomely paid, and again, mostly left alone to do their jobs.

Then, there are other technicians, like the sound guy and the camera operator, who are your **group coaches**. Fireable if they pissed anyone off, but no one else knows how the camera works, so basically, they are left alone.

Then, below all these people, is the **kicker**. The kicker is the **writer**. Insanely fireable for any reason. After all, it's just kicking. Anyone can do that. If this guy doesn't kick it the way I want him to, I'll just get another kicker. There are loads of them, just dying to take the job. Every time the kicker makes a tough kick, does the city throw him a party? Do they, hell! But, when the kicker misses a field goal in the dying seconds, was it anyone else's fault they lost? The quarterback? The coaches? The defense? Anyone else who failed to secure the win? No. It was the kicker. The kicker lost the game. It was their fault. Let's fire them and get another kicker. After all, ANYONE CAN KICK A BALL!

But, NFL kickers are paid pretty well, and so are screenwriters. NFL kickers have a pretty cool life, as do screenwriters. But, they are not important in the hierarchy, and if they think they are, they will find themselves losing that career very quickly.

A small, select group of writers will amass a little bit of power, but usually not until they step sideways into dual roles as writer/director or writer/producer. Only then can they start to truly take control of their work and their destiny. As long as you are okay with this situation, then you can enjoy a long and successful career as a screenwriter, but if you are someone who needs to be in charge, or will flip out on anyone who tells you what's wrong with your work, then maybe you should start preparing for a different career, because it's going to happen a lot.

Stage 7:
Professional Level Writing

55.

Our 6th Screenplay

Our sixth screenplay (and all that come after) is our third and final *major* benchmark to reach in our writing journey. We would hope to start this script *roughly* two years after we started.

It took me over five years to finish my sixth screenplay and that was a lot of time wasted. I was writing, but as I mentioned, I took a short detour into TV comedy writing for a while. That was how I justified the time I lost on my screenwriting, but there was no reason for me to stop writing screenplays as well. I just enjoyed the time off, safe in the knowledge that I could still call myself a writer. I was making money from writing during this time, but still never enough to support myself without another job, so it was just lazy and stupid. Such a gap can derail us completely.

Do me a favor. Go back to the first script you ever wrote and read it straight through. Don't stop, no matter how difficult it is.

Are you back?

I'm going to bet you couldn't even make it to Page 30 without being shocked at how unreadable it was. I bet you're even quite impressed anyone else *did* make it all the way through.

However, there were probably at least four or five moments that really impressed you. That's because our first script was written purely on instinct and natural talent, and what we generally create is of a poor quality, but every so often we hit on a moment of genius that we can find it hard to recreate once we begin to understand "the rules" and how to craft a story properly.

Now re-read the rest of your scripts in sequence. Try and do this in one afternoon if you can.

Back again?

Each one gets much better, right? They are better stories that are properly structured and more proficiently written. But also, I bet some of them feel a little stale. A little over produced. Technically they are leaps and bounds above your first script, but in doing so you have lost some of the sparkle, some of the raw surprise that writing from the heart can create.

At this stage, we become very aware of why our past scripts didn't sell. Even if people responded to them positively, we can now understand that ultimately, they weren't good enough to stand out or break us in.

Our subsequent scripts are a very different part of our journey. We now know how to write. We don't need to study this book or any other book to craft a story. We can just do it by sitting down and thinking about it. We can tell when something is working or not working, and we can be critical about our own work during rewrites. We have all the technical skills screenwriters need. What we need to do now is *relearn* how to write on instinct.

Once we can write on pure instinct—combined with the technical skills of story and structure—then we have the chance to write something truly wonderful.

From here on out, every script has a shot at being great. Every script has the potential to be the one that breaks us in. Interestingly, it is not necessarily true anymore that each subsequent script will get better. We have now mastered most of the screenwriting *craft,* and we no longer have to fight to make our script look and feel professional. Now, we are fighting to make our professional script stand out in a world of other professional scripts from other professional writers, and the only way to do that is to create something unique, original, and surprising. Unfortunately, we don't do that every time—nor do the best writers on the planet, by the way.

Think of your favorite writers, be they novelists or screenwriters. Is every book or film they write better than their last? No. Not even close. Many people think *Carrie,* Stephen King's first novel, is still his best. (And please read Stephen King's book, *On Writing.* It is half autobiography, half textbook on how to write properly. It also details the very real struggle of a man, who is clearly a genius, to get that genius published.)

Feedback, analysis and coverage of our work should now be generally positive. Gone are the days of "…. too many problems with character motivations…" to be replaced by "…a good story with a solid structure, but too much like other films in its genre…"

This is all very positive stuff, but at the same time it raises the bar of what we need to achieve. With our first script, we thought we were going to be competing with the big boys. Now we look back and realize we weren't even close, but now we really are competing with them, and that means we must be as good as Lawrence Kasdan, or Andrew Kevin Walker, or Tony Gilroy, or Ed Solomon, or Drew Goddard, or Terry Rossio, or J.J. Abrams, because if we are not as good as them then why would anyone hire us?

Now is the time to become as good as we truly believe we are.

I would also suggest that now is the time to start utilizing any insider and industry contacts that we had before this journey started or have cultivated during the journey.

Had we sent them our early scripts their response would most likely have been polite but underwhelming. They would have been very unlikely to read future work or to send it on to their own contacts.

Things are different now. We are not only much more aware of the quality of our own work, but likely producing pieces that receive positive feedback. When that is true, any such contact could be just the magic door that we need. Their response may still be that they don't want to pass it on. That is their prerogative, but believe me when I say that they will expect it to be terrible, so when they are quietly surprised by the quality of the work they are regularly more than happy to do us a favor and put it into someone's hands. It still may lead to nothing, just as many of our marketing efforts may lead nowhere, but such is the journey we have chosen to take.

A key question that new writers ask me is: "How many scripts do I need to write to break in?"

The answer? As many as it takes!

It might be 6; it might be 20. Remember, this is the same as professional writers having to write 10, 20, or even 30 scripts, before they finally get one into production. They're making money for their work, but that's the only difference. Don't think of this as time wasted; think of it as practice and preparation for the next stage of our career.

A good barometer number is 10-15 scripts, which is a solid average if you speak to enough writers who managed to break through and sell a script or get representation.

Some writers are lucky with a much earlier script, but in many cases that one script can turn out to be a fluke. The writer had not mastered their craft enough to write subsequent scripts to the same standard, and as such their success can be very short lived. Many writers break in with a much later script, and in my experience, these people were always much happier (in hindsight) that it took so long.

The more scripts we write, the more we have learned. We have fought to make our stories work. We have been bombarded by negative feedback. We have rewritten and rewritten, sometimes making our work better, sometimes making it worse, but all the time learning. And lastly, we have become at least a little battle hardened. We have become ready and appreciative of success when it appears. We will be much more professional in meetings with agents, managers, studios and producers. We understand their feedback and why they may want to change certain elements. We are more willing to try and work within the system than to fight against it. We are ready for our career.

I said at the beginning of the book that we should expect our journey to screenwriting success to take *about* 5-7 years. That is if we do the right things, make the right choices and fight as hard as we can. We will not be a millionaire, Oscar winner at the end of five years. That five years is to break us in; to get a script sold, to get an agent and to start making a name for ourselves. That has been our investment.

It is generally accepted that once we break in, we still have another five years before we build anything resembling a real career. And that is if everything falls into place in the way we want.

Where are you now? Are you still on your journey? Have you dropped off? Dropped out? Given up? Working at 50% capacity? Waiting for the phone to ring rather than getting out there and meeting people?

Remember, I failed! Plain and simple. I can say it now without the embarrassment and regret that I carried with me for years. I didn't work hard enough, and I failed. Please, don't be me!

Don't ever give up.

We can write 30 scripts that are ignored and ripped to shreds by every person who reads them, but our next script might be *Whiplash* (Damien Chazelle). We don't know what brilliance we have in us—and other people *certainly* don't know—so we should never listen to anyone who tells us to give up or end our journey.

A fantastic script will always be recognized if we get it into the hands of enough people. It may not get made, but it is never ignored. It's just too potentially valuable to ignore.

56.

Should We Move To L.A. Now?

If our goal is to have a career as a *Hollywood* screenwriter then we should be seriously thinking of making the move. In their book, *Writing Movies for Fun and Profit*, uber-successful screenwriters Robert Ben Garant and Thomas Lennon correctly discuss the need to be in the heart of the industry. Studios, agents, and producers will need us to be available at a moment's notice for meetings, pitches, rewrites, and more.

However, we *don't* need to be in L.A. to work in indie movies, and we don't need to live in L.A. while we are writing a screenplay that is good enough to get us noticed. Remember, it may take us years to have something good enough, so moving to L.A. now could be the most depressing move on Earth.

Once there, we will realize everyone is trying to be a screenwriter. Waiters, accountants, pool cleaners—they all have a script they are working on. To be one of that crowd can be very disheartening, as we struggle to get by in our bill-paying job.

On the other hand, being around so many people who love movies and are pushing each other to be better can be just the drive some people need. It's also very nice to be in a place where saying we are "working on a screenplay" is not dismissed as total folly. Plus, everyone we meet has connections of their own. Those connections will be invaluable when the time comes to get our masterpiece read.

Being there means we will learn the realities of the industry. We learn its job titles and its opportunities. We see the reality behind the dreams when we see the homes of star writers and realize that in Los Angeles they can still only afford a 2-bed condo in West Hollywood. We will realize the opportunities as a television writer and meet many people who moved that way and made a great living.

We can sell a script from anywhere, of course. A producer who loves our script may not care where we live. But it would be hard for them to work with us to rewrite and develop it. Therefore, they may simply buy the script outright with the intention of getting other writers in to continue the work. We may be paid handsomely. But, one script sale is not a career. To build a career, we need representation, relationships, and a brand. The only realistic way to get those things is to be in Hollywood.

It would be great if there was a single repository to which scripts could be submitted. One email address where we attached our script. Then a computer read it, scored it out of 100 and anything over 90 was sent over to the agent whose client list most closely resembles our script, or to the correct producer or studio who is looking for that exact material.

It doesn't work that way I'm afraid.

Instead, Hollywood is like making friends. Past the age of 23, everyone thinks they have enough friends. No one goes out for a drink with their friends, desperately hoping they make a new one. Quite the opposite, in fact. When a stranger approaches your group and tries to strike up conversation, you are all wary of this newcomer and—though polite—you are really waiting for the first opportunity to turn away, push them out of the group, and go back to your *real* friends. That's like Hollywood. Agents already have their client list set up. If they add to that list it will become too difficult to service the clients they've already got. They've got their friends, and they don't need us.

But we do make new friends, just as agents do sign new clients, and studios do form new relationships with new writers. And just like making new friends, it happens when we have something that is so attractive to people that they can't help but invite us into the group. For writers, that something is our spec script.

With that in mind, although there cannot be an exact answer of when the time is right, here are some key things we might have in place to start seriously thinking about making the move:

1) An agent is ready to sign us (or who has already signed us)
2) 2 or 3 agencies who are not ready to sign us but have had real, substantial conversations with us about our work and potential.
3) A script sale of any sort, even for a low figure option.
4) A script sale for a high figure deal.
5) A win or high placement in one or two high profile screenplay competitions.
6) A strong desire to stop pretending and get on with being a screenwriter.

The last one is probably the most important and requires none of the other things to be true but will be aided when combined with any of them.

Some of us may have very lucrative careers, and therefore, we are naturally loath to quit our jobs and move to L.A. with no hope of work. I understand that. I was in a similar boat. If you simply cannot move to Los Angeles, then you need to find another route in. Sending your script out and saying, "Sorry, I live in Ohio and can't come for meetings," is just not going to cut it. Get financing, shoot your film, and make a name for yourself on the indie circuit. Then, agents and studios will come calling and wait for you to travel.

On the other hand, if our work is still developing—and if feedback is still predominantly about how to improve our craft—then a move to L.A. may be premature. Only you really know whether it is the best move.

Once there, if we need money, we should do everything we can to get a job *inside* the industry—if possible, as a reader—just as many have done before us.

The point is that breaking in is now feasible, realistic and should be the primary driver for us. It doesn't replace the writing. Even if we do break in, we need a couple of other scripts that are at least as good to back up whatever script got us in the door, so that people know we are not a one-hit wonder and can repeat that success.

Right now, we have our best script, and we probably have one other good script. Our earlier scripts are most likely below par, so we must keep writing, but we are no longer writing for the sake of writing. Writing with no end goal is just a fun hobby. We are now writing to make the move from hobby to career and if Hollywood writing is your goal then Hollywood needs to be your home.

Star writers, who command huge paychecks and respect, can move away at some point, safe in the knowledge that the phone will keep ringing, and people will wait 24 hours for a meeting.

I hope that will be you one day, but for now, stay where you are if you need to. But, if you are ever lucky enough to get someone who genuinely wants to buy your script, or an agent who wants to sign you, then the answer to the question, "Do you live in Los Angeles?" should always be, "I've actually just rented an apartment there and am moving in at the end of the week."

57.

How To Create a Believable World

Escapism is why movies exist. Escapism is why *stories* exist. Escapism transcends genre, budget, location, and stars, and it touches on something people can feel—no matter who they are. It speaks to the core of why people have gone to the movies since they were invented:

To escape from the normality of their own lives if only for a short time.

We do this by taking them to new and interesting worlds.

One day, while watching *Top Gun* (Jim Cash & Jack Epps Jr, based on an article by Ehud Yonay), I was thinking about how sexy it made the world of fighter jets. Reports suggest that recruitment for naval aviators went up as much as 500% after the movie came out. So *Top Gun* is an obvious escapist movie. It makes us a part of a world that is noticeably different (and more attractive) than our own.

But as I continued to watch the movie, I tried to work out why it worked so well. How do we create successful escapism? Does the movie have to be about something sexy like fighter jets? Does it have to be filled with beautiful people? Must the hero be as super human as James Bond?

No. It doesn't, and they don't. If that were true, then *American Splendor* wouldn't work as escapism. Or *8 Mile* (Scott Silver), or *The Social Network* (Aaron Sorkin, based on the book by Ben Mezrich). However, they *do* work. So, what are all these films doing?

They all create a believable, contained "world" that we really want to experience.

It can be any genre, funny or scary or depressing, if the movie manages to create a contained, believable "world" that we really want to experience then we have somewhere to escape to. If it doesn't do those things then we either don't want to escape there, or we don't know to what world we are supposed to be escaping.

Top Gun achieved this perfectly. It portrayed the contained "world" of the Top Gun flight school, where the best of the best compete against each other and Viper. Did we want to experience that world? Who wouldn't? Hence the staggering increase in people trying to sign up.

Without those elements, we may enjoy the story or the characters, but we cannot escape anywhere. All we've done is watch a story unfold. A good story becomes great when we feel we have truly become part of the world that the characters are experiencing, rather than just watching them from afar.

**Create a believable, contained "world" that
we really want to experience.**

Let's break it down.

1) Create a believable world

Believable doesn't mean *real*. It means that our world has its own rules, and its own internal logic that is strictly maintained for the whole movie. We can have ghosts, aliens, time-travel, godlike powers, talking toys, or monsters—as long as the rules of this world are established early and adhered to for the rest of the film.

The "world" of *The Full Monty* (Simon Beaufoy) is just as believable as the "world" of *Men in Black* (Ed Solomon). Audiences have an innate ability to suspend their disbelief. That's why they come to the movies. They *want* to be introduced to a new world that is slightly, very, or totally different from their own, but once the rules of this world have been established, the audience cannot and will not accept those rules changing to suit the writer/filmmaker's whims.

I hate to criticize films, because in general it is easy and cheap, but to understand these ideas it is necessary to look at some films that I would argue didn't achieve them successfully.

I especially hate to criticize the greatest filmmaker who ever lived, Steven Spielberg. I could only ever dream of having 1% of his movie talent—along with ridiculously-talented writers, David Koepp and Jeff Nathanson—but I must argue *Indiana Jones and the Kingdom of the Crystal Skull* is a high-profile example of a world the audience did not *believe*.

Up to this point, Indiana Jones movies had all created wonderfully believable worlds. Indy was super human, in that he was the best version of a manly-man that could possibly exist, but what he and his comrades did was still firmly within the realm of human ability. And although the "worlds" (Cairo, India and Turkey respectively) all included magic, that magic was based on religious and mythological tales; the lost Ark of the Covenant, the Hindu Sivalinga stones, and the Holy Grail.

The audience with which I watched *Crystal Skull* lost faith in the believability of the world of this latest installment in the first few minutes. Indy finds himself right inside the heart of a nuclear test site and survives the blast by hiding inside a lead-lined fridge. I'm sure this fridge may have had some ability to shield him from the immediate blast, but the fridge is thrown hundreds of feet into the air and tumbles over many, many times. Indy then gets out of the fridge—without a scratch on him—and watches the mushroom cloud right in front of him. The next shot is of Indy happily having a shower, implying that this shower was all that was necessary to rid him of the staggering amounts of radiation and searing heat that he was patently exposed to.

Even if we did stay with the movie after this, which I really wanted to, it lost me completely later when Indy's son finds himself swinging through the trees with a bunch of monkeys, with cartoon-like speed and skill. This bore no relation to what could be done by any human being on the planet. This was not the world of Indiana Jones that had been set up three movies earlier and adhered to until now.

And lastly, the crystal skull ends up belonging to aliens. Aliens are directly contradictory to the magic and mythology that the series of movies had been built upon up to this point.

The Ark of the Covenant and the Holy Grail are both relics that are intrinsically tied to the belief and existence of the Christian God. And both relics were "real." The Ark of the Covenant did exactly what the Old Testament said it would, and an immortal Knight had protected the Holy Grail. So, if they're real then God and Christianity are real. But if Christianity is to be believed then aliens don't exist.

I'm not a religious person at all, but I'm a movie fan and I was now completely lost as to the rules of the world of Indiana Jones. It had lost believability.

A film that does achieve perfect believability, however, is *Wayne's World* (Mike Myers & Bonnie Turner & Terri Turner). The reason I chose this as an example is because it is one of a small group of anti-logic movies from recent decades that manages to depict real life but does it while breaking all the rules of real logic—and even movie logic. For instance, movie logic dictates characters can't break the fourth wall and talk to the camera, but Wayne and Garth can. They can narrate or hypothesize with the audience whenever they want. However, *only* Wayne and Garth can.

Once this logic is set up, it can't change. The movie understands its logic so well, that when Glen, the diner manager, tries to talk to the camera, Wayne stops him and literally reminds him (and us) of the movie's own logic, "Only Garth and I can talk to the camera."

These are writers who understand how to create a believable world that sticks to its own rules, no matter how illogical that world may seem at first glance.

2) Is the world contained?

We must understand the physical or character boundaries of the world that we are escaping to. The final and key world of the movie may be introduced straight away, or it may be introduced anywhere up to the end of Act One. After that, we must stick primarily with this "world" for the rest of the movie. Moving out of this world after that will confuse the audience.

The world can be contained physically, such as the Horace Green prep school in *School of Rock*, or Kevin McCallister's house in *Home Alone*, or the city of *Monstropolis* in *Monster's Inc.*, or Harvard Law School in *Legally Blonde*, or Florin in *The Princess Bride*.

Even *Star Wars Episode IV: A New Hope* is contained within that single galaxy. A galaxy is a big area of physical containment, I'll grant you, but containment all the same. And they put it right up front, "A long, long time ago in a galaxy far, far away." Okay. That's the world we are now a part of.

Or, the world can be contained by a time period, such as the 1920s in *The Sting*, the 1950s in *L.A. Confidential* (Brian Helgeland & Curtis Hanson, based on the novel by James Elroy), the 1970s in *Anchorman* (Will Ferrell and Adam McKay), or the 1980s in *The Wedding Singer* (Tim Herlihy). This is why period movies are so desirable to filmmakers and audiences alike. It immediately creates a firm base on which to create a world that is different from our current reality and—thanks to the rose-colored spectacles of nostalgia—is usually more desirable than our own.

Lastly, the world may have no physical limitations but is seen through the *contained* point of view of one person, or a very small group of people. Examples include the world of the FBI profiler in *The Silence of the Lambs* (Ted Tally, based on the novel by Thomas Harris), the world of the super-rich in *Wall Street* (Stanley Weiser & Oliver Stone), or the world of investigative reporters in Boston in *Spotlight* (Josh Singer & Tom McCarthy). In each case, whatever we see, we see it through the same eyes and the same point of view.

In *Spotlight*, we see the world through the eyes of journalists trying to expose abuse by the clergy. Although their ambition is honorable, their "struggles" could seem justifiably insignificant if we open out the world to show the myriad of other social ills around them at any moment. We never cut to a childless, disabled woman who can't get a job, who says, "Who cares about the struggles of well-paid journalists? They have to stay up late to fill in spreadsheets? Boo hoo! I can't even afford food." That's the same physical world, but a completely different philosophical world, and it would be jarring.

The Hundred Foot Journey, (Steven Knight, based on the novel by Richard C. Morais) featured the wonderful and contained world of a small French village, where two restaurants exist straight across the road from one another (100 feet apart, in fact). Late into the second act, after a very enjoyable battle of the restaurants, the young chef protagonist moves to Paris. It completely upsets the balance of the movie. Paris has nothing to do with the world we experienced for the whole movie. Opening up the world so late in the story simply highlighted how petty the entire film had been up until that point. The childish battle of two aging restaurateurs was very enjoyable, until we were reminded that a huge world exists outside this little village, a world of poverty, disease, misery, and a million other restaurants—in which case, who cares about these two?

Another movie that I believe suffered from a confused world was *Julie and Julia,* (Nora Ephron, based on the books by Julie Powell, Julia Child and Alex Prud'homme) the semi biopic of Julia Child. Half of the movie was set in the 1940's/50's following Julia Child in France as she discovered cooking and went on to write her most famous book. The other half of the movie followed Julie Powell, a blogger who set about trying to cook every recipe from Child's book in 2002. The two worlds had nothing to do with each other and barely crossed over. Which world was supposed to seduce us? For me personally, I found the world of 1940/50's Paris seen through the eyes of Julia Child to be fascinating. On the other hand, I found the world of a blogger in 2002 whose sole claim to fame was to cook someone else's recipes to be inanely dull. Therefore, every time we were shown the blogger's world, I became angry that I was being taken away from the world that I *did* want to experience. Maybe other people may have enjoyed the world of the blogger more than that of Julia Child. Either way, by confusing the world of the movie it was confusing to the audience.

The world can be contained either by time period, location, or point-of-view—or it can be a combination, such as the world of Los Angeles in the 1970s, as seen through the point-of-view of the porn industry in *Boogie Nights,* or the physical world of Hill Valley, circa 1955, in *Back to the Future.*

We have now given the viewer a world that they both *believe in* and *understand.* The last part therefore is to make it a world that we desire.

3) Do we really want to experience this world?

This is where it gets interesting, because we can feel a desire to experience a world for many reasons. Let's start with some obvious ones.

i) The world could be more exciting than our own

This is true of spy movies such as the Bourne and Bond movies. Or "high octane" movies like *Point Break* (W. Peter Iliff, story by Rick King & W.E. Peter Iliff), or its unofficial remake *The Fast and the Furious* (Gary Scott Thompson and Eric Bergquist and David Ayer). It is also true of many movies based on certain exciting careers like *Top Gun* or *The Silence of the Lambs* or *Dirty Harry* (Harry Julian Fink & R.M. Fink and Dean Reishner) or *Sicario* (Taylor Sheridan).

Or movies that depict a similar world to our own but with one exciting difference, like *Ghostbusters* or *Night at the Museum* or *Ex Machina* (Alex Garland). It is also true of comic books and comic book movies, which is why they have been a source of escapism for children (and adults) for over a hundred years.

ii) The world could be sexier than our own

"Sexy" is used here in the physical or aspirational sense. Bond movies again fulfill this criterion, but so does *Ocean's 11,* or *Goodfellas,* or *Out of Sight* (Scott Frank, novel by Elmore Leonard), or *Get Shorty* (Scott Frank, novel by Elmore Leonard) or *Iron Man* (Mark Fergus & Hawk Ostby and Art Marcum & Matt Holloway) or *Rush* (Peter Morgan); worlds that we may daydream about, even if we know that in reality, we are not brave, driven or stupid enough to live in them. That's why we want to enjoy them vicariously.

iii) The world could be funnier than our own

The best comedies are enhanced by elements of tragedy or sadness that we experience in the real world but present them in a world where such things can still be potentially funny. Being dumped at the altar is funny in the world of *The Wedding Singer*. Getting a stranger pregnant is funny in the world of *Knocked Up*. (Judd Apatow) Being the nerdiest guy in school is funny in the world of *Napoleon Dynamite* (Jared Hess and Jerusha Hess). Having a girlfriend at death's door is hilarious in the world of *The Big Sick* (Emily V. Gordon & Kumail Nanjiani).

It's also why, when a comedy movie fails to amuse us, we are so angry about it. We go to see dramatic films for any number of reasons, and we can be entertained by them for any number of reasons, but we go to comedy films *primarily* to laugh and experience a world that is funnier than our own. When it fails to achieve that, it has quite obviously failed at its primary function.

iv) The world could be more romantic than our own

It can simply be a world where love exists in the manner we all desire, such as in *Titanic*, or *The Notebook* (Screenplay by Jeremy Leven, Adaption by Jan Sardi, based on the novel by Nicholas Sparks) or *Brief Encounter* (Noel Coward). If you haven't watched *Brief Encounter*, track it down. It's worth it, I promise.

Or, it can be combined with a funny world to create the classic "romantic comedy," such as *When Harry Met Sally* or *Bridget Jones's Diary* or *Annie Hall*. The romantic comedy genre cleverly combines two separate genres that classically appeal to men and women separately, but by combining them gives us a movie that any couple can enjoy together. "Romantic action" movies are very few and far between, but when done well such as *Speed* or *The Bodyguard* (Lawrence Kasdan), or even *Deadpool* (Rhett Reese & Paul Wernik) they are legitimate money-spinners. I can only assume that if anyone ever nails the "romantic horror" genre that there will also be great spoils available.

***

If those are the obvious ways to make a world appealing, what are the less obvious ones?

v) The world could be scarier than our own

At first glance we may wonder why a world that is terrifying is appealing, but the historical success of the horror genre says otherwise. That is because a world that is truly scary allows us to live out our darkest fears and fascinations in the safety of a movie theater. Horror is a genre of catharsis.

But more often than we'd think it depicts a world that we would like to physically experience.

The Amityville Horror (Sandor Stern, based on the book by Jay Anson) is based on the killings at a real house in Amityville, New York. Do you think people stay away from that house in droves? Hell no. It's one of the most visited tourist spots in the state, and if the current owners wanted to, they could rent out rooms to people desperate to stay in the murder house and have a healthy income for the rest of their lives.

If Camp Crystal Lake existed, it would be jam-packed with movie fans every summer.

What about *The Shining*? It's terrifying. But I believe the world of the Overlook Hotel 100%. A world that is perfectly contained by the winter; the snow stops anyone getting in or out. I really, really want to be there when it happens, and I am desperate to go into room 237, pants shittingly terrified as I may be.

Other examples are *Saw* (Screenplay by Leigh Wannell, Story by Leigh Wannell and James Wan), *The Conjuring* (Chad Hayes & Carey W. Hayes), and *Get Out* (Jordan Peele). These are all examples of wonderfully contained worlds we would really like to experience—if only for a short time.

vi) The world could be *less* appealing than our own

I know this seems counterintuitive, but bear with me. This does not work if the world is *slightly* less appealing than our own. Then we're just watching a movie about a life that's much like our own. However, if the world is *significantly* less appealing than our own, then we are intrigued enough to live vicariously through someone else's misery for a short time, knowing we can return to our own much more appealing "real life."

Precious (Geoffrey Fletcher, based on the novel by Sapphire) is a perfect example of this. That movie depressed the living hell out of me. It was a harrowing portrayal of the "world" of Precious and her abusive mother, contained in Harlem, circa 1987.

I felt pity, sympathy, anger and helplessness all the same time. I wanted to reach into the screen and pull Precious out of it.

Similarly, in *American Splendor,* (Robert Pulcini & Shari Springer Berman, based on the comic book series by Harvey Pekar and Joyce Brabner) we are taken into the world of Harvey Pekar—mostly, inside his messy house, and his amazingly-boring office job, for that is the world of Harvey Pekar, the world that has been depicted for decades in the popular comic-book series, *American Splendor.* The world is dirty, underpaid, sick, and miserable for great patches of time. This makes it *significantly* less appealing than our own (although perhaps more similar than we would like to admit).

By the end of the movie Harvey's physical world has not changed. He is in the same dead-end job (although retiring) with the same oddball friends, and his house is just as dirty and dilapidated as ever, but an element of redemption comes from the people in his life, specifically the daughter he has adopted who has finally brought him some true happiness. What's so clever about this movie is how jealous we are of Harvey and his world even though he is so poor, sick and miserable.

vii) The world could include a character that we aspire to be

We should always identify with our protagonist and other key characters, but that doesn't necessarily mean we want to *be* them.

However, if we can genuinely create a character that people aspire to be, then we are making the world in which they live even more appealing. Therefore, we can combine this idea with any of the ideas above to create a doubly appealing world.

Again, *Top Gun* achieved this perfectly. Not only was the world of the Top Gun flight school incredibly exciting and sexy, but Maverick is somebody that every 16-year-old guy aspires to be. As does *Fight Club* (Jim Uhls, based on the novel by Chuck Palahniuk) and *Star Wars Episode IV: A New Hope* (in Han Solo, not Luke Skywalker) and *Iron Man,* and *Guardians of the Galaxy.*

However, aspirational characters do not exist just to appeal to teenage boys. Films have created aspirational characters for all sorts of people including *The Hunger Games,* or *Home Alone,* or *Mean Girls* (Tina Fey, based on the book by Rosalind Wiseman), or *Hidden Figures* (Allison Schroeder and Theodore Melfi, based on the book by Margot Lee Shetterly), or *Toy Story.* After all, who didn't want to be Buzz Lightyear?

***

This is by no means a definitive list of reasons that we may want to experience a world. Indeed, finding new and surprising reasons that we want to experience a world is one of the key skills of a great screenwriter.

Let's look therefore, at some movies that unfortunately did not successfully create a world that we want to experience.

One would be *Tomorrowland* (Damon Lindelof and Brad Bird, story by Damon Lindelof & Brad Bird & Jeff Jensen). It created a wonderfully unique "world" of Tomorrowland, a futuristic world where innovation, experimentation and the furtherment of humankind were the goal.

It should therefore have been more exciting than our own, and sexier than our own and more fun than our own. Three good reasons to really want to experience this world. Except here's where I think the movie really fell down; the film's called *Tomorrowland*, but we never really go there. We see an "advert" for it, but 80% of the movie is spent on Earth, and not a very exciting or interesting version of Earth.

When we do finally get to Tomorrowland, it's abandoned and empty, a dilapidated version of what it once was. This makes it impossible for the viewer to fall in love with, or even understand, the world we came to see. I walked out of the movie frustrated and angry about never getting to go to Tomorrowland.

I fear other people felt the same, which contributed to its poor word-of-mouth. How could we fall in love with a world we never got to experience?

Let's go right to the top of the Hollywood movie chain. I now believe that the reason James Cameron is a living genius is that he is better at creating worlds than anyone else on the planet. Let's look at his two box office behemoths.

Titanic:

Does it create a believable world?

Yes. The world of Titanic. The ship of dreams.

It is faithfully recreated visually, but more importantly we learn of all aspects of this "world." We see its first-class decks and their super rich inhabitants. It's steerage decks and the working people desperate to make it to the new world. We see its crew, from the men who feed the boilers to its tea-drinking Captain. We see its storage decks filled with fancy cars and luggage. We see its dining rooms and boiler rooms and crow's nest. We are at one with the whole world of Titanic by the Midpoint of the film.

288

Is it contained?

Yup. As soon as the ship sets sail, Titanic is the only world that we, and the passengers, know. There is no getting off or switching to a different world.

Do we really want to experience that world?

Amazingly—yes. And we know it's going to sink. Why did 12-year-old girls go and see that movie 10 or 20 times? They loved it because in the world of Titanic true love could exist in a way that would be impossible anywhere else. Jack and Rose fell in love because of the enclosed but magical world of the ship. Being rescued on the bow. Making love in the secrecy of the stowed away cars. Clinging together as it slid into the water.

Admit it: While watching it, you wanted to be aboard the Titanic, even though *you knew it was going to sink, and everyone was going to die.*

What a piece of writing.

Avatar:

Does it create a believable world?

Absolutely. The world of Pandora. A lush, bountiful planet filled with wonder and flying horses (or whatever they are), currently inhabited by the Na'vi, the sexy, blue aliens. It feels completely real, realistic and believable from the moment we arrive.

Is it contained?

Once again, after we land on Pandora that is our whole world. We never go back to Earth or any other world again. All we know is the beauty, problems and battle that is taking place on Pandora.

Do we really want to experience that world?

So much so that there were regular reports at the time of people considering, or *actually* committing suicide because they couldn't live on Pandora. That's how desirable the world was to people. A tragic side effect for Cameron of being too good at his job.

***

Go away and study your favorite movies. What is the world they create? How is it contained? How do they make it believable and why do we want to experience it? I'm sure if you try hard enough you will find some popular exceptions to the rule, but it will be harder than you think.

Create a believable, contained "world" that we really want to experience.

If a reader puts down our script, thinking, *"Damn, I wish I could experience that world,"* or *"Damn, I wish I could be like that character,"* or even, *"Damn, I'm glad I'm **not** like that character,"* then again, we have massively increased our chances of getting recognized, signed, or hired—and maybe even creating a film of real quality and longevity.

58.

When is it Okay To Break The Rules?

We can only break the rules once we understand them. That's why we've spent all this time learning them.

However, if we can do it, breaking the rules and showing something truly original is a tool that could lift us above the pack. Something more than a flawed protagonist with an interesting inciting incident, well-structured obstacles and a satisfying conclusion.

This doesn't mean we create a story with no goals, no obstacles and no resolution. That's not breaking the rules, that's just idiotic storytelling.

It means that we create something that shows we understand screenwriting so well that we can deliver what an audience wants in a way that no one has done it before. This can be quirky and arty, such as *Memento* (Christopher Nolan), or it can be action packed escapism like *Pulp Fiction*.

Breaking the rules can be very advantageous for our spec script if we can do it well. Such a script may be even less likely to get into production with a studio where the mantra of "the same, but different" prevails, but getting the script into production was never the goal of our spec script. The script is to get us noticed, and one that stands out by breaking the rules in a clever and unexpected way can do just that. Screenplay competitions love scripts that try to be different. But if we break the rules in an unskilled way then I'm afraid we fall back into the pile of amateur scripts by people who didn't understand the rules in the first place.

So, how do we break the rules in the right way? I wish I could tell you. If I knew that, I would be a very rich man. Andrew Kevin Walker knew how to do it when he wrote *Se7en*, and it *did* go into production, and he quickly became the go-to writer when a studio was looking for someone who understood storytelling but would present it in an unexpectedly dark or twisted way.

Therefore, although I can't tell you how to break the rules, we can look at some films that broke the rules effectively and successfully and analyze how they did it.

Forrest Gump (Eric Roth, based on the novel by Winston Groom) is a fascinating case study of how to break the rules. By any textbook definition of storytelling, *Forrest Gump* shouldn't work. It has a flawless protagonist (or at least, he has no major flaws to be fixed by the end), who learns and changes very little throughout the whole story. Things keep happening *to* Forrest, and he takes a very passive role. He doesn't even really come up against any obstacles. Everything Forrest tries to do—be it becoming a college football star, winning the Medal of Honor, or becoming a national hero by running cross-country—he does surprisingly well, either because of innate skill, or because his naiveté and lower-than-average IQ stops him from seeing the potential pitfalls. The problems he *does* encounter are solved by coincidence, rather than actions taken by Forrest, such as the storm that launches the Bubba Gump Shrimp Company. This should be the dullest story ever. So, why did it resonate with so many people and earn nearly $700M around the world?

It works because Forrest's story is played in parallel with that of Jenny, his childhood friend and love of his life. For every good thing that happens to Forrest, the setback happens to Jenny. She is abused as a child. She is used as a sexual plaything by her boyfriends. She abuses drugs and alcohol. She is the victim of domestic violence and thinks she deserves it. She ends up playing nude guitar in a titty bar. She contracts AIDS.

Jenny is the counterpoint to Forrest's story, and so we want Forrest to keep succeeding. And we want them to finally get back together and complete each other once more, "Like peas and carrots." I don't know the book well enough to comment on the source material, but I do know that Eric Roth clearly understands storytelling well enough to know how to deliver what we want in a way that surprises and delights us.

Psycho (Joseph Stefano, based on the novel by Robert Bloch) should always be remembered when speaking about breaking the rules. It opens as a rather familiar, if entertaining story about Marion Crane, a young secretary who steals $40,000 from her employer and goes on the run. We have a solid protagonist with a clear goal, an exciting inciting incident and all the makings of a fun road movie.

At the end of Act One she checks into a motel; The Bates Motel. There we meet its young manager, Norman Bates, who has all the hallmarks of an interesting supporting character.

292

A few scenes later our young protagonist is murdered in the shower in one of cinemas most memorable and shocking scenes. Was it shocking because of its graphic nature? Partly. Such scenes were not as common as they are today. But mostly it was shocking because everything the audience understood about storytelling had just been turned on its head. The movie was about Marion Crane. And we just spent 30 minutes with her. How could she be dead?

With Norman now the protagonist, the rest of the movie goes on to have many wonderful shocks, scares and surprises that earned it $30m at the domestic box office (or $370m in today's money) and a legitimate place in the annals of movie history.

It's a Wonderful Life is also an interesting example. The structure is relatively simple. Our protagonist is George Bailey. The inciting incident is when his uncle loses $8,000 from their building and loan business. George, distraught and scared, contemplates suicide so his family can get the insurance money and avoid ruin. He is visited by Clarence, his guardian angel, who wants him to see the value of his life, and so gives him the chance to see what life would be like if he had never been born. He resists at first (of course), but then visits all the people in his life who are all now much less happy than they were with him around. His brother is dead. His wife is now a spinster. His uncle is in an insane asylum. The town has been taken over by the vile Mr. Potter.

George, realizing the value of life, begs to have it back. When he returns, the community that he has served for so long comes to his rescue and donates enough money to save the business. What a lovely movie. Except that everything described here takes place in the last 40 minutes of a 130-minute movie. The whole rest of the movie is one long flashback simply to explain the set-up. What most movies do in 10 minutes, takes 90 here. So why isn't it boring?

First, the incidents in that flashback are filled with drama, revelation, and character change, so they have everything they need to be interesting, but it works because we need all that time to fall so madly in love with George and the townspeople. Without all that setup, the ending wouldn't mean much. It would be nice, but we wouldn't know what George sacrificed for them. We wouldn't know just how much he means to them, but with it, that last five minutes are the most magical, emotional, and overwhelming you will ever see, making it the enduring Christmas classic it has been for over 70 years.

More recently, a film that successfully broke the rules was *The Lego Movie*. It is unforgivable at the end of the second act of a movie to completely break the internal logic and reasoning of the story into which we have invested 80 minutes of our lives, but that's exactly what Phil Lord and Christopher Miller did, and it works impeccably.

I believe they managed to pull it off because they not only understand story structure perfectly, but they also clearly understood what Lego fans wanted from a movie. As such, showing the relationship between the Lego world (which we totally believed) and the real world was not jarring. True fans of Lego have always created worlds with those little colored bricks that they felt were completely real, but those worlds lived alongside and intertwined with their own lives. To portray that so perfectly in the movie was a validation of our own feelings toward Lego. I would love to know how many people tried to talk them out of that ending!

Election, is an outstanding screenplay. It's also a rule breaker.

It is the story of a high school senior, Tracy Flick, who is trying to win the election for student body president, but in a perfect twist of screenwriting it is told from the point of view of her teacher Jim McCallister.

Unknown to him, he is the villain of the movie. He is her antagonist. He doesn't like Tracy, for various reasons, and spends the entire movie trying to stop her winning the election, even encouraging another popular student to run against her and ultimately cheating her out of the win.

By the end of the movie, Tracy is a successful Washington power player. Jim has lost his job, his credibility, his reputation and has to move towns to escape the shame. And all the time, he still doesn't realize that he is Blowfeld to Tracy's James Bond.

And lastly, I'm going to add *The Big Sick* into this group of rule breakers. It's a romantic comedy where one half of the romance spends the lion's share of the movie in a coma. We don't even see her that much. This leaves the male lead to spend the movie falling in love with her parents, and they with him, but it is as romantic and funny as any romantic comedy since *When Harry Met Sally*.

Rules, as they say, are meant to be broken. Breaking the rules in a way that satisfies the needs and expectations of an industry while showing people something truly different is unbelievably hard to achieve, but if we do achieve it, it could be just what we need to make our name and kick-start our career.

59.

Are We Hitting The Right Tone?

Getting the tone right across the whole of our screenplay is tricky—and by the *right* tone, what we are talking about is a *consistent* tone.

But what is tone? Tone is difficult to nail down exactly, but it is a combination of the following things:

1) The genre of our story
2) The rules of the world
3) The actions and reactions of our characters

Let's look at each piece and how they affect each other.

1) The genre of our story

Let's say we have written a *raucous family comedy*, and for 60 pages, we have family fun with pies, dogs, and children, but then, on Page 61, one of the children dies in a graphic car accident, and the next 20 pages are a funeral with no jokes. That is a drastic change of tone within a recognized genre, and one that will throw the reader completely.

However, if we write a comedy and our first five pages are funny, but then a major character dies off screen, and we have a funeral with a couple of jokes, then it is not necessarily out of tone. The reader knows by page 10 that this is a *black comedy*. If we keep up that dichotomy of humor and tragedy for the rest of the script then the tone is consistent with the genre.

Similarly, if we open on a remote farmhouse at night where a masked killer stalks and murders the residents with an axe and there's nothing funny about it, then we are firmly in the *horror* genre. It is almost impossible to go anywhere else after that without completely confusing the audience as to what sort of movie they are watching. It is the reason that the *horror/comedy* is very difficult to pull off. If the audience is having fun, how can they be scared? And if they are truly scared then how can they laugh?

The immediate and obvious genre therefore sets the first piece of expectation within the reader as to the tone of the script.

2) The rules of the world

We must make many choices to define the rules of our world, and they must all be completely consistent with one another throughout the whole script.

Below is a selection of potential questions that we could ask of ourselves before we start writing.

What is the world of our movie? Is it the real world? An alien world? The 1920's? The modern world? The dark ages? Roman times? A world of monsters? A world full of superheroes?

When somebody gets shot, do they bleed out there on the sidewalk and die? Or is this a comic book world where people can get thrown across the room through a plate glass window and get up with barely a scratch on them?

Is it a fantasy world where magical or mythical creatures exist? Or a world that looks like our own but with different beings?

Can characters talk to the camera? Can they learn world class Kung Fu in three weeks? Or, are they bound by the exact laws of physics and logic that govern our own universe?

Can they fire a gun with assassin precision the first time they pick it up? Or do they not realize it has a safety catch on it?

When their boss fires them, do characters retort with witty banter and insults or do they walk out into the street and cry, realizing that their life has just fallen apart?

Are all characters impossibly attractive—even though they're supposed to be FBI agents? Or are all characters schlubby and coffee-stained *because* they're FBI agents?

Do people own fast, expensive cars but seemingly have no jobs to pay for those cars?

Can a masked killer just disappear even though they went through the door two seconds before we got there?

Can all people fight like MMA fighters even though they're accountants?

Can our characters still run after being shot, or do they have to sit down and wait for an ambulance?

This list of questions is a fraction of what we need to ask ourselves to understand and set out the clear and consistent rules of our world. Once a rule is created it cannot be broken for fear of confusing the tone of the whole script.

3) The actions and reactions of our characters

When Doc Brown unveils the time machine Marty doesn't say, "Oh jeez, you got me up at 1am for this, you nutbar? Time travel isn't real and never can be. Go read some Einstein!" Why? Because the Doc shows him the flux capacitor, which is what makes time travel possible. Once that is established it now dictates the actions and reactions of all characters for the rest of the movie. Time travel is never questioned again, by anybody, across all three movies.

In a comic book action movie, our hero can blow up their enemy and move on to the next problem safe in the knowledge that the bodies will just be disposed of somehow and that no one will really question them about it. After a whole city has been destroyed no one will say, "Gosh, I understand that the bad guy needs to be stopped, but what about the trillions of dollars of damage and many dead people left in the street you just destroyed?"

However, in a small family drama, if our protagonist guns down his enemy in the street, the rest of the film better be about that moment because in the *real* world, that act has *staggering* consequences that need to be dealt with: Ambulances, police, morgues, families in distress, arrest, trial, and years in prison.

***

There is no right or wrong tone for our script. What's important is once a rule is established, it must remain *consistent* throughout the rest of the film. A consistent tone means the world and its rules—as well as the expectations and reactions of our characters—never change.

A regular problem I see with drama scripts is that the writer feels it necessary to have some light relief in amongst the drama and after 60 dark and somber pages I am suddenly reading a scene with a quirky bellhop, or an incompetent lawyer. Such characters are nearly always out of place and incompatible with the tone that has been created.

Men in Black, *E.T. the Extra-Terrestrial* (Melissa Mathison), and *Alien* (Dan O'Bannon, story by Dan O'Bannon and Ronald Shusett) are all films about aliens, but they have a dramatically different tone to one another.

Alien is very "real." The characters are space truckers. They speak and act the same as truckers on Earth right now, they just happen to be in space.

When the Alien turns up there is nothing funny about it. They are surprised. Killer aliens are not a part of their world as they understand it. They are now stuck in space with something trying to kill them. They are terrified and we as an audience know that the alien is as real as any human killer, just deadlier. The humans involved have nothing beyond their own human wit and skill to outsmart it.

E.T. the Extra-Terrestrial is "real" in the sense that it takes place in a recognizable suburban world in the 1980s, but from Page 1, it is also magical as see the alien immediately (or, a little bit of him, at least). However, it is not a whimsical world. When the trucks turn up, the aliens are terrified for their lives. The bad guys may be human, but the threat is very real and quite scary. We now know magical things can happen if they involve the alien, but there is also the possibility of tragedy and death.

Men in Black, on the other hand, is whimsical from the start. We open on the scene in the desert as K and Z track and find the illegal "alien." The alien is funny. The action is over the top. K kills the alien with an entirely implausible gun that explodes the alien into blue goo but without any real emotion about the death. People have their memories erased with the flashy thing. The aliens in this version of Earth are comical and expendable. Many unreal and implausible things will happen if they are funny. There will be a lot of death, but it won't have any real lasting effect.

All three films work perfectly and maintain a consistent tone for the entire film. Once the world, its logic, and its tone are established they must remain consistent for every encounter, every line of dialogue and every action and reaction.

The tone of our script may change as we develop during rewrites, so we can end up creating tonal problems for ourselves by holding onto scenes or sequences that we love. These scenes may no longer fit the tone of what the script has become. This is similar to the problems we create in our dialogue when we write a line that we love.

We must be continually aware of the overall tone and make sure that every scene fits into the rules that we have created.

Ghost (Bruce Joel Rubin), has a fascinating tone, as its genre changes three or four times across the run time of the movie, but its tone is always consistent.

It opens in modern-day New York. The world is real, as we know it to be. It is amusing and charming from the moment it starts. It wouldn't be called "funny" in the traditional sense, but the characters and situations are very light and lighthearted, and it is primarily a "romance" movie, in that we are following the relationship of Sam and Molly.

It then takes a massive left turn when our protagonist, Sam, who we have grown to love, gets murdered in the street in a vicious and quite bloody way. This should be completely out of tone, except for one thing—the movie's called *Ghost*. Rubin knew what he was doing and put the expectation right in the title. So, it's not a shock that the film is going to feature someone who dies and becomes a ghost.

The next few pages are dark—and supernatural. Sam becomes a ghost and follows his body to the hospital, where he sees the woman he loves distraught by his passing.

Nothing supernatural has happened up until this point, but the reason it works is the world Rubin has set up has not changed. The *real* world is still the real world—just as real as it was before. All Rubin has done is created a *new* world: The world of the dead, a world that has its own set of rules. Ghosts can see and talk to each other. Ghosts can walk through doors and walls. Good people are taken away to the light, and bad people are taken somewhere else. The rules are explained to us by a "quirky ghost," which retains the humor and lighthearted tone of the opening—even though we have just watched Sam die.

We then follow Sam as he tries to watch over Molly, and to work out who murdered him. The murderer even visits Molly's apartment. Sam cannot stop or catch him but he follows the murderer to the "bad" end of town. There, he sees the workplace of a psychic, and for fun decides to visit. Inside we meet Ota Mae Brown, who we quickly learn is a fraud. Except that when Sam talks, she can hear him.

They don't meet until the end of the first act. The next 40 pages are outright comedy, with an odd-couple relationship: Black con-woman paired with white, male banker, working together to solve a crime. Totally different genre than the first and second movies we have been watching, and yet… *completely consistent in tone*. Why? Because Molly doesn't take part in any of the "funny" scenes. Her character and role are still that of the brokenhearted woman who lost her husband. In fact, the scenes between Ota Mae and Molly are tragic and heartbreaking, as Molly thinks Ota Mae is conning her.

By speaking to the dead, Ota Mae is the physical crossover between the two worlds, but Molly is the tonal crossover. She interacts with Ota Mae and the funny/magical worlds of ghosts while reminding us that, back in the real world of New York, her life is in very real and very immediate danger.

Then the movie turns dark again as the real killer, Carl, is discovered and goes after Molly and Ota Mae threatening to kill them unless Sam returns the money.

Sam overcomes him, even though he is dead, and Carl dies when a window smashes and a massive shard of glass pierces his stomach. Then the black beings come and take him away. This moment is genuinely terrifying.

But then, the final seconds of the movie are some of the most romantic you could ever see as Molly gets to see Sam one last time as he is taken away to the light.

Bruce Joel Rubin won the Oscar that year and deservedly so, if for no other reason than having created a movie that has no logical balance to its genres while keeping a single, consistent tone through every single page. It is truly incredible.

This is a script that we should all read, watch and study to understand, but it is a wonderful exception to the rule. The easier rule for our own writing at this stage is: pick a genre and stick to it.

We must understand the tone we are trying to create and make sure *nothing* conflicts or confuses it.

60.

How Do We Write Female Characters?

This is not the 50's, where female love interests had almost no purpose in the story beyond looking good, doing what the male protagonist told them to do, and needing to be saved every so often to show off how heroic our male protagonist was. Such characters are the classic "damsel in distress" and should have disappeared completely from movie making by the 1960's. Amazingly, they haven't.

A *lot* of script readers are female, and nothing is going to turn them off quicker than female characters who are introduced with more detail about their bodily assets and what they're wearing than why they might be a real person with a story of their own.

I'm not suggesting that we have to always pass the Bechdel test, but we should at least be conscious of each female character.

In case you are not aware of it, the Bechdel test was created by Alison Bechdel, an American cartoonist, after a conversation with a friend. The test is this: Does the movie in question have at least two female characters who are named, and do those characters talk to each other about something other than men?

Think of some films yourself and put them to the test. You will be shocked by how few films pass, even those starring women or created for a female audience.

Movies with female stars have always existed, even if those female stars weren't paid *quite* as much as their male counterparts, but there has been a noticeable industry shift more recently to seek out material with female leads. Thanks to some outstanding writing by, and for, women in films such as *Bridesmaids* (Kristen Wiig & Annie Mumolo), *Pitch Perfect, Trainwreck, Sisters* (Paula Pell), *and Spy* (Paul Feig), among many others, it is finally being accepted that movies can star primarily, or exclusively, women and make a huge amount of money with male audiences.

With this industry shift in mind—and just to make sure we are the best writers we can be—we should think about how we write our female characters. This chapter is not just aimed at men. I do think it's harder for men to write women well, just as it's harder for women to write men well. We are more familiar with our own group, and the group we have spent the most time around, but just because you're a woman doesn't mean you write great female characters. Everyone—male or female—has been raised on a near 100% diet of stereotypes from the moment we were born, including toys we were supposed to play with, jobs we were supposed to do, and roles men and women played in movies. It's harder than we think to break out of these stereotypes—even if we are the most enlightened person in the world.

Therefore, paying attention to our female characters and exactly what we are trying to achieve with them is a useful exercise.

I am happy to admit that I did not have a natural feel for female characters or their dialogue when I started out. For my first few scripts every woman I wrote sounded like either Sally Albright or Annie Hall. Woody Allen himself admitted that he found it very hard to write female characters until he met Diane Keaton. She was his muse that allowed him to give a real and natural voice to women.

The first way to help ourselves is to think of actresses that we admire in the role as we write it, and don't make them the latest "hottie" actress. Pick one that we know can hold their own on screen against anyone. Then, when we write a particularly shallow or stupid line, imagine it from the mouth of Meryl Streep or Jennifer Lawrence or Noomi Rapace. We will catch ourselves and think, "She'd never deliver that line. It's pointless and stupid—or just boring."

Second, we must make sure that if we *do* have a female love interest, she has as many flaws as (or more than) our male protagonist. Even though she is a supporting character, we must give her just as many things to fix; that way, she can't exist simply to be eye candy, or a weak ally of the protagonist. She will have to have her own story, and her own obstacles and revelations. The example in the chapter on subplots in *The Italian Job* is a good one.

Speed, is another perfect example. It's Jack Traven's movie, but it gives Annie (the love interest) all the actual driving to do. She is a clear partner in the story from the moment it starts. If made only a few years earlier that would have been a man doing the driving and sharing the movie with Keanu Reeves, and Annie would have been just an attractive woman on the bus.

Or Catherine Banning in the remake of *The Thomas Crown Affair* (Leslie Dixon and Kurt Swimmer, Story by Alan Trustman). It's Thomas Crown's movie, his name is right there in the title, but his success or failure is intrinsically linked to the choices that Catherine makes, and she goes through just as much turmoil and change by the end of the movie, if not more.

Third, we need to be aware of our own biases expectations for females and female characters. If any female character starts becoming what a man might describe as the "perfect woman," we must stop ourselves immediately and realize we are writing a male fantasy, not a real person. Here are some of the characteristics or things to look out for and worry about:

1) She's incredibly beautiful but loves gaming/sci-fi.
2) She's incredibly beautiful but drinks beer and loves sports.
3) She's incredibly beautiful but is not attracted to looks herself in any way.
4) She is the most sexually adventurous character in the movie.
5) She's bisexual.
6) She falls for the protagonist despite rampant misogyny, because he is slightly charming sometimes.
7) She ignores/adores the drinking or drug use of the male protagonist, despite taking no part in these activities herself.
8) Anything else that women don't really think or do in real life.

We should love female characters for the same reason we love male characters: *Because* they are flawed and imperfect, not because they adhere to any stereotype of male-perceived perfection.

A last tip: We don't need to mention in female character descriptions that they are "beautiful," "gorgeous," or "a real knockout." It's redundant. *Of course* they're beautiful; they're going to be played by movie stars. *All* movie stars are beautiful. Do we really think if we leave out the description of the "gorgeous brunette," any reader or executive is ever going to imagine someone ugly in the role? They are imagining the same movie stars we are. Our problem will never be getting beautiful women to fill the roles in our script; the only problem we will ever have is ending up with actresses who are too beautiful for the "dowdy receptionist" character we wrote.

Just because most scripts or movies don't do this very well, doesn't mean we shouldn't try. Just think how much more attractive our project could be if a male *and* a female star become interested.

61.

Why is Comedy The Hardest Genre?

It's not, of course. No genre is harder than any other to write well, but there is a misconception that comedy scripts are easy to write because they are just about being funny. Not true. In fact, quite the opposite. Comedy scripts must be just as skilled as their dramatic counterparts. They must be just as conflict-driven, with characters who are just as interesting and flawed, and have character arcs that are just as believable and emotionally enthralling, and it must have a structure that is just as precise and surprising—*and* after all that, it has to be funny!

It is a great shame that for as long as movies have existed, it has been believed within the awards community that straight drama deserves more recognition than comedy.

Comedies get a lot of criticism—especially comedies that are funny. Ironically, the funnier the comedy film, the more people feel it to be unworthy of dramatic praise. It's no accident that a comedy has almost never won Best Picture at the Oscars. *Annie Hall* (Woody Allen) is the funniest film to ever win, but it's very highbrow comedy set in the world of NY intellectuals. They will sometimes let comedy script win the Best Screenplay category, with *Juno* (Diablo Cody) being a great example of a screenplay that made no attempt to hide its "comedy" credentials and still win.

Comedies are easy to dump on at a dinner party without anyone challenging us, because to defend them makes us look like we are defending *all* comedies—some of which are awful—but to defend one particular drama does not make somebody say, "Ugh, you don't like *drama* films, do you?"

But the truth is that most dramatic and "worthy" movies would be lucky to be as thematically sound as a lot of "stupid comedies."

Let's look at some movies that were dismissed by many (or most) as being simplistic and cheap and see why they are quite fantastic in their theme and structure.

In *Happy Gilmore* (you can tell I have a bit of a soft spot for this film), Happy is an underachiever who is desperate to become a hockey player. Why? Because his dad loved hockey and died when Happy was young.

Happy is a terrible hockey player except for a powerful slap shot. This skill becomes potentially useful when he realizes that he can drive a golf ball over 400 yards. This happens at a time when his grandma, who he loves dearly, is kicked out of her house on account of owing $275,000 to the IRS. Happy must get the money, and his new-found golf skill is the way to do it. Grudgingly, he joins the pro tour and comes in dead last in every tournament but becomes a blue-collar star.

The current golden boy, Shooter McGavin, tries to get him kicked off the tour and even buys Happy's grandma's house to blackmail him out. Happy challenges Shooter to a challenge; whoever wins the tour championship gets the house.

Happy finally practices and studies golf and arrives at the tournament ready to beat Shooter. He suffers a setback when a crazed fan, paid by Shooter, runs Happy over with a Volkswagen. Happy starts to lose until his grandma arrives and tells him that everything will be alright. The house is not important; she just wants Happy to be…happy.

Now Happy can finally relax and just play for himself. And he wins.

Happy Gilmore is the story of an underachiever who stumbles into being good at golf, but what it's *about* is fulfilling your destiny and doing things for yourself, not to please or impress other people. Happy is somebody who does everything for other people. He wants to be a hockey player to honor his father. He only becomes a professional golfer to save his grandmother's house. When he finally realizes he can do what is best for him while still being loyal to those around him, he becomes truly great and truly happy.

Shooter McGavin is his antagonist and his thematic opposite. Everything Shooter does is for himself and for fame and money. He believes he should win the tour championship because its his turn. This man will never fulfill his destiny or be truly happy.

If we take this theme—and all the elements that build it—out of the screenplay, then sure enough, all we're left with is a story about a guy who hits golf balls really hard, and we would indeed have a stupid and shallow movie. With them, however, we have a thematically sound movie that happens to have a lot of stupid (but funny) jokes in it.

As an aside, I have no idea if Tim Herlihy chose the name "Happy" as a statement of theme, but it would make sense either way.

Let's look at a more recent comedy that was also written off by many as shallow and childish. In *21 Jump Street* (Michael Bacall, Story by Jonah Hill, based on the television series by Patrick Hasburgh and Stephen J Cannell), Schmidt and Jenko, two former high school enemies, join the police academy at the same time. Realizing the other has skills they need they befriend each other, partner up and both qualify the academy. They are placed on mind-numbingly dull duty until their youthful looks get them signed up to an undercover program to infiltrate a drug gang at the local high school.

Jenko was a high school star, Schmidt an unknown loser, but at the new school their roles are reversed as times have changed and academic prowess and the ability to two-strap your backpack are now considered admirable qualities.

Their partnership (and their friendship) starts to break down as Schmidt falls deeper in with the dealers and the cool kids, leaving Jenko ostracized and hanging out with the geeks. They are about to blow the case when they realize that they can't do it without each other. They again partner up to take down the dealers and in doing so catch the maker of the drugs and the biker gang they failed to arrest properly at the beginning. In the process, Schmidt has exorcized the demons of his loser years at high school, and Jenko has proved an academic ability that he didn't know he had.

21 Jump Street is a hilarious movie about undercover cops, but what it's *about* is friendship. All events and supporting characters display a different element of friendship, and its effect on the leads. As we leave the theater, we do not doubt what can be accomplished if we have friends in our lives, or what will happen to us if we let those friends go. It's fantastic and very funny.

However, for those of us wanting to write comedies, let this be a warning: a few jokes do not a comedy script make. As stated above, our script must be as dramatic and perfectly structured as any script out there. In fact, the more "stupid" or "infantile" the humor, the more we need to be airtight on our story, structure and character arc to justify it.

Airplane is a fascinating case study. When the Zucker brothers and Jim Abrahams set out to make this comedy they bought the rights to the classic, 50's disaster movie *Zero Hour* (Arthur Hailey & Hall Bartlett & John Champion) so that they could legitimately and legally copy the characters, structure, and even exact scenes of the original movie. In doing so, they gave themselves an airtight structure of a real disaster movie onto which they could then build a perfect retake of the original moments in a way that drew out the underlying absurdity of the genre.

"We have to find someone who can not only fly this plane, but who didn't have fish for dinner," is an exact line from the original movie. The result is not only one of the funniest films ever, but a perfectly enjoyable disaster movie.

Many people who are very funny in real life are not necessarily funny writers. Stand-up comedians, who can hold a room of thousands of people in raucous laughter for over an hour, cannot necessarily transfer that skill to movie writing. A stand-up joke is a very different skill from writing a comedy screenplay.

Conversely, people who are not necessarily a riot in conversation can be fantastic comedy writers. By their own admission, the Farrelly brothers are not particularly funny guys. They have spoken in interviews about the fact that old school friends were shocked to find out they were now millionaire comedy writers as this was not their reputation in their youth.

There is always a premium on truly great comedy writing. Comedy will never disappear as a genre of demand by young, theater going audiences. Musicals came and went. Horror films go through waves. Comic book movies are here now but will soon die out; however, comedy will always endure. Why? Because it covers every other genre. We can have funny musicals, funny comic book movies, funny love stories, black comedies, absurdist comedies, spoofs of other movies. There's simply no end to comedy.

Some comedies are built on their situation, others are built around the characters and their actions and reactions. Therefore, some comedies "sound" funny in their tagline.

A wannabe rock guitarist pretends to be a substitute teacher at an uptight, private elementary school—School of Rock

This dramatic premise is inherently funny. We can immediately see where the primary source of jokes will come from.

However, other comedies are not necessarily built on a comedic premise. The premise might be quite dark.

A middle-aged couple decide to investigate when their neighbor drops dead—Manhattan Murder Mystery (Woody Allen and Marshall Brickman)

There's nothing inherently funny about this at all. It sounds to all intents and purposes like a standard mystery plot. And it is. The humor derives from the characterization of the middle-aged couple and their interactions with each other and their allies and enemies, but if we take out the jokes, *Manhattan Murder Mystery* is still a good mystery movie.

As a last little note for this chapter, we spoke earlier on about the problem caused by writing a great line or a great moment. That is never truer than for comedy writers. Writing a truly great joke is the worst thing that can ever happen to us. The whole film becomes about keeping that one great joke no matter how little it suits the characters or situation. We are going to have to learn to let it go and delete the funniest thing we've ever written. And it still won't work if we try to insert it into our next script. Or the one after that. It is dead and must be killed, never to return.

So, comedy is not really the hardest genre, but it is also not the easy, lowest common denominator genre that some believe it to be. It requires as much skill, time, patience, dedication and talent to do it well. We won't win awards, but we might get rich.

62.

Creating Movie Moments

Think about your favorite movies in the world. Even the ones you have watched many times. (For my sins I have watched *Tootsie*, *When Harry Met Sally*, and *Midnight Run* over 200 times each.) We don't instantly remember the whole movie. We remember moments. Moments that can stick with us for years.

Moments are what work colleagues recall to each other when they discuss a movie. Moments create word of mouth.

And the same is true of our script. Moments will make it stand out. They will get it recognized and remembered and talked about. We want moments. The problem is—they are very difficult to create.

Here are some famous movie moments:

Jaws: Hooper diving in the sunken fishing boat as the head rolls out.

When Harry Met Sally: The diner/orgasm scene, specifically the last line of the scene— "I'll have what she's having."

Raiders of the Lost Ark: The sword wielding attacker accosting Indy, only for Indy to shoot him and get on with the story.

Great moments! If you've seen the movies (and I hope you have), you remember them. And you know what? None of them were in the original scripts.

The head moment in *Jaws* was added as a reshoot because Spielberg decided that there was too long without a scare. The, "I'll have what she's having" line was added on set (and delivered by Rob Reiner's mother), and the Indy script called for a long and impressive sword battle, but Harrison Ford was tired and sick and suggesting shooting the guy instead.

This proves that there is no magical formula for movie moments. Many times, they happen accidentally in a way that we simply cannot predict.

However, that does not mean we cannot try and create them in the script.

A great example is *American Pie*, sold as the spec script "East Great Falls" by new writer Adam Herz for $750,000 (See? Miracles do happen).

That script is choc filled with moments. Jim masturbating into the sock as his family walk in. Jim seducing and embarrassing himself in front of Nadia as it is broadcast over the internet. Jim and the pie (obviously). Stiffler drinking the beer with the surprise in the bottom of it. Finch making his fateful toilet trip. Finch seducing Stiffler's mom. And of course, the final payoff band-camp/flute joke, which I think made me laugh more in a movie theater than any other gag in my life.

There was no way that anyone could walk out of that movie and not be desperate to go and tell someone what they just saw. Hence the terrific word of mouth it received. But before that, there was no way that readers weren't dying to tell their boss what they just read, causing a bidding war that put the purchase price up to $750k.

Do moments have to be funny? Not at all. Think of the moments that have stuck with you forever from *The Shining*, or *Moonlight*, or *Get Out*, or *Saw*, or *Batman Begins*, or *A Few Good Men*, or *Hidden Figures*, or *Whiplash*, or any other movie from any decade or any genre.

The Shawshank Redemption is another movie that found its real audience and success on video. The movie is built around regular moments that are funny, sad, charming, sinister, down-right horrifying and ultimately uplifting.

Just think how many come to mind right now: Fresh fish night, the tarring of the rooftop, Brooks committing suicide, the opera in the courtyard, the murder of Tommy, and of course the escape and the comeuppance of Hadley and Warden Norton. On and on they come at us and every one of them makes us rush with emotion.

That's what creates longevity in a movie, and what can create longevity in a script.

"Why does a script need longevity?" I hear you ask. Because scripts take years to get made. And everyone involved in those early stages (producers, directors, stars, studios) have many projects on the go in the hope that one of them will get the financing it needs and get into production. And humans get bored. A script that someone loves today could seem tired six months or a year from now when a newer, fresher screenplay comes along. What is going to keep them fighting for our script?

Moments are one of the things that will keep it front of mind. They can still feel fresh and powerful even when a producer is reading the twentieth draft.

They are easy to recall out of the 20-30 projects that some star producers have in development at any given moment. They are potentially moments that movie stars know will make them look good and get their fans excited.

And they will get us other jobs. A producer may not buy our script but if they remember moments from our script then they may think of us when a job comes up. A better overall script with no real moments is more easily forgotten than an average script with two truly great and memorable moments.

I know I'm asking the (almost) impossible of us here, since if we knew how to create wonderful movie moments, we would just do it and become rich.

We should not be creating our story around moments. We should create a story that we believe in with characters that are as honest as we can make them, but it is no bad thing to look at our finished script and think, "What are the moments that people will remember? What are the moments that people will talk about? What are the moments that might make my script stand out?"

And if there aren't any, why not? Have we given our story every interesting moment that we could have given it? Is it just a collection of things happening or is it a collection of moments that people will remember?

Create moments and we can create gold. Literally.

63.

Are Adaptations a Different Skill?

Yes. That was easy.

You want more? Oh, okay. Why is it different? The key difference with an adaptation is that we are creating the best possible version of someone else's idea. For a lot of writers this is near impossible. Some of us have neither the desire nor the capability to work from anything that we didn't create ourselves.

Adapting material is not a skill we necessarily must achieve to be a working screenwriter, but it is a skill that could be very useful as it opens a new stream of potential work.

It is not easier to work on an adaptation—or, for that matter, any more difficult—it's just different.

When we are at a point where we are creating original material of a very good/excellent quality, then having a go at an adaptation can be a valuable exercise to not only develop new skills, but also to develop our skills in writing original work.

Those who are masters of adaptation are masters of many of the core skills of screenwriting; brevity, and the ability to visually display elements that might otherwise be invisible to the viewer.

If we took a standard 400-page novel and adapted it directly into a screenplay; i.e., we wrote out every scene as it happens in the book and transferred every line of dialogue that is spoken aloud, we would finally end up with a screenplay that would be at least 400 pages long (if not longer) and which wouldn't make any sense to the reader, since many of the key elements of a novel are within characters' minds and are never spoken aloud.

To get that down to 110 pages and have every element make sense in a visual medium we need a hell of a lot of skill.

First, we are going to have to lose *at least* 50-60% (or more) of what happens in the book. It is for this reason alone many book adaptations are doomed to failure with its original fans. There is simply no way even the greatest screenwriter can transfer the story from the page to the screen in a way true fans of the book will like. Some favorite scene or moment of theirs from the book is going to get cut out or changed.

TRUE FAN
It was alright, but they cut out
the scene with the violin. That
was the best bit of the book. Why
would you cut that out?

Why? Because massive amounts had to be cut and you're the only person in the world who thought the violin scene was so good.

It doesn't mean we lose 50-60% of the scenes from the book, but it does mean that the more scenes we keep the more we will have to lose from each of those individual scenes. Personally, I am big fan of the Harry Potter novels, and I think Steve Kloves (who adapted six of the seven books to screen) did as good a job as anyone could possibly do with those adaptations. The novels are dense with story. There are setups in the first book that pay off later in the book but also pay off in books two and three and beyond, and as such those moments must be kept even if they don't affect the story of the first movie. But I was still pissed at some of the stuff that was lost or changed. The more beloved the novel the more we are destined to annoy people when we adapt it.

Second, after losing vast amounts of material, we need to find ways to portray internal thoughts or narration onscreen in a way readers and viewers will understand.

Let's say the novel is about a hitman who has been hired to kill a target. All he's given is a location and time. When the person walks through the door at 4pm he is to kill them, no matter who they are. He waits with his sniper rifle and on cue the target appears. We've never met this person before as the reader, but the hit man has. It is his ex-wife. The book now describes in detail exactly what the hit man is thinking. He is shocked and conflicted. Who has hired him to kill his ex-wife? Can he do it? What happens if he doesn't? What happens if he does? She is getting closer to the next door and will be gone. What does he do?

How on earth do we show all of that on screen? All we would see is the person appear at 4pm. We don't know who they are. The hit man doesn't shoot them, and we don't know why. Unless the hit man explains it all for us:

```
                    HITMAN
        Oh no! That's my ex-wife! I
        wonder who hired me to kill her.
        I'm not very happy with her right
        now, and she is bleeding me dry
        with alimony so killing her
        wouldn't be so bad. But she was
        my wife at one time, and I do
        still have feelings for her.
        Gosh, I'm conflicted.
```

Which, I think we can all agree, is the worst writing ever. If this is a key dramatic moment in the story, then to fix the problem the screenwriter might have to go right back to the beginning and create additional material earlier on that sets up these characters in a way that the audience now knows who she is when they see her, and everything they need to know about their relationship and his state of mind. Then, when we see a look of shock on his face, and a pause before he pulls the trigger, the emotions that he feels make sense.

Therefore, we are not only going to *lose* a huge amount; we may even have to *create* material to explain the moments we want to keep.

In other cases, we may flat out disagree with the dramatic choice that the original writer has made and believe that there is a much better way to present the moment. However, that scene may be one of the "famous scenes" that lovers of the book all adore, in which case we may have to keep the beloved moment while fixing the issue.

As part of our editing we are also going to have to lose whole characters and sub plots. Again, this will piss off original fans, but in many cases, we need to keep some element of what this character provided—without keeping the actual character themselves. Therefore, the help or hindrance that this character provided must be transferred to another character that we are keeping.

You can see how this starts to get very complicated and very stressful, but also immensely satisfying when we feel it working. When we genuinely manage to take 150 pages of novel and turn it into a slick and perfect, 25-page Act One we feel staggeringly proud of ourselves. And in doing so will have taught ourselves a great deal about editing our own work and just how much we can lose when we need to, while preserving the story.

And that is why I want to push you to try your hand at an adaptation at this stage in your journey. It would be great if someone was offering to hire you to do this, but in the absence of that we can do it on our own.

There is a *huge* number of novels out there, and very few of them have been picked up by major studios for adaptation. That means there are a lot of novelists who are waiting for the phone to ring for their big payday. If we get there first, we may convince them (and their publisher) to give us the rights to adapt their work for a very small (or maybe no) fee. This isn't always an easy sell, and I'm not suggesting superstar writers here. Don't bother asking John Grisham if you can adapt his latest novel. That's already been locked down in a multi-million-dollar movie deal. I'm talking about the thousands of novels from working writers who are making a living—but that's about all—from their work, because here's the kicker: The novel doesn't need to be fantastic. All we need is a novel with a fantastic *idea*. It might be really crappily handled, but we are going to fix that in our adaptation and bring the core idea to life in a way that the novelist failed to do.

Then, when we try to sell the script, if the idea is enticing and the script works, nobody will care whether the book was particularly brilliant. However, the fact that it's adapted from a published novel may just be enough of a hook to make it stand out to the agent or production company as worth putting on the top of the pile.

Lastly, if we do reach out to a bunch of novelists and they all tell us to go away then we do have one final avenue. Remember earlier, when I told you to leave others' work alone? Well, you can ignore that if the work is in the public domain. The law around this is a little complicated but in general anything published before 1927 (as of 2020) is in the public domain and its perfectly legal to not only write an adaptation, but also to try and sell that adaptation to a studio.

And remember, an adaptation is not always about the straight translation of the words on the page. *Clueless* (Amy Heckerling) is an adaptation of *Emma* by Jane Austen. *10 Things I Hate About You* (Karen McCullah & Kirsten Smith) is an adaptation of *Taming of the Shrew* by William Shakespeare. *Bridget Jones's Diary* (Helen Fielding and Andrew Davies and Richard Curtis, based on the novel by Helen Fielding) is a slightly looser adaptation of *Pride and Prejudice* by *Jane Austen*. *Easy A* (Bert V. Royal) was an adaptation of *The Scarlet Letter* by Nathaniel Hawthorne.

A lot can be done with classic novels if we put in the time and thought.

If you feel you are best served by creating another original script instead of worrying about adaptations, then do that, but for many of us the act of adaptation will be beneficial in more ways than we expect.

Stage 8:
Breaking In

64.

Success is Where We Find It

I bet you're sick of writing for no reason by now, but remember, we never know when we will write that truly great script which gets us recognized, so we must keep writing. But we also want to be ready at any moment to break over that threshold and into the club.

First, let's see if anyone has broken in. If you have sold a script, got signed by an agent or hired by a legitimate studio or production company for an original script or rewrite please put your hand up.

If your hand is up—a *huge* well done. It doesn't mean you're set for life as a screenwriter, but you have overcome the most difficult barrier: Breaking in. Once you are inside, things are lot easier, not *easy*, but *easier*.

Most of us will not have achieved those things yet, for two reasons:

1) Six scripts is not a lot, when considering how far we must develop as writers.
2) Even if we do create something wonderful it's still hard to get enough of the right people to read it and get "discovered."

The key to success as a screenwriter to is to realize that success is not the only success. I know that sounds weird, but what I mean is that selling the script is not the only goal that makes us successful. If we think that way, then we are setting ourselves up for failure. Doctors study for many years and then take one big set of exams. If they pass, they are a doctor—for life. We don't get that luxury. We must think differently.

Getting someone to read the script is success. That person replying to us in any form is success. That person being happy to read future scripts is success. That person being willing to speak to us by phone or in person is success. Getting an agent or manager to call us and chat about our script— even though they don't want to sign us—is a *massive* success.

I once sent out a script (my seventh, if you're interested) to some agents. A couple of them had invited me to send in my work based on a previous script, others I sent in with a cold query letter. From one of the cold inquiries I was invited in for a meeting by a partner agent at a large, if second tier agency. I figured this was my ticket. I'd finally done it. It took seven scripts but here I was. He was going to sign me, and I would be making million-dollar deals by the end of the week.

I went in and we had a good chat. He was supportive and encouraging and told me all the good things about my script and some things that I could change to improve it. His insights were thoughtful and right on the money. He also gave me some general career advice, which again was insightful and useful.

After about 45 minutes he thanked me for coming in, we shook hands and he asked me to send him my next script.

I walked out and was lost, confused and angry. Why hadn't he signed me? In fact, why had he never even mentioned the idea of signing me? As I re-ran the conversation in my head, I realized that he had quite deliberately avoided any conversation that even hinted at the idea of signing me. Had I done something wrong? Had I screwed up my big shot? What should I have done differently? Should I have been bolder and asked him to sign me? Maybe he wanted writers that were proactive and confident.

When I did write my next script, I sent it to him as requested and this time received a standard "Thanks, but no thanks" reply signed by his assistant. (The script wasn't very good, by the way. I sent it out far too early, desperate to capitalize on the success of my last, much better script).

I was pissed, and I wrote directly to the agent with a snotty email asking why he had asked me to send my next script if he wasn't even going to read it. Suffice to say, I never heard from that agent again. My immaturity and lack of understanding of the process had burned a bridge that could have been very valuable to me. It showed a terrible lack of respect for someone who had given me their time and support when they had no reason to do so.

I will never know exactly what his intention was in calling me in that day. Maybe if I'd somehow "blown him away" he might have signed me, but I now believe that signing me was never his intention. He was feeling me out, assessing me as a potential future client if I continued to produce work worthy of representation. I have since met numerous writers who are now represented by agents who did something similar. The agent read a script they enjoyed and wanted to know more about the writer. They didn't fall in love with the script enough to sign them then and there, but they were willing to give up an hour of their time, support the writer's growth and start building a relationship that could be beneficial to them both somewhere down the line.

Any meeting like that with an agent, production company, or producer is a *big* win. I saw the lack of a sale—or the lack of being signed—as a *failure*. Completely the wrong way to see it—and we are going to stay here for a moment because this misunderstanding of "success" is one of the major reasons potential star writers are knocked off their screenwriting journey.

To quote Winston Churchill: "A pessimist sees the difficulty in every opportunity. An optimist sees opportunity in every difficulty."

If we take the pessimist's viewpoint of the things that happen to us, then I guarantee that we will fail.

This journey is one long series of things *not* happening the way we want them to. We cannot see things for what *didn't* happen. Instead, we must go looking for every small thing that *did* happen and capitalize on it immediately.

This was a core failing of mine, as well as many, many writers that I have met and worked with. Successful writers can dump the failure from their mind, go looking for any nugget of opportunity and use it to make something happen.

What should I have done after the meeting with the agent? I should have seen the potential. I should have been buzzed and excited about getting to work on my next script knowing that somebody of importance was happy to read it. I should have used that connection, small as it was, to get meetings and conversations with producers. I should have nurtured the relationship with the agent and thanked him for accepting my subsequent script, even though he (or his assistant) hated it, thus keeping that avenue open to me. I should have been shouting all over town, "I've finally got important agents giving me their time! Well done me!"

But I didn't. I bitched and moaned about not getting signed, and didn't tell anyone about the meeting, convinced that I should be ashamed of the outcome, that it somehow meant that I was an even bigger failure than I was before the meeting. I set myself back 2-3 years because I went looking for failure.

We cannot and must not do this. We must be proud about any success, no matter how small. We must tell people at parties about our meeting with an agent. Speak with pride and confidence about the fact that we really wanted them to sign us, but even though they didn't, that we have made a major jump forward in our career journey. Someone at the party will think we're a dick. They will mutter under their breath to other partygoers about us being some idiot wannabe.

Is that annoying? Yes, it's annoying and embarrassing, but there might be someone else at the party who has a friend who is looking for a script, and maybe—just maybe—they'll ask if they can forward it along for us. Or perhaps there is a new agent there, just starting out, who is looking to bolster their own roster, and they *do* know who this agent is, and they know such a meeting is not easy to come by.

Or maybe no one at the party gives two hoots about us or our career. That's fine, but we should still be the living embodiment of an optimist about our own career. Everything—and I mean *everything*—is an opportunity.

Plus, even if things did always work out the way we wanted, instant success is not all it's cracked up to be. Don't believe me? Watch the fascinating documentary *Overnight*. It follows the rags-to-riches tale of Troy Duffy, the bartender whose script for *The Boondock Saints* was bought by Harvey Weinstein for $300,000 and given a $15m budget with Duffy attached as director. It's every writer's dream—instant Hollywood success, signed by William Morris, meetings with movie stars. Weinstein even bought him the bar he used to work at.

And then—it all falls apart. Duffy is naïve at best, absurdly overconfident and dickish at worst. He alienates his friends and family, and more importantly the executives at Miramax as the deal starts to fall apart, until almost inevitably the movie is dropped by Miramax and put into turnaround.

What we can all see, that Duffy can't, is that the success was too instant. He hadn't earned it and so he didn't know what to do with it. His almost comical over-confidence helped him get through doors and make the deal, but he lacked the years of relationships and struggle that temper that overconfidence into experience. He had instead been handed the keys to Hollywood with little to no idea of the way it worked. Trust me when I say that many, many other writers and filmmakers have made the same mistakes, just without the cameras.

No one in the world expects to get every job they interview for. We know that most job interviews will not lead anywhere, but we will keep going until we finally get a job we love. Same thing here. All this work is just an extended job interview for one of the most sought-after jobs in the world.

I don't care who you are, all this rejection is hard and sometimes we just want to crawl back into bed and be left alone for a year. How can all our hard work be so viciously received? What have these other writers got that I don't? Am I just bad at this?

It's even worse when people we love ask how it's going. What are we going to say?

<pre>
                    YOU
                (grinning)
        It's going great. Every agent has
        ignored me. One development exec
        told me it was, quote, "the worst
        thing he's ever read," and I went
        out in the first round of a
        screenplay competition no one's
        ever even heard of, but don't
        worry, because Hywel says that
        I'm not a failure.
</pre>

Instead, with a *real* smile, I want you to confidently say the following:

<pre>
                    YOU
        The response has been what I
        expected for this stage of my
        journey. I'm already working on
        my next script, but I'll keep you
        up to date when things happen.
</pre>

You will be angry. You will be lonely. You will be frustrated. You will be embarrassed. And that's' why we need to grip onto the positives.

Enjoy every element of success, no matter how small it may be.

If we don't, we will give up and drop off our journey very quickly. And you will never know what could have been.

Anyone who is seen as successful in any field was simply better than their counterparts at dealing with the failure and enjoying each small moment of success. Be one of them.

65.

How Do We Have a Meeting?

You got a meeting with a producer? Great! That's a big step. Every meeting is a potential job.

We all think we know how to meet people, but very few of us know how to do it well.

The rules of the meeting exist in every industry in the world, so you may have learned some of this from other jobs you have done, but the best job to help us learn is as a salesperson. I know we writers think we are artists, but we're not, we're salespeople. We are selling ourselves and the stories that we write. We are selling them to agents, to managers, to producers and to studios. If you think you are doing anything else, then get over it now and understand what your real job is. It's selling, just as much as it is writing.

Here are the rules to successful meetings when we are the one selling. (The rules are very different for the person who is buying. They can do anything they want.)

1) Be five minutes early

That is five minutes early to the office of the final person we are meeting. Not five minutes early on site.

We should be onsite with *a lot* of time to spare—especially if we are lucky enough to get a meeting at a studio. The studios have hierarchies to their parking, and we are a nobody, so we will be lucky to even get a parking pass on the studio lot. If we do, it will be a long way from where the meeting is to take place, so we should be there with lots of time to get lost and still get to the final location five minutes early.

The reason to be five minutes early for the arranged meeting time is it is the perfect time to set the correct expectations. If we arrive 30 minutes early, then the exec's assistant may call them and tell them we're waiting. The exec's first thought will be: *"Already? Our meeting's not for another half an hour,"* and now our presence in the office is bugging them for the next 30 minutes.

Any later than five minutes early and she'll be thinking, "Where the hell is that stupid writer? Our meeting's starting in one minute."

Obviously, never be late. That's game over completely. If something out of our control happens and we are late, the *first words* out of our mouth when we meet the exec or producer should be, "I am *so* sorry for being late." If appropriate, give a very quick explanation why—"A tanker blew up on Melrose," etc.—and hope they can get over it enough to listen to us. Don't be surprised if they just cancel the meeting.

Arrive on location early and then mosey around. Go to the bathroom, grab a coffee, but don't arrive at the exec's office till five minutes before the meeting.

Plus, getting into this habit means that we are much less likely to arrive completely stressed from getting stuck in traffic. We need to be at our most relaxed in these meetings and getting stressed on the journey is the last thing we need.

2) Dress appropriately

This does not always mean "dress smart." That is true of most job interviews in the world, but we are trying to create the right ambience of "working writer" here. Too smart and we look like a frustrated executive. Too scruffy and we look like we don't care or are being disrespectful.

"Smart casual" is what we're going for. Smart jeans are good. Polo shirts are okay. Long sleeve casual shirt is better. Relatively smart shoes are good. Sneakers are okay if they are new. If they're your 15-year-old "round the house" sneakers, then leave them at home.

The more famous we get the scruffier we can be. Until then, be smart but more casual than the executive.

3) Be nice to everyone you meet

I mean *everyone*. This is a good rule for life in general—after all, why be a douchebag?—but it is specifically true on the day of a meeting. We don't know who is going to be in our meeting, so we must treat everyone we meet as if they might be the decision maker, and that includes security personnel, assistants, receptionists—anyone! We don't know whom the decision maker listens to. They may love our pitch, but if they also love their assistant, and their assistant tells them we were a dick, then goodnight. The job's gone.

I have ended up chatting with people in elevators who turned out to be the boss of the person I was pitching to. (On the topic of elevators—always hold the door open for anyone who wants to get on—again, you never know.)

I worked with a writer once who was excited to get his first real pitch at a studio. On his drive to the studio a car pulled in front of him sharply and nearly hit him. Incensed, the writer honked at the guy and then drove round him and gave him the finger. As the writer approached the studio, the dickish driver stayed behind and turned into the lot. Now the writer started to worry. Sure enough, the guy stayed behind him for a while until he turned into a VIP parking space. Obviously, he was someone important at the studio.

Guess who was sitting in the room as the writer walked in to pitch?

It's just not worth the risk. Anyone annoys us, just let it go. Be polite, courteous and professional with everyone. Plus, we want to stay calm, remember? So why get angry with people? It's only going to hurt us.

4) Go the bathroom right before the meeting

Either while you are killing time on site before going to the exec's office, or in the five minutes we have given ourselves once there. Two reasons:

1) We want to make sure we are not sitting in the meeting desperate for the bathroom. Asking to leave to use the bathroom is a big no-no. It just leaves the exec sitting there like an idiot.

2) We want to make sure we look okay and don't have some rogue food on our face.

A friend of mine once turned up for a job interview. The assistant very kindly pointed the way to the bathroom, but my friend did not need the bathroom and did not take her up on the offer. He then sat in an hour's interview before travelling home and seeing himself in the mirror for the first time. He had chocolate all over his face from a muffin he had eaten for breakfast. The very sweet assistant was trying to help him out as politely as she could.

Once in the room, no one will tell us that we have the proverbial chocolate on our face. They'll just remember us as the idiot who couldn't eat a muffin properly.

Go to the bathroom and make sure you look good.

5) Go in with the right attitude

No matter who we are meeting, we should be projecting four simple things:

1) Passion
2) An opinion
3) Ability and willingness to change our opinion
4) Gratitude for the opportunity

That's it.

This is not just true of screenwriters, this is true for everyone in every meeting in the world that is trying to sell something, be it salespeople, entrepreneurs seeking investment, or even just an employee asking for a raise. These four elements, correctly combined, give the other person everything they need to make it as easy as possible to say yes.

If we lose any one of these elements, we are just giving the person all the ammunition they need to say no.

Without passion, we are boring. Without an opinion, we are a pushover. Without the ability and willingness to change our opinion, we are difficult, and without gratitude, we are entitled and irritating. But *with* all these things, we are giving them a chance to judge our writing, and if we lose out because of our writing, then so be it. Next time, our pitch needs to be better.

I had a fascinating meeting once at a TV studio. It was with the writing team I mentioned earlier, so there were five of us as writers who were meeting with the VP of production. The producer who had been shepherding the project through the studio was in the room, but this was the first time we had met with his boss. One of our group was running late so the four of us went in.

From the moment it kicked off, the meeting went down the shitter. We were all nervous and intimidated by the seniority and manner of the VP that we were there to impress. We were comedy writers but none of us were being funny, or even interesting. We were fumbling our words and mishearing what he said. At one point the VP even looked over at the producer with a "What the hell have you brought me?" look. We all knew we were about to be asked to leave, at which moment the fifth person in our group arrived and burst into the room.

He was by far the most overconfident of all of us. A quality that wasn't always positive, but from the moment he entered the room the whole atmosphere changed. He grabbed the VP of production by the hand and started recounting his dreadful journey and why he was late. He was speaking to the guy as an equal. Not disrespectfully, just as an equal.

For about five seconds I think the rest of us all had the same feeling of, "Oh my God, what are you doing?" but suddenly the VP's manner switched, and he started laughing. Our colleague's energy and humor immediately rubbed off on the rest of us and we all came to life. My colleague had no idea what he'd walked into and luckily, he didn't care.

The meeting ended up being an hour long—doubling the 30 minutes we'd been allocated—and we discussed not only the show we came to pitch, but also the opportunity for another series. This VP ended up being our biggest champion at the studio—all thanks to one of our group not caring about seniority.

Interestingly, at this time in our lives, the five of us did not singularly possess *all* the qualities I have listed above, but combined, we possessed them all. The overconfident person had passion and an opinion but little ability to change that opinion. I was the diplomatic one who had the ability and willingness to change and could convince the others to do so as well. Another of our group was always the person who remembered to say, "Thank you for the meeting," and express gratitude. Between us, we were like one perfect writer.

We need to learn to do it all, I'm afraid—or, at least, if you are a writing team, then you must share the load, and have it all covered.

6) Have three goals for the meeting

This is another trick to steal from sales. We should go into every meeting confident that we can come out with the sale, but if we don't, then what are the acceptable alternatives?

For instance, let's say we are meeting with a producer about our script. What is our first goal?

i) Sell the script

That's what we're there for, right? That's the best outcome, so that should be what we are working towards. If we start out hoping for a more meager goal, then we are just taking away the chance to get what we want.

However, life is more complicated than that. The producer may not be able to say yes right now. Or maybe he or she is just checking out new writers they admire for upcoming projects.

Therefore, when it becomes clear that the immediate goal is gone, we want a second outcome to move to. Importantly, don't return to the first goal. If the producer has stated outright that they can't buy the script, then going back to it again in any way will just annoy them. Instead, move on to the second goal.

ii) To come in and pitch for a current project

If it becomes clear that there is no potential sale for this current script, then the second goal could be to make sure that we are considered for immediate and current projects. If we move straight to, "Oh well, never mind. Thanks anyway. See you later," then we are pissing away a chance at a realistic job right now.

Remember, very few "meet and greet" meetings are about buying our spec script. It is a chance for someone who liked the writing to check us out as a person and a writer. Ask them what else they are working on. When you hear the project most suited to you as a writer or rewriter, get excited and ask if you could pitch for it.

However, they might not have any projects currently in development, or nothing that they feel you are suitable for.

Therefore, our third goal may be:

iii) Get another meeting about a different project you are working on

Always have other projects you are developing. A good working writer never has just one script. They don't have to be complete and final drafts. They might just be outlines, but we want to have at least three or four other potential projects.

Take the opportunity to pitch the idea now. Choose the one that you feel fits the exec or the output they have been discussing. If they like the idea, then try to lock them down for a meeting to come in with a full outline and a chance to pitch it properly. Don't be pushy but if they are willing to put it in the calendar right there then we are much more likely to make that meeting happen. Once we are out of the room, we are starting all over again.

The same idea of having three goals is true no matter who we are meeting. If it's our first meeting with a potential agent, then our three goals might be:

1) Get signed.
2) Pitch another finished script you have and get them to read it and agree to another meeting to discuss it.

3)   Get them to agree to read our next script whenever it is finished.

Always start with our most desirable goal, and don't move down a goal until it is clear that the first goal is not going to happen.

Make the third goal something useful, but also something entirely realistic. We have properly screwed something up if we don't achieve the third goal before leaving the room.

We may achieve more than one goal. We may sell the script, get the chance to come in and pitch for a current project *and* get another meeting for a different project. If so, great! But only one goal achieved is still a good meeting.

7) Follow up in the right way

Our follow up to the meeting will depend on the person we are meeting and our situation. For instance, if we do have an agent then they should look after the follow up to see how it went and what we can do moving forward.

If we were lucky enough to get the meeting on the strength of our script and are unrepresented then ask them in the meeting how they would like us to follow up. By phone? By email? If so, what email? Direct to the exec or through their assistant? It's not rude to ask, it just means that we are trying to work in a manner that suits them.

With this situation in mind, a good third goal for a meeting with an exec or producer, if we are unrepresented, is to ask the exec for their recommendation of an agent and ask if it's okay for us to use their name when making contact. Such a name drop could open a door with an agent who would otherwise ignore us.

***

Seven rules that outline the key principles to having a successful meeting. Most business decisions in the world are decided in meetings like this. Get ready to have a lot of them.

66.

How Do We Have a Meeting With An Agent?

When the time comes, and we get the chance to sit in the office of an agent or manager who may sign us, we need to be more than just someone who wrote one good script. We need to show we truly understand the business they are in, and we want to be in that business *with* them—the business of movies.

It is naïve and idiotic to think that we write movies in a vacuum; that we are artists and other people must worry about the money. We are all part of this business and although we might not write the checks we need to not only understand where the money comes from and where that money goes, but we need to show that we can make artistic choices that fit within the reality of modern movie making.

Nothing irritates me more than new writers talking about how they would never make any creative choices based on budget or audience testing. And they would never write anything to accommodate product placement.

In fairness to them, they are correct, they never will have to compromise their vision, because they will never get a movie made. The first time they make such a comment in front of an agent or studio exec they will be politely escorted from the building, never to return.

It's okay to worry about and fight for the artistic integrity of our script. It's exactly what we *should* do. It's *not* okay to think this is the only factor involved in the decision-making of the film. There is no industry in the world in which a single product costs $50M-$200M to make but has only one creator, and one person who gets to make all the decisions. That would be ludicrous. Think about what else costs that much to make: Buildings, planes, tanks, bridges, and hospitals. Only an idiot would believe these are the artistic visions of one person, or the architect is the only person who gets to decide the best way to build a skyscraper, and they can stomp off in a little huff if the structural engineer suggests a different product that is just as strong, but cheaper.

On the other side though, "Yeah, whatever you want," suggests that we are someone without an opinion. Our opinion needs to be as useful as the opinion of everybody else in the chain. And to have that opinion we need to understand the business. If we are arguing to keep a scene, or for an expensive stunt, then we need to show that we can argue for the artistic benefit against the problems and costs it may incur.

YOU

> He has to blow up the school.
> That's the key scene in the
> movie. I won't lose it.

Is very different from:

YOU

> I know the school explosion is
> expensive, but it's pivotal
> moment in his journey to destroy
> the place that created his hatred
> of learning. Plus, who doesn't
> want to see their high school
> blow up? It'll be a scene that
> teenagers tell their friends
> about.

Therefore, we must understand every aspect of the process. We don't need to understand the marketing of movies as well as the Head of Marketing. That's their job, and they should know it *way* better than we do, but we *should* understand the basics of how their choices are made. The same goes for funding, casting, production, special effects, visual effects, editing, test marketing, distribution and many, many other steps in the journey from script to screen.

Here are some wonderful books to get us started:

Casting: *A Star is Found,* by Jane Jenkins and Janet Hirschenson.
Acting: *If Chins Could Kill,* by Bruce Campbell
Producing: *You'll Never Eat Lunch in This Town Again,* by Julia Phillips/ *The Kid Stays in the Picture,* by Robert Evans
Financing and distribution: *The Hollywood Economist,* by Edward Jay Epstein
Production: *From Reel to Deal,* by Dov S-S Siemens
Cinematography: *Cinematography,* by Blain Brown

Editing: *When the Shooting Stops, the Cutting Begins,* by Ralph Rosenblum and Robert Karen

Primarily though, we need to understand the business of screenwriting. That's what we're here to do and we should be clued up. Again, it's okay to not know everything. Asking questions is good, but we should have a wide area of knowledge from which to pull our opinions. Here is an initial list of books about filmmaking, from the writer's perspective, that I believe can help us build the wealth of knowledge that we will need.

1) *Adventures in the Screen Trade,* by William Goldman (Obviously)
2) *Which Lie did I Tell?,* by William Goldman
3) *Tales from the Script,* Edited by Peter Hanson and Paul Robert Herman. (This has a wonderful accompanying documentary)
4) *Writing Movies for Fun and Profit,* by Robert Ben Garant and Thomas Lennon. (Even if you read it before, read it again. It is invaluable for you at this stage)
5) *Oscar Winning Screenwriters on Screenwriting,* by Joel Engel
6) *Breakfast with Sharks,* by Michael Lent
7) *Good in a Room,* by Stephanie Palmer

Breakfast with Sharks is a window into the realities of creating and maintaining a relationship with an agent, as well as many other types of relationships you will need over the years.

One important opinion we must have in our initial meetings with agents and managers is what *type* of writer we want to be. "A screenwriter" is not good enough. Like it or not; we will get pigeonholed. Everybody does. They don't hire the writers of *Deuce Bigalow: Male Gigolo* (Harris Goldberg & Rob Schneider) to rewrite the latest Clint Eastwood prison drama.

We will be known for a certain type of script, so get pigeonholed in the *right* hole right now. Know the genre and market you want to write for (and this had better be the genre of your spec script). Know the other writers in the market whom you admire and why. Know the directors who work primarily in this genre, and *all* their films.

It's okay to aspire to other genres, but we must explain why we believe we can make that move in logical and realistic terms.

Also—and this is a biggie—we must be available for all types of work. A mistake a lot of new writers make is thinking their career will be only about writing original scripts. No one makes a living that way anymore. We must be immediately available and willing to go to meetings for assignment work for projects that producers are trying to get off the ground. It doesn't mean we will say yes to every single meeting. We should still believe in the value of the project and that we are the correct writer for it—but thinking our career will be made by writing screenplays on spec is deluded. For our agent to make money, *we* need to make money, so any writer who is not willing to take assignment work is not going to make it onto their roster.

Next, we need to show that we are going to work just as hard as them (if not a lot harder) at selling our work and selling ourselves. Yes, the agent is there to find avenues to get us hired, but an agent is primarily there to make the deal. The best deal they can. A good agent will get us way more than the 10% we are paying him or her, but they need us to continue to take responsibility for our own career. We still need to be out there meeting people, pitching our ideas, trying to get meetings, trying to get ourselves known, fighting for our scripts. When people are interested, we can point them to our agent to pick up the conversation.

Ultimately, an agent or manager will sign us when they feel that we are a valuable commodity to them. Our spec script got us in the door, now we need to show them that we are the type of person who will make money for them quickly and continue to do so. We need to be someone with whom they want to be in business.

67.

How Do We Pitch?

At some point we are going to have to "pitch" our project.

This is one of the key areas where even great writers fall down. They just can't get it together in the room. Public speaking may not be your thing. It's very few people's "thing." In fact, it is the number one fear in the world—over death. If you are one of those lucky people that loves being in the room and performing, then you have a huge leg up here.

We talked about taking acting classes to get better at dialogue. Those classes will also be a massive benefit to us when it comes to pitching. It is, after all, a performance.

Being great at pitching is a combination of several skills, very few of which have anything to do with writing. No one can definitively tell you how to pitch your own projects. You need to develop a style that fits you as a writer. However, there are some principles that will aid all of us in becoming as adept as possible at pitching.

1) Practice, a lot

The actual pitch we are requested to do may have to fit anywhere from 5-20 minutes. Therefore, a good place to start is practicing and perfecting a 10-minute pitch, which we can later adapt to the time slot offered to us.

The 10-minute pitch should start with a 60-second topline summation of the whole story without giving away major plot twists or the ending. An extended logline, as it were. Then, we will spend the next 8-9 minutes starting at the beginning and filling in the details and elements that make our story and characters truly unique.

Write it out, if that helps you, but you eventually need to get to a place where you can deliver a succinct 10-minute presentation—*without notes*.

I can feel most of you bristle at the very idea of standing in a room by yourself, giving a 10-minute pitch aloud repeatedly. If you don't want to do it, don't do it. Go in with a crappy pitch, like other writers who never get the career they want. If you want to be a screenwriter, then get over it and get used to practicing by yourself or in front of friends and family.

This is a place where working with a partner can be useful. It's way more natural to practice something like this with a partner whose financial future also relies on the success of the pitch. However, if one of you is dull in front a crowd then give pitching responsibilities to the person who can bring the material to life. Maybe give the partner a few lines of dialogue to add in when necessary.

If you really feel like an idiot just speaking to yourself, then set up a camera and film it. It gives you an instant audience, plus the chance to watch it back and assess its success.

2) Forget everything you practiced

The key to a truly great pitch is making the audience feel that this is the first time we've ever delivered this pitch, and that it is truly spontaneous. The story is just pouring out of us.

The point of practicing it so much is so that we can deliver it in a manner that feels spontaneous and passionate, while hitting all the key story elements.

This is very hard to do. If it was easy, everyone would be great at pitching, but they're not. Think about how many truly great public speakers you've seen in your lifetime. Not many. Fortunately, we are not striving to be Dr. Martin Luther King, but don't underestimate how much a great pitch can sway a buyer. The exact details of our pitch become less important than the emotion they feel while listening to us.

3) Never be annoyingly self-deprecating

A little self-deprecation is fine. We don't want to come across as cocky. But don't use self-deprecation to cover your shortcomings. This includes saying anything such as, "I'm not very good at this to be honest," or "I didn't sleep much last night, so I'm not at my best."

You may think that by setting expectations low you now have the chance to exceed them. That's not how it works.

Very few people are 10/10 at public speaking. Producers know that. They want energy, confidence and passion and they will work with writers whose primary skill is writing and not speaking. But they will get annoyed by people trying to apologize their way out of the pitch before they've even started. Be confident in the skills you have, not worried and embarrassed about the skills you don't.

4) Know your beginning and your ending

Don't start with, "Errr, right…. Okay, so… er…Yeah, it's about a doctor in Nazi Germany…" Instead, start with, "It's about a doctor in Nazi Germany…."

And end clearly and definitively. Don't just trail off with, "I never know how to end these things." Know your last line and deliver it perfectly.

Everything in the middle can be much more "off script" and freeform if we nail our beginning and our ending.

5) Make sure the key story elements are covered

This sounds obvious but it's amazing how many times I've heard a writer pitch their story only to get to the end and have them say, "Oh, and he's also blind. Sorry, I forgot to tell you that at the beginning."

A great place to start for the structure of our pitch is our nine story questions:

1) Who is the story about?
2) What is their flaw or flaws?
3) What happens to them that changes their life for better or worse?
4) What must they now achieve?
5) What are the major obstacles that get in the way of that goal and how does our protagonist overcome them?
6) What's the worst thing that happens to the protagonist?
7) What does the protagonist do to turn this around?
8) How does this story end?
9) What is the theme?

This is everything we need them to know to understand the core story and character arc of the movie.

In terms of theme, we may want it to come out in the subtext, or it may be suitable to state it outright at the beginning or end of the pitch. That needs to be a judgment call we make according to our story and the audience.

6) Tailor the pitch

Every pitch is different. It will depend on how long we have to pitch and what we are hoping to achieve. If we have 30 seconds with a producer then we may just pitch an extended logline which includes the protagonist, the inciting incident, their goal and what stands in their way. That may be enough to whet their appetite and make the story sound attractive enough to read.

However, if we have been invited in for a pitch proposal on a project, and 10 people are in the room for a 60-minute meeting, then we will most likely be expected to deliver at least a 5-10 minute (or more) pitch that includes a clear depiction of all our story elements.

How do we know how long our pitch should be? Ask. Don't be subtle.

WRITER
Let me tell you about my story.
To make sure I tailor this
properly, what sort of detail
would you like here? Do you want
the two-minute version, or the
10-minute version?

And whatever they say – deliver that. And no more. Otherwise, we can end up giving them far less (or far more) than they want (or need), before they decide. Nothing is worse than having them cut you off or ask you to speed through the rest of your pitch so they can get to the next meeting.

7) Include dialogue if it is key to the story, or funny, or fantastic

The pitch is primarily to bring the *story* to life, but in doing so, we may want to include the odd line of dialogue. Any such inclusion should be brief and necessary. It is not a chance to show off our amazing dialogue skills by reciting both sides of a three-minute conversation.

Introduce it quickly and easily: "As Henry says to Angela, "I married you once, I'm not making the same mistake again.""

If it's a line that is truly funny or wonderful, or it explains a big chunk of story, or it's a line that will be in the trailer then include it, but they should be sparse throughout the whole pitch. Make them feel special.

8) Don't give them any more story than they need

Include only the sub plots that are necessary. People will get lost if they are trying to keep track of too many stories.

Obviously, the longer the pitch the more detail they expect, so tailor it to what is required, but use the skills we have developed in our writing to be as brief and succinct as possible.

The worst thing is getting 16 minutes into our 20-minute pitch and realizing we are barely at the midpoint, and suddenly having to rush through the last half of our movie. Better to end a few minutes early with a story that makes sense than a few minutes over with a huge story that was confusing.

9) Vary your volume, pitch and energy

Not being one-note and monotonous is not enough. This is about truly using our *entire* vocal range. It's about being bouncy and smiling one second, and stable and quiet the next, to make sure our tone matches the emotion our story is conveying at that moment. The audience should *feel* our story, not just hear it.

Don't worry about being too big. However big you think you're being; it feels smaller to the audience; I promise.

10) Find a way for the audience to keep track of characters

They won't tell you when they've forgotten a major character. And if they do, it'll be embarrassing.

Make sure characters are as defined and visual as possible. In their book *Writing Movies for Fun and Profit*, writers Thomas Lennon and Robert Ben Garant, suggest introducing characters in your script with a magic "Think." E.g. "Paul is a mountain of a man. Think Dwayne Johnson."

Personally, I don't like doing this in the script, especially a spec script, as it can potentially make us look a little naïve about the casting process (but then what do I know, those boys are millionaires many times over), but I do think it's a good idea in a pitch. It gives the audience an immediate image and makes it a lot easier to keep track of characters if they have a known star in mind.

If we bring a character back after an absence, give the audience a quick reminder of who they are; "Then he runs into Jake again—the boyfriend who hit Suzy—and they face off in the bar…"

11) Don't get gimmicky

Have you seen *Shark Tank*? Don't do that. As the series has progressed the entrepreneurs on that show have clearly been convinced by public opinion, and the show's producers, to include gimmicks and "hilarious quirks" in their pitches. In real life we just look like a dick. The people in the room want to hear a great story, well told. That's it. That will impress them way more than bringing someone along in costume, or a bizarre object that you introduce and place in their hands.

Whenever the idea of any sort of gimmick enters your head, don't think about how amazing it will be when they love your gimmick. Instead, imagine how embarrassing it'll be, and idiotic you'll look, if the idea bombs. Because that's most likely what will happen.

12) *Always* have a bottle of water

In most cases, when we arrive at a meeting, someone will politely offer us a drink, but not always, and that's fine for them; they are not about to get up and talk for 10-20 minutes without stopping. We are, and we'll be nervous and excited, so our mouth *will* dry up.

Always have a bottle of water in your bag. If someone gets you a drink, just leave it in the bag. If they don't, take it out and *use it*.

Therefore, we now need to learn a new skill; how to drink water and stay hydrated without interrupting your pitch.

Remember that video of Marco Rubio delivering the Republican rebuttal to the President's 2013 State of the Union address? (Google it if not!) That is a masterclass on how *not* to drink water while delivering a speech.

Want to learn how to do it properly? Watch a truly great stand-up comedian. They're on stage for up to 90 minutes without a break. They need to stay hydrated without ever upsetting the timing of a punch line. The best of them can make the water part of the routine before finally delivering a killer punch line and then taking a drink. It's a joy to watch.

13) One of you take the lead

This is only relevant if you are pitching as a pair, but if you are then one of you needs to be the primary pitcher. And the secondary pitcher needs to leave them alone. Otherwise you get the following:

```
               PRIMARY PITCHER
     She tracks down the killer to his
     hideout, but he's not there.

              SECONDARY PITCHER
     Well...
```

All eyes in the room turn to the secondary pitcher.

> SECONDARY PITCHER
> Well, he IS there, but he's
> hidden himself so that...

> PRIMARY PITCHER
> Yes, I was just getting to that.

> SECONDARY PITCHER
> Oh, okay. Keep going.

> PRIMARY PITCHER
> So, it SEEMS like he's not there,
> but he is.

The primary pitcher needs space to make choices, and tailor the pitch to whatever has been requested *without interruption*. The secondary pitcher should be ready to be invited in at any moment or to deliver pre-prepared pieces of dialogue or additional details.

***

Pitching is one of the key talents we will need to learn to make it as a successful screenwriter, and to be blunt, it's hard.

It's like telling an accountant, "Sure you're a genius with numbers, but I'll only let you be my accountant if you get up in front of the room and pitch to me, in less than five minutes, the story of my money. Oh, and by the way, it needs to be really entertaining and surprising and enjoyable, even if the story of my money is a depressing one."

Any accountant would just laugh at you and walk out of the room, but that is what screenwriters need to do. We need to write the greatest screenplays in the world *and* bring those stories to life in 10 minutes in front of a room full of people we don't know—but when it works, we can book a gig without ever writing a word.

68.

How Do We Make The Deal?

This is what this whole journey has been about, so what happens when we get there?

First, it's perfectly possible to sell scripts and get work before you get an agent. One does not have to follow the other. Indeed, one does not *necessarily* follow the other. If you do sell scripts or get hired for work, then agents will come calling; believe me.

Second, we are going to count a script "option" as a sale at this point in our career.

A script option can be for anything from $0 to a few thousand dollars. Whatever the offer, you must weigh up whether the fee is worth it. You are never going to get a great sum of money from an option. An option gives the producer the legal rights to sell the screenplay to a studio for an agreed period, usually six months to a year. If they make a sale in that time – great! Everyone wins. If not, then the rights revert back to you as the writer allowing you to sell it to someone else or renew the option with the producer for another set period.

Many new writers without any credits will regularly receive $0 option offers. The producer knows you are desperate and with $0 down they have no risk on their side whatsoever.

I am going to argue that at this stage in our career that we should option our scripts anytime we get the chance. Even for free. There is a very legitimate argument made by some writers that to option a script to a producer for no fee is a folly. The argument goes that if the producer can't even raise five hundred or a thousand dollars to pay an option fee then how are they possibly going to raise the millions of dollars needed to finance the film. This is a fair and reasonable argument. But on the other side, a script sitting on our desk doing nothing is worthless. If someone wants to put their name and reputation behind our script to try and get it made, then let them. It gives us time to get on with our next (and probably better) script and gives us a nice way of making an introduction to an agent or other producers; "I currently have a script optioned by X producer or Y production company," sounds a lot better than "I am a new writer with no contacts or credits."

There are a raft of very hardworking producers and production companies that are trying to break in themselves, that simply can't afford the fee to every script they want to represent. At this level, the chances of our script getting into production are very small; they are relatively unknown producers pitching a script from an unknown writer. But at least it's getting pitched around the industry. What good is it doing gathering dust on our shelf? We never know who might read it, and it will very likely get into the hands of people that we could not get to ourselves. Name recognition is huge so let's give our script any exposure we can. Just make sure than any option agreement allows us to take back ownership of the material at the end of the option period whether the producer wants to renew it or not, in case a better prospect comes along.

So, the question to ask is not really, "Is this $0 option worth it?" as financially it clearly isn't. Instead the question should be, "Will this producer work hard for my script and get my name out there?" If that's not true, then hold out for someone else. But if they have any sort of track record or they are genuinely passionate about your script and appear keen to make it happen then give them a go. Absolute worst-case scenario is that you get your script back.

However, there are two numbers you should always have in mind as you go into these negotiations.

1) The option price (even if you are sure it won't be available).
2) The purchase price.

Successful producers and production entities will happily pay an option fee and a good rule of thumb is up to 10% of the purchase price. Whether the film gets picked up or not, you keep the option money, but only get the balance if it goes into production.

So, what should the purchase price be? I'm afraid it gets even trickier here. If we are a member of the Writer's Guild of America, then minimum WGA fees apply. Since we are new and trying to get our career off the ground, we are most likely not WGA members. Therefore, the fees can be anything. If we are selling a relatively low budget script, which is not looking to be funded by a studio, then we may never get into WGA territory. If the script is relatively high budget and will need studio involvement, then they will probably work to WGA fees if only for legal safety.

However, the WGA minimum fee for an original screenplay is anywhere from $50k - $100k. If this is a high-budget film, then you might want (and expect) more than that. If your script ever got into a bidding war, then you would get more than that. Without such a bidding war though, we must be realistic.

A good rule of thumb is that outside of minimums, writer's fees should be around 1-5% of the production budget. 5% is for low budget films (1% of a $300k budget is basically pointless), or for big name writers. The 5% of high-budget films may pay for numerous new writers throughout the whole process, who will each get a small portion of that 5%. Therefore, the lower end of 1-2% is more realistic. On a $30m movie the total writing fee should be around $300-$600k. If the film is in the $150m range, then it *should* around $1.5m-$3m. However, both those scenarios are very rare for new writers unless many studios are biting your arm off for the script. Be prepared for the producer and the studio arguing that as a new writer with no track record you are entitled to nothing more than the WGA minimum. Again, this is why a good agent or manager are well worth their 10%.

But without any of these entities on our side we are fighting a David vs. Goliath battle. Do we take a WGA minimum offer for our script?

We should fight and negotiate, but ultimately, like the zero-dollar option, an unsold screenplay sitting on your desk is valueless. A film that may get into production can give us a career, so in most cases, I say yes. During the period after sale and into production you could build the career you always wanted from the buzz that this sale creates. After that, the exact dollar amount you made from this first sale won't matter anymore.

However, be warned. Whatever money we make does not come in one batch. Even at the low end of WGA fees, $50k sounds like a good chunk of change, especially if we have the grand total of $0 from our screenwriting career up to this point. Or, let's play the dream game and say a studio wants to buy it for $600k. In either case, just like the option fee you don't get all that money up front. Initially you will only get a small portion of that. You will receive another chunk after you turn in your rewritten draft. Maybe more money if they want more rewrites. Eventually, the balance will be paid on the day that production starts.

You may have heard about script sales where they talk about, "$200k against $600k." That meant that the writer got $200k up front (at least once they had turned in their first draft and rewrites) but will only make the remaining $400k if it goes into production.

The WGA breaks down their minimum fees as follows:

	Low	High
Original Screenplay, excluding treatment or sale/purchase of original screenplay	$48,819	$99,937

Installments for Employment:

	Low	High
Delivery of First Draft Screenplay	$37,703	$54,519
Delivery of Final Draft Screenplay	$11,116	$27,735

There are more stages for screenplays pitched at the treatment stage, and different fees for selling stories/treatments or for rewrites.

Either way, it's very unlikely that we get rich off our first script sale. More realistically it will keep us alive and motivated as we dive back in to writing and selling our next script.

However, without an agent, here is the most important advice for all of us at this stage. The moment anyone starts talking to you about options, purchases or contracts:

Get a lawyer!

I argued earlier that very few producers will take the risk of stealing material when they can purchase it so cheaply. But they will take every advantage they can to get that material as cheaply as possible and keep as much of the studio's money for themselves.

As soon as a good lawyer is involved in the process then two things happen:

1) The producer knows that they can't take advantage of you and will start being more reasonable in terms of expectations and deals.
2) The money you are to receive could increase dramatically.

I know this doesn't help you when you're struggling to fill your car up with gas, and a lawyer is asking for $300 an hour to read an option agreement, but it is so important that it is something that you should start preparing for now.

Ask everyone you know for recommendations of a lawyer. Specifically, an entertainment lawyer. If you are in Los Angeles then this will not be hard. Many lawyers will offer a quick introductory call before dolling out advice. Find one that sounds knowledgeable and that you trust and that you can ultimately afford at this stage of your career.

A writing teacher I had many years ago had two lawyers. One, very reasonably priced, was the person he went to when a contract needed checking or amending slightly. The second, who was much higher priced, was the one he turned to when negotiation was needed. His Pitbull; expensive, but worth it when deals are being made.

We can't possibly be as knowledgeable and savvy as we need to be with a world that is so fraught with pitfalls, so get help.

69.

How Do We Build Our Own Career?

Even after we get an agent we are still responsible for our own careers.

Getting a script optioned or sold is a wonderful thing, but a single script is not a career. A script is a job. A job that, if we are lucky, will make us a noticeable to significant amount of money at some point down the line.

To have a real career we need much more than one great script. We need many scripts at various stages of development with many different outlets and producers, so that money is coming in regularly (even if it is in small amounts) until a bigger payday comes.

This is obviously part of an agent's responsibility for their client; to make sure that they can pay the bills and keep working. However, before we have representation, we need to make this happen for ourselves. Plus, agents are not magic. They can't just make jobs appear from nowhere and even if they could they can't guarantee that we are going to book the gig, so they are much more likely to take on a client who understands that finding new work is just as much the responsibility of the writer as the agent.

Get involved in any project. Nothing is beneath us. Meet anyone who needs something written. We can't commit to writing everything that is asked of us, especially if people expect us to do it for free (which many will), but there is very little lost by meeting people. Some low-budget projects will seem amateurish, but when we meet the people involved, they may present themselves as professionals who are trying to get something good made on a low budget. These are useful people to work with. Short films made by such people can propel everyone involved forward into features with some real money behind them.

As a working writer we are a small business. A small business of one. Our day must be made up of all the things that a small business needs to do, and like any business only a small fraction of that is the work for which we get paid.

The three key activities of any small business are:

1) The work. In this case, writing.

2) Marketing.
3) Selling.

We've covered number 1 so let's look in more detail at the others.

Marketing

Marketing is making ourselves known. Advertising the fact that we exist and that we are a writer who may deliver a valuable product. It is raising our profile and building our brand.

Therefore, marketing activities include:

- Writing introductory emails and letters
- Connecting with people on social media
- Sending out our script
- Meeting people at industry events
- Managing our screenplays on networking sites like Blacklist or Inktip.
- Entering screenplay competitions
- Building and promoting a website (Keep it simple and elegant. Basic details about who we are. Maybe a blog, and potentially access to a writing sample. We are new, and we need profile, but we don't want to look tacky and amateurish.)

These are all valuable marketing activities. They should not be used as a reason to avoid writing, but should be carried out every day while we continue to write new and better scripts, so that when the latest script is finished we will have avenues of legitimate distribution.

Our brand in the industry is much more important than we think and begins being formed a lot earlier than we think. Each time we interact with someone they are evaluating us. Were we intelligent? Were we capable? Were we professional? Did we understand their business? Did our demeanor and attitude fit the script we were selling? (comedy writers need to be amusing in the meeting.) Do they think they would enjoy working with us? Did we seem honest and authentic?

After that, every time they talk about us to a colleague or friend they pass on their opinion of their experience and interaction, which forms the first impression in the mind of the next person, and so on.

Therefore, we must consistently embody our brand. And our brand right now is "hard working, enthusiastic writer looking for a break." Don't write angry, pissy emails to people. Don't post social media comments and

347

reviews about industry insiders. Bitching about movies and moviemakers is for trolls and teenagers, not those of us who are genuinely trying to work alongside them.

When we receive a rejection letter or email immediately write back with a "thank you" note to the person for taking the time to read your work.

Every time we meet someone new, tell them loud and proud about the current script we are working on and the other projects we have, no matter where they are in the process. AND ASK IF THEY'D LIKE TO READ IT.

They don't give a shit? Who cares? We've lost nothing—but if we tell enough people we will eventually meet someone who *does* care, and who might just be a potential buyer. Lots of people with money *want* to get into the movie business, but they don't know where to start. Maybe our script is just what they need.

We are going to market the shit out of ourselves. Otherwise we are just another person with 100 pages of paper held together with brads on our desk.

Selling

Marketing and selling are *not* the same thing.

Marketing is raising our profile; selling is when we get a potential buyer on the phone or in person and convince them to hire us. Marketing is passive. Selling is active. Marketing creates the opportunities for us to sell, but marketing without selling is pointless.

As I've mentioned earlier, when I tried to get my writing career off the ground, I was forced to take an office job to pay the bills. That job was selling. In this case, selling advertising space. Initially on trade magazines and later at the Financial Times newspaper. (Some of you will be too young to remember newspapers, but the FT was arguably the most famous newspaper in the world in 2001 when I started there).

The FT was easy to sell. Everyone knew it and respected it. It was a brand with which people wanted to be associated. Everybody took my call. Everybody liked what I had to sell. Everybody wanted to buy it, so it only came down to whether they had the money at that moment, or if their money was allocated to other things. I assume that this is the equivalent of Aaron Sorkin selling his latest effort.

However, selling unknown trade magazines was very different. People were incredibly difficult to get on the phone. The name meant nothing. And if they did know it they weren't impressed by it. They had very little money and many places they could spend it. They needed massive bang for their buck to warrant the expenditure. They would fob you off with a myriad of excuses as to why they were too busy to talk, or to read the materials you sent over. Even if they were interested, they were still difficult to nail down for a meeting. And then they wanted discounts and extras thrown in for free.

This is the equivalent of us selling our screenplay at this stage of our career. Nothing about it is going to be easy. I'm glad I had that job, as without it I would have no idea how hard real selling is. Anyone who sells a big brand name has no idea. Selling an unknown entity is hard.

There are a thousand books out there on selling, but I would point you towards *The Sandler Rules: 49 Timeless Selling Principles and How to Apply Them* by David Mattson. It's a relatively quick and easy read for people new to selling and gives tips that are easy to use in real life.

The reason to read it, or any other book on selling, is to demystify the idea of sales. Remember, production companies and producers need scripts to survive. We are not bothering them by offering them a script. We are offering them exactly what they need to keep their business going. But so are lots of other people. Do they buy 10 "great" scripts from new writers, 3 "good" scripts from writers with credits and a track record, or save their money for one script from a star writer. They need to get meetings, too, and the script from the star writer will get them into a studio quicker— regardless of quality—than a great script from an unknown. We need to convince them that our script is worth the investment, but we also need to convince them that we, as a person, are worth the investment. That being in business with us as a writer is a smart move on their part.

Did you send out a script to a producer or agent and get no reply? Don't bitch and moan about it – call them up. You'd be amazed by how many producers pick up their own phone. But even if their assistant does pick up, don't be deterred. Be polite and honest but get them talking and try to make an impression. Give them a reason to mention us, the call, and the script to the producer. We may just get a call back.

If we do manage to get the producer on the phone, then get in immediately and explain who we are and describe our script. Don't waste their time but get them talking. No closed questions.

> YOU
>
> Hi, Mr. Geisland. This is Alex
> Writer. You requested my script
> *The Long Goodbye* about the blind
> hitman. What did you think of the
> script?

If it's an immediate no, then ask for any feedback they can give us and then say, "Thank you for taking the time to read it and for giving me such useful feedback. Is it okay if I send you my next script?"

If the producer is even remotely positive about our script, then thank them and try to close them for a meeting. The industry is still very face to face when it comes to new relationships. Therefore, the goal of any sales call is not realistically to get the script sold or optioned, the goal is to get a meeting.

> YOU
>
> That's great. I was wondering if
> I could come in and speak to you
> about this script and other
> projects you have going on. Maybe
> you have something in the
> pipeline that I could pitch for?

Every minute of every day that we have available, that is not spent writing or working to pay the bills, should be spent either marketing or selling. Will it mean that we miss out on some fun parties? Yes. Will it mean that we are tired when we get up for work? Yes. Will it mean that we have very little social life? Yes. But this is what is necessary to get noticed and get in the room. Thousands of writers can finish a screenplay, and some of them will be excellent. But only those writers that can market and sell that screenplay will make any money or build a career.

70.

How Do We Take Notes?

If we are lucky enough to sell or option a script then we are very quickly going to get notes—from many, many people. We will get notes even if we don't sell something. An agent or manager may give us notes to help us improve a script or make it more sellable.

Therefore, we need to know how to take those notes in a positive and useful way.

Remember when we got feedback on our very first screenplay? How annoying it was? How upset we were? Well, getting notes from people who are paying us money (or representing us) can be even more annoying and upsetting because these people may expect us to make the changes they request, whether we agree with them or not, and we are going to disagree with *a lot* of notes.

We need to learn how to react positively to ideas with which we disagree, and how to argue against them without causing friction or negativity. Also, how to make only the changes that we feel are correct while still satisfying the note giver.

A useful piece of psychology to understand for these meetings is the theory of "ego-states" made popular by Eric Berne.

The theory states that as humans we adopt one of a few emotional states at any moment and behave accordingly. In simple form the states are:

Controlling Parent   **Nurturing Parent**

Adult

Adapted Child   **Natural Child**

This has nothing to do with being a parent (although if you are you will recognize these emotional states very easily) but instead is to do with our reactions to people and events around us and the behaviors that they cause. Let's look at how we act in each state:

Controlling Parent: We are controlling (as it states). We issue orders and make demands. We are rigid in our thinking and will not change opinion. We are taking a dominant position.

Nurturing Parent: We are helpful and kind and caring. We are sympathetic and tolerant, even if someone has done us wrong, or upset us. We are taking a supportive position.

Adult: We are rational, fair-minded and realistic. We see others as equals and treat them as such. We do not let emotions take over. We are taking a logical position.

Adapted Child: We follow the rules. We understand and adapt to the expectations of others. We are "well behaved." We are taking a socially acceptable position.

Natural Child: We are spontaneous and imaginative. We don't worry about the "rules" and want to create our own way of doing things. We are imaginative and pleasure seeking. We are taking a rebellious position.

Each ego state has its own positives and negatives. If we are a parent or caregiver, then we have been in a position where a child has been about to do something dangerous, like grab a hot iron or run out into a busy street. That is no time for a rational Adult-to-Adult discussion about the potential dangers of such an action. It's time to jump to Controlling Parent and scream, "STOP!!!" and pull them back.

Similarly, the Nurturing Parent in us can be a wonderful part of our personality, but when overused, it can be smothering and annoying. An example is when we are in the middle of getting something off our chest only to have our "helpful" spouse/partner jump in with their commiserations and possible solutions. But that's not what we wanted. We just wanted to talk it out, but people (primarily men) love to fix things and our Nurturing Parent takes over.

As one person in a situation adopts one of these states, we can be triggered to a potentially conflicting state. Remember back to when you were a teenager. When your mother took a Controlling Parent state and told you not to do something, what did you do? You wanted to do it even more, right? Even if you didn't really want a tattoo at first, the moment you are told you can't have one the desire increases tenfold. That is because when faced with a Controlling Parent (literally in this case) you moved instinctively to the Natural Child and took an opposing, rebellious viewpoint. One that was going to lead to an argument between parent and child.

What we learn from all this is that the primary ego state for any such notes meeting (and at moments when we are pissed with our loved ones) is the Adult state. The logical, rational, unemotional state. Why? Because the person giving the notes will be hovering around the Controlling Parent state. They are used to giving directions and getting their way. That's why they wanted to be in charge.

They won't say, "It felt to me like our guy should win that fight, but hey, what do I know, I've never written a script in my life. You're the writer, what do you think?" They'll say, "Our guy needs to be more heroic. He should win that fight."

However, we spent months writing this script and thinking about exactly why he loses that fight, and how it affects every single scene after it. If he's the kind of guy who *wins* the fight, then he's a *totally* different character, and it's a *totally* different film.

What's our natural reaction going to be? Which ego state will we want to jump to? Natural Child, right? We will want to stop them and argue, "Are you a fucking moron? Did you even read the script? You've completely missed the point of the whole fucking thing." Then, we'll throw water in their face and storm out—and, of course, we'll never work again.

Or, we can be driven into Adapted Child, which will see us seething on the inside while smiling on the outside. We will write down the notes word for word and then we go away and think, "He clearly just doesn't understand this and never will. The film's fucked whatever so I'll let the guy win the fight. Who cares?" And we turn in the draft exactly as requested, causing everyone who reads it to say, "But this makes no sense. That guy would never win that fight." And soon the script is dropped, and we're forgotten about forever and we never work again.

So, how do we react? What's the Adult reaction? Remember the qualities we wanted going into the sale meeting?

1) Passion
2) An opinion
3) An ability and willingness to change that opinion
4) Gratitude

These are all Adult qualities and we want the same ones going into a notes meeting.

As an Adult, we say:

> WRITER
> Yes, I see what you mean. I love
> the idea of making him more
> heroic at this stage to really
> get the audience on his side. He
> could win that fight, or perhaps
> he gets into the fight because
> he's protecting someone. A woman,
> maybe. That way, we see his
> heroic side, but if he loses the
> fight, then we still have the
> setup for the third act when he
> wins the fight against his
> neighbor, which is a scene I know
> we all like. Could that satisfy
> what you were hoping to achieve?

They may say yes, they may say no. Some battles we are going to lose no matter how passionate and logical we are. We're not in charge. But such a response puts us in the best place to get what we want for the script while satisfying the needs and position of the person giving the notes.

A tool for how to phrase our response is a game called "Yes, and…." When anyone asks us a question or asks for our opinion there are three ways we can respond:

1) No
2) Yes, but…
3) Yes, and…

"No" shuts the conversations down cold and puts the other person immediately onto a defensive back foot. For instance:

> EXEC
> I think she should poison him
> rather than stab him. What do you
> think?
>
> YOU
> No.

There is a horrible silence in the room.

> EXEC
> What do you mean, "no"?

"Yes, but..." is better, but still basically says, "Yes... but now I'm going to explain why you're wrong." It still puts the other person in a defensive position where they feel they must repeat or stand by their argument for whatever they want, even if it was just a musing at first.

> EXEC
> I think she should poison him rather than stab him. What do you think?
>
> YOU
> Yes, but stabbing is more visceral. More visual as well. It fits the character.
>
> EXEC
> I think she's more calculating than visceral. She would poison him.

However, "Yes, and..." builds on what the person said. It means they are never wrong, and all we are doing is taking their idea and adding in our own ideas and thoughts on top.

> EXEC
> I think she should poison him rather than stab him. What do you think?
>
> YOU
> Yes, I love it. And it's so calculating. She's a calculating person. The stabbing was very visceral, and I do like the idea of that on screen as well. Did you like that visual of the blood dripping down onto the white wedding dress?
>
> EXEC
> Yeah, that was good. I like poisoning too though. Have a

```
think about it. See if poisoning
adds anything.
```

By building on, instead of arguing against their idea, we have given them an out to express and process their opinion without feeling like it must become gospel. All they want to know is that we respected their position and their opinion and that we gave a thoughtful response that was open to the idea of changing.

Again, the response might be, "No, she poisons him. And if you don't change it, I'll get a writer who will." In which case, let's be pragmatic and make the choice we feel is best for us and for the film.

In most cases, writers end up getting angry and frustrated about notes they feel are wrong or stupid, but their frustrations stem primarily from their own reaction to the notes. If taken more positively, and with a "Yes, and…" attitude you will be pleasantly surprised by the degree to which people are willing to discuss it and let us make our own choices. Or at the very least give us the chance to argue our side and suggest alternatives.

Screenwriters like to think that they are unique in having people in power force changes to their work. They are not. This is no different from most jobs in most industries. No matter what job we do, at some point our boss will turn up at the last minute and offer his or her "insights," which are ludicrous, ill-informed and usually just flat out wrong. The only way to develop as a writer is to expect it, plan for it and react as positively as possible.

If we become skilled at this then we will get more work and stay in jobs for longer than writers who throw tantrums. We will also be happier and healthier. The alternative is a lifetime of stress—I promise.

71.

When is Our Journey Over?

This whole book has been designed to get us to the stage of "breaking in." Are we signed by an agent yet? Have we sold a script? Have we been hired to write or rewrite something?

If not, then we're still going, but even if we have achieved those things, that is not "the end". Remember, there is no "end" in the same way as other careers. We don't get our diploma and a job for life.

We are now fighting the same fight as career screenwriters: Making our script so bankable that saying no is not an option. But there are *so many reasons to say no*.

Saying no is not difficult. Saying no is very unlikely to get anyone fired. Saying no will create no additional work whatsoever. Saying no allows them to go to bed on time. Saying no won't even really embarrass them when someone else disagrees.

However, saying yes is real work. Saying yes means they are putting their reputation on the line with this script and you. Saying yes means they must justify their choice with provable reasons. Saying yes *can* get them fired, if someone more senior disagrees.

Why would anyone ever say yes? Because saying yes to the right script can make a career. It can lift them from the assistant pool to an agent's desk. From the mailroom to a junior executive position. Putting their own money behind the script can get them a studio deal and first dollar gross profit share. It can make them more money than they ever dreamed of.

People will say yes when it is in their best interests to do so. We must make it impossible for them to say no. And we must get many people to say yes:

1) An agency reader must read it, love it and "Recommend" it.
2) The agent's assistant might then have to read it and love it and recommend it to their boss.
3) The agent must read it and love it and decide to represent and sell it.

4) The studio reader must love it enough to pass it up to their superior.
5) The studio exec must love it more than all the other successful writers' spec scripts and pitches.
6) And on up the studio to the top.

In many ways, what we are doing now is not that different to what the rest of our life will be if we are lucky enough to break in. There is no such thing as a guaranteed job. No such thing as being promoted and knowing how much money we'll make next year. This is not that type of career. We'll never know if there is another job around the corner. We will need to fight hard for every job we are lucky enough to get.

This is what it's like to be a working screenwriter. The fact that we haven't made any (or much) money yet is irrelevant. Hundreds of represented writers haven't made any money this year yet either.

If we don't enjoy this, then we'll never enjoy this life. Go and have a long hard think about whether this is really what you want to do. You won't be quitting because you can't write scripts of quality or because people don't recognize your genius. Instead you are making a much more mature choice as to whether this is really the life for you.

Let's say we write a terrific script and get signed by a huge agent at WME. She sends us out on meetings, and we get hired to write the new *Bourne* movie. Is our journey finished? No. Sorry. Because we will potentially be fired after we turn in our first draft, and we'll have to start all over again.

There is no end to this journey, just a series of new beginnings. If we get signed, then we start our journey to sell our first script or get our first writing assignment. If we fulfill that journey, then we start a new one to get a film into production. If we fulfill that, then we start a new journey to win awards, or at least be recognized for work that we truly love and admire, and so on.

Plus, filmmaking is a fickle industry. Even star writers fall by the wayside. One movie that bombs can easily spell the end of our career. A change in studio personnel can mean that all our champions disappear in one go. There's so much we can't control.

Let's concentrate on what we *can* control. We can always write, either on spec or assignment. We will never get worse as a writer if we keep writing. We can work harder than anyone else to build and maintain a profile and reputation with the people who matter. In our early stages, that is just to get ourselves recognized, so these people know we exist. Later, it is to remain a popular and successful client on our agent's roster, or a go-to writer for a studio.

We can create a plethora of movie ideas—even if we don't write the whole script. We can have a bunch of treatments for potential movies in our back pocket. If an agent/buyer asks, "What else have you got?", then pick out the idea that most closely suits what you think they are looking for.

We can be ready and open to any opportunity that may come our way. Again, the opportunity is not going to be Scorsese calling to say he's read our script and wants us on set the next day. It's very rarely that grand or that obvious. It's many little opportunities that build up over time; a phone call here, a recommendation there, the name of someone we should chat to, even if they seem irrelevant or unimportant. Never pass up an opportunity to move forward. We never know what it might lead to or what is hidden behind it.

If we have broken in and are making a living, then one of the best things we can do is pass our knowledge onto others. In doing so, we will become more aware of our own talents and successes. Mentoring new, talented writers is one of the nicest things you can do.

Wherever you are and whatever you are doing just make sure to keep moving forward. If we stagnate in this industry, we die.

So, to go right back to where we started, how do we become a working screenwriter? We write a fantastic script, and we fight as hard as we can to get people to read it. And we keep fighting until someone recognizes our genius. And if we do, the filmmaking community will eventually pay attention to us, whether we are 21 years old or 70, whether we are brand-new or have three Oscars to our name. No one cares. They just want a fantastic script.

Go write it!

Index of Books, Movies And Writers

About the Author

Hywel Berry has written for theater, film and television, producing two plays, and selling three TV pilots.

He was hired to write three screenplays, none of which ever went into production. He really wanted to be a working screenwriter, but like many people who start this journey he made some money, but never a living.

Needing to clothe and feed his two children he started working as a public speaker and now delivers keynote speeches and workshops to Fortune 500 companies all over the world. A job he loves.

Realizing how many other people were dropping off their own screenwriting journey Hywel decided to help new writers to avoid the same stupid mistakes that he made. So, he wrote this book, and offers live and video classes to writers all over the world at:

www.ScreenwritingJourney.com

You can contact him with anything you like at:

hywel@screenwritingjourney.com